Seafood and Health

Joyce A. Nettleton

Seafood
and
Health

Joyce A. Nettleton

Osprey Books
Huntington, NY 11743

Published by
Osprey Books
P.O. Box 965
Huntington, New York, 11743

Design and illustration by Lorraine Brod, Centerport, New York
Composition by New Age Typographers, Inc., Huntington, New York
Printed and bound in USA by BookCrafters Inc, Chelsea, Michigan

Library of Congress Cataloging-in-Publication Data
Nettleton, Joyce A., 1944-
    Seafood and Health

    Bibliography: p.
    Includes index.
    1. Seafood 2. Cookery (Seafood) I. Title
TX385.N49   1986   641.3'92   86-23467
ISBN 0-943738-22-2
ISBN 0-943737-21-0 (pbk.)

There are no limits to Jeeves's brain-power.
He virtually lives on fish.
P.G. Wodehouse

Contents

List of Recipes

Appetizers

Soups and Stews

Salads

Entrées – lean fish

Entrées – rich fish

Entrées – shellfish

Sauces

Acknowledgements

Few books come to life without the help of colleagues and friends and this one is no exception. Many people patiently argued details with me long after their interest in the subject had waned. It is no exaggeration that their suggestions and insights transformed this work. These special people are: Carol Jean Suitor, Linda Hachfeld, Raquel Boehmer, Margo Woods and Robin Orr.

Several people reviewed sections of the manuscript and provided thoughtful, rigorous comments. Their work improved the accuracy and discussion of the material. Warm thanks go to Carol Jean Suitor, Alice Shapiro, Margo Woods, Mary Etta King, Carol Morgan and my husband, Arie Derksen for their help.

Developing, adapting and testing recipes for publication is a project that taught me lessons I had been reluctant to accept. The talents of Nancy Stutzman, Linda Hachfeld and Raquel Boehmer improved the efficiency and flavor of the recipes in the book.

Estimating nutrient content is more difficult than it appears and many assumptions must be made. Caroline Roy carefully performed the calculations for estimating the nutrient content of the recipes and found errors I would have overlooked. She is both a competent nutritionist and a reliable colleague.

For contributions of recipes and permission to adapt their own creations I am indebted to many people. Among these are: Raquel Boehmer, Ralph Boragine, Maxine Hegsted, Sheryl Julian, Kay McCarthy, Robin Orr, The Catfish Institute and Steven Foster Smith, Jan Kerman of Evans/Kraft Bean Inc., The Fishmonger's, Cambridge, Massachusetts and Lisa Foppiano of Connors Brunswick Inc.

Seafood and Health is my second book published by Osprey Books. It plies new waters for both Osprey and me but its course has found fair winds. It is my continued good fortune to have a publisher and editor who is both patient and skilled. Thanks to Ian Dore.

Joyce A. Nettleton

Foreword

William P. Castelli, M.D.
Medical Director, Framingham Heart Study.

Half the people who go to read this book will die from a process called atherosclerosis which is a collection of cholesterol and extra tissue, like scar tissue, that will block the blood flow through their coronary arteries producing a heart attack, or block the flow through their cerebral arteries and produce a stroke, or block the flow to some other organ that will destroy the health of that individual. Actually two-thirds of all Americans die with this process in our arteries and even if they didn't exactly die from this process they may have suffered much ill-health from such a process.

Well then, are there societies in the world that don't suffer so much from these cholesterol and fat deposits in their arteries? Actually about two-thirds of the people that live on this earth don't die with these lesions in their blood vessels. They live in Africa, South America, Asia; they live outside the big cities. They subsist largely on whole grains. Bring them to this country and they don't change their genes on the boat over here but they sure do change their diet and they start living and eating like us and that spells big trouble for them. Not that genetics or inheritance doesn't play a role in whether you get heart attacks or strokes, it certainly does. But there is little you can do to change your mother or father. However, you can change your diet, and there is ample evidence that if you do you will change your chances of a heart attack. Take all the diet (and for that matter, all the drug) trials ever done in the history of medicine and they all show the same thing. For each 1 percent the cholesterol was lowered in these trials the subsequent heart attack rate fell 2 percent.

Today when your arteries fill up with these deposits we have bypass surgery to go around the blockages, we have balloon angio-plasty (we stick a balloon in the narrowed blood vessel and blow it up to crunch the atherosclerosis and improve the opening), and we are soon to have laser guns so we can blast the atherosclerosis to bits. However, recent evidence (about 15 studies) from clinics where they repeat the X-rays of these vessels after bypass or whatever have shown that for 80 percent of the people who underwent one of these procedures the lesions are worse two to ten years later. Yet in every one of these studies a certain proportion of the patients did not have an increase in their lesions and in a few there was reversibility. What was so special about these people? They all had a fall in their serum cholesterol levels.

In our studies in Framingham we know that over half the people in America have a cholesterol that is too high and if you measure the fancy total cholesterol to HDL cholesterol ratio these people have a ratio over 4.5. We are about to have a crusade in America on cholesterol. With new technologies it is possible to take a drop of blood from your finger, stick it in a machine and three minutes later tell you if your cholesterol is too high. If your total cholesterol is over 200 mg/dl you exceed the goal of therapy: the Europeans are picking 200 as a goal as well.

Well, how do over half of Americans lower their cholesterols? Other than exercise and drugs, the corner stone of a healtheir life is diet. But no one wants to go on a diet, eating is one of the last joys of life. The trick of course is to find foods that don't raise your cho-lesterol and that don't give you heart attacks and one of the foods in that category is fish.

The evidence that eating fish is good for you goes way back. Dr. Ancel Keys did a study called the seven country study. He went around the world and found countries with the highest through the lowest rates of atherosclerosis and heart attacks. What country had the lowest rates? Japanese fishermen on the island of Kyosho. Stud-ies of the Eskimos who eat nothing but meat show their arteries to be clean of lesions; the meats they eat are mostly fish, or animals that eat fish. Finally we have the Zupthen study from Holland, a society not too unlike our own, where those who ate fish twice a week in the sixties and seventies had half the heart attack rate of the people from that town who didn't eat fish.

That's where this book comes in. Not only will it explain some of the reasons why you should eat more fish but it will help you learn how to cook fish at home with tasty recipes. Most Americans eat fish out in restaurants but they need help to cook fish at home so it doesn't have a fishy smell. This book will help you do just that.

While eating fish just a couple of times a week could have an important impact on whether you get a heart attack the newer information on fish indicates that it will help people with other diseases such as phlebitis and rheumatoid arthritis, prevent certain cancers, lower blood pressure, help in migraine headache and so on. Why not just pop a few fish oil capsules a day? Because there is no evidence that doing that is as safe as eating fish. We have lots of studies that indicate that eating fish (even all the shell fish now are good) results in lowered rates of the degenerative vascular disease but we don't know the safety of eating the oils.

Besides, eating fish can be one of the joys of eating. Cook a few recipes and find out how easy it can be!

Chapter One

What Makes Seafood Different?

People who customarily eat seafood are less likely to develop heart disease, diabetes, arthritis, bronchial asthma and psoriasis, and they have fewer occurrences of certain cancers. Why?

The seafood and health story began with the observation, first published in the early 1970s, that Greenland Eskimos living the traditional way of life had virtually no heart disease. They ate plenty of fat, protein and cholesterol just as Americans and Europeans do, but were apparently protected from *atherosclerosis**, the leading cause of death in America. The findings among Eskimos have been supported by observations in Japan, the Netherlands, Sweden and the USA.

Scrutiny of the Eskimo diet, however, revealed that the kind of fat eaten differed from the fat found in American and European foods. Eskimos, living mainly on sea animals and fish, consume fats that are more highly *unsaturated* than the fats we eat from animals and grains. The fats in Eskimo foods have certain *fatty acids* called *omega-3 fatty acids* which are not found in plants or land-based animals. The question was, could these omega-3 fatty acids be protecting Eskimos against heart disease?

The answer appears to be yes. Finding out how these omega-3 fatty acids are working in the body is now occupying hundreds of scientists worldwide. The search has led to new understandings of

---

*Words printed in italics are defined in the Glossary at the end of the book. Only the first occurrence of the word is italicized.

1

how different fats are handled by the body, how cells interact and communicate with each other and how diet influences cellular activity. What began as a search for ways to discourage heart disease has opened new frontiers not only in heart disease but also in immunology, cancer, infectious disease, headache and cellular metabolism.

Seafood has captured headlines because of its unique health merits. Newspapers, magazines and talk shows have carried the message from the May 1985 *New England Journal of Medicine* that eating fish regularly can help fight heart disease. Proclaimed the prestigious medical journal: "Consumption of as little as one or two fish dishes per week may be of preventive value in relation to coronary heart disease."

Fish Oil Is Unique

Like us, fish and shellfish use components of *fats* to build cells and provide energy. The fatty acids in fats are used to make hormones and a group of substances called *eicosanoids* that govern cell activities. Fish obtain their fattty acids mainly from the plankton and sea creatures they eat. Fish devouring other fish accumulate fats that the smaller fish obtained from plankton. As a result, the fatty acids from plankton become concentrated through the food chain.

Unlike the fats in plants and land based animals, the fats or oils (oils are fats that are liquid at room temperature) in fish have their constituent fatty acids derived exclusively from sea life. These special fatty acids are called omega-3 fatty acids. They differ from plant and animal fatty acids in their chemical structure. They have longer carbon skeletons and they have fewer hydrogen atoms, making them more unsaturated than the fatty acids in plants and animals. These differences in chemical structure cause the fats to behave differently in the cell. It is also thought that these highly unsaturated oils enable the fish to remain flexible in extremely cold waters.

In comparing fish oils with those from plants, we have mentioned that fish oils are more highly unsaturated – that is, they are missing more hydrogens. And from our studies with vegetable oils and heart disease, we would expect these highly unsaturated oils to be heart healthy and to lower our risk of heart disease. They certainly appear to have protected Eskimos and others from heart disease, but they do so in ways completely unlike vegetable oils. It is the latter discovery – the way omega-3 fatty acids work – that is one of the most exciting parts of the omega-3 story.

This is what we think happens. When we eat seafood with omega-3s the fatty acids are taken up into cells just like other unsaturated fatty acids. They are stored in the membranes of different kinds of cells. There they are available to participate in the metabolic activities going on inside the cell or to influence what is happening on the surface of the cell. Because they are structurally different from the other kinds of fatty acids in the cell membrane, they are preferentially called upon for certain activities. As a result, the kinds and amounts of substances produced inside the cell or at its surface are different from those usually made when no omega-3s are around. These seemingly small chemical changes apparently underly the enormous differences observed when omega-3s are involved. Just how they might be helping in heart disease and other health situations is the subject of Chapter Two.

Seafood Is Nutritious

Our thinking about what makes a food or the way we eat nutritious has become more sophisticated over the past several years. We not only want to have the nutrients we need for health, we also want to be free from harmful substances. It sounds simple. But it is a question of degree. "A little is fine; more is usually worse." That dictum is almost certainly true for fat, calories and sodium but it is less easy to determine for other nutrients, substances and food habits. The classic recommendation has always been variety and moderation – sound advice if we could be a bit more precise about it.

Nutritious foods are those generous in the nutrients we need and stingy in those substances we do not need. Seafood has high quality protein and a wide assortment of vitamins and minerals without much fat, *cholesterol* or sodium. Because most Americans have abundant food, we are more concerned about avoiding those components that undermine health – fat, sodium and cholesterol – than with obtaining the nutrients we need. Yet, in spite of plenty, some groups of people do not get enough iron, calcium, certain vitamins and protein. By concentrating on eating the most nutritious foods prepared in healthful ways we ensure sound bodies and fewer health problems.

Topnotch Protein

Seafood's traditional importance in good eating has been its high quality protein. It compares favorably with chicken, beef, eggs and cheese for top honors in supplying us with all the amino acids we need for tissue building and repair. That makes it an efficient source of protein for meeting our basic needs. Seafood is especially digestible because it has very little connective tissue. For that reason fish is recommended in many special diets.

Many popular protein foods have drawbacks associated with other nutrients they furnish. For example, chicken, an excellent source of protein, is high in fat if the skin is left on. Without the skin it is a lean and valuable food. Beef, pork and lamb, however, are relatively high in fat even when trimmed. The unfortunate part about these meats is that their fat is mostly of the *saturated* kind, the kind that promotes heart disease. That is why it is wisest to consume meats in modest amounts and cooked in ways that leave the fat behind.

Look at the chart below to see how seafood compares with other popular favorites as a source of protein. It holds its own.

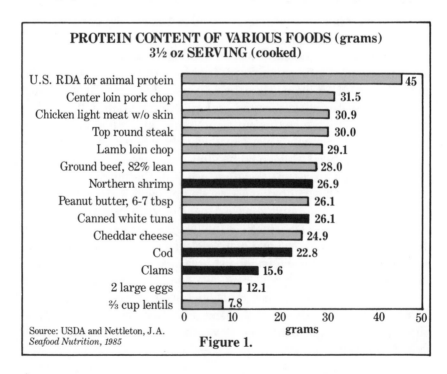

Figure 1.

Most animal foods have what nutritionists call complete protein. That means they supply all the amino acids we need to make proteins. Certain of the amino acids we need cannot be made by our bodies. Those we cannot make ourselves, the essential ones, we must obtain from foods. Most animal proteins supply all the essential amino acids.

Vegetables and grains also have protein but are usually short in one or more essential amino acids. We can make up for these shortcomings by eating a wide variety of foods so that none of the essentials is missing. Eating small amounts of animal foods in a largely vegetarian diet ensures that protein needs will be adequately met. This consideration is especially important for children whose small appetites and erratic eating habits may compromise their nutritional well-being.

Including seafood in a predominantly vegetarian lifestyle is wise not only in meeting protein needs but also in furnishing other scarce nutrients like iron and vitamin B_{12}. Many vegetarians find seafood an acceptable substitute for or addition to grain and vegetable dishes. It is tasty nutritional insurance.

Seafood Oils Are Good For You

As a mealtime mainstay, seafood outshines most of its protein rivals because it comes without any detriment from its fat. In fact, its oils are beneficial. Not only are most species of fish low in the total amount of fat they have, they are low in saturated fat, the kind of fat that promotes heart disease. People can enjoy generous servings of seafood without consuming large quantities of fat that supply excess calories and raise blood *lipid* levels.

Figure 2 (next page) shows how some popular species of fish and shellfish compare with poultry, red meats and cheese in terms of fat. Most of the richer species of fish have no more fat than the leanest meats. Most fish have less than 5 percent fat while all shellfish have less than 2 percent fat. Only skinless poultry can compare with that. With weight and health considerations influencing many people's food choices, the fat advantage alone puts seafood at the top of the list.

Seafood is not just low in its total amount of fat, it has the kind of fat that is health-promoting. Most animal foods are rich in saturated fats – the kind that raise blood cholesterol levels and encourage the clogging of blood vessels. Seafood is low in such saturated

5

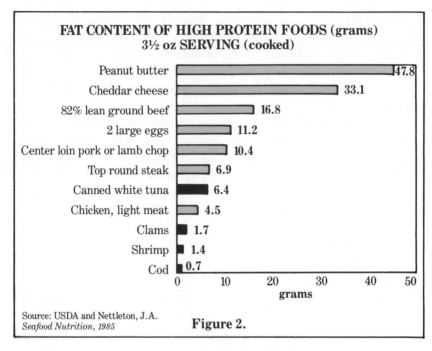

FAT CONTENT OF HIGH PROTEIN FOODS (grams)
3½ oz SERVING (cooked)

Peanut butter — 47.8
Cheddar cheese — 33.1
82% lean ground beef — 16.8
2 large eggs — 11.2
Center loin pork or lamb chop — 10.4
Top round steak — 6.9
Canned white tuna — 6.4
Chicken, light meat — 4.5
Clams — 1.7
Shrimp — 1.4
Cod — 0.7

grams: 0 10 20 30 40 50

Source: USDA and Nettleton, J.A.
Seafood Nutrition, 1985   **Figure 2.**

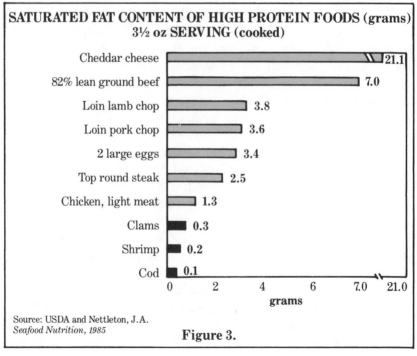

SATURATED FAT CONTENT OF HIGH PROTEIN FOODS (grams)
3½ oz SERVING (cooked)

Cheddar cheese — 21.1
82% lean ground beef — 7.0
Loin lamb chop — 3.8
Loin pork chop — 3.6
2 large eggs — 3.4
Top round steak — 2.5
Chicken, light meat — 1.3
Clams — 0.3
Shrimp — 0.2
Cod — 0.1

grams: 0 2 4 6 7.0 21.0

Source: USDA and Nettleton, J.A.
Seafood Nutrition, 1985   **Figure 3.**

fats. Instead it is rich in unsaturated fats – the kind that lower blood cholesterol and lipid levels. So the oils in seafood actually help you in two ways: they are present in small amounts so they do not provide excess calories, and they are the most favorable kind. They work for you, not against you. The chart opposite shows some comparisons.

This sounds like a paradox, because it is. On one hand a major advantage of seafood is that most of it has very little fat. On the other hand, its fat is highly desirable because it apparently protects against certain diseases. Should you be seeking more of it?

Many people answer this question with a resounding yes. But right now the answer is more complicated than we would like. For instance, if fat intake remains as high as it is for most Americans, could the consumption of omega-3s from fish be helpful? We really do not know. How beneficial these fats may be in the face of an overwhelming amount of fat from grains, meats, dairy foods and vegetable oils is simply not known. In low fat lifestyles, however, there is evidence that such oils are beneficial. Probably we need to seek less fat from all foods along with a greater share of our remaining fat intake from seafood.

We do know that using more seafood instead of meats, poultry and dairy foods can effectively lower total fat intake, something most of us need to do. Seafood will only lower total fat intake, however, if you do not fry it, or sauce it up with rich toppings. Eating seafood in place of poultry, cheese and meat also shifts the balance of fat in the omega-3 direction. With plenty of fish in the diet you ensure that your body has a steady supply of omega-3s to influence its cellular activities. There is every reason to believe that it is highly favorable.

Where's the Fat?

Fish handle their body fats in different ways, depending on the species of fish and environmental conditions. Many fish store fat only in their liver. The muscle tissue of these fish, the part we eat, is very lean. Examples of such fish are cod, pollock and flounder. Some fat is stored under the skin and along the lateral line but much of this is removed in filleting.

Other fish store fat throughout the muscle tissue, particularly in sections with red muscle fibers. Such fish as mackerel, swordfish and salmon are known as rich-fleshed fish for this reason.

7

LOCATION OF FAT IN THE FISH AND RETAIL FORMS OF FISH

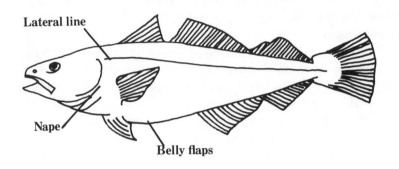

- Belly flaps
- Nape
- Sections closest to head

- Dark red portions
- Lateral line
- Just under skin

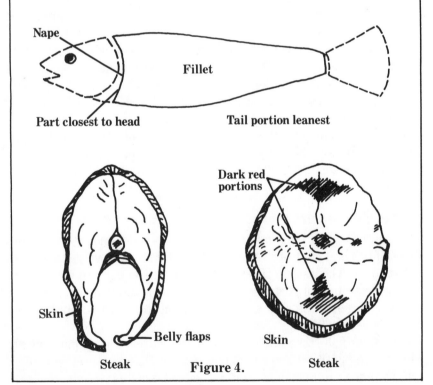

Figure 4.

Regardless of the species, some fat is usually found just below the skin and along the lateral line. The belly flaps and nape area just behind the head are also higher in fat but these may be cut away when the fish is filleted or steaked. (These sections may be used in some processed fish products). The diagram in Figure 4 shows the locations of the fat in most fish.

If you are trying to obtain as little fat as possible from fish, choose the lean species (see Table 1) and shellfish. Trim away the skin after the fish has been cooked and do not eat the red muscle or belly flap sections. Select portions closest to the tail as these are the leanest. And do not fry.

Except for the dark red muscle fibers, color is not a reliable guide to fat content. Fish vary enormously in their total fat content – as much as twenty fold – according to species, sex, season, geography, sexual maturity and environmental conditions. Most estimates of fat content are averages of widely differing values. The individual fish you buy can have an amount of fat entirely different from that given in tables of nutrient composition.

Farm-raised fish are more uniform in body composition than those captured from the wild. That is because they are fed a uniform diet, have limited mobility and a short life span. Their body composition does vary, according to sexual maturity and feed.

Usually the diet of farmed fish is based on cereal grains and cereal oils, not sea life. Not surprisingly, the fats of such fish are often very low in omega-3 fatty acids. Depending on the species of fish the feed may include some sea products but details of the diet and body composition of farmed fish are scarce.

Cholesterol Content of Seafood

This subject is discussed in detail in Chapter Four. In summary, most fish are very low in cholesterol, even the fattier species. They are comparable to or better than most protein rich foods we eat in abundance. Virtually all fish is excellent for heart-healthy eating. Most shellfish too are not high in cholesterol but there are notable exceptions to this general statement.

The most recent change in our thinking about cholesterol and shellfish pertains to certain shelled molluscs: clams, oysters and mussels. These animals, once thought to be high in cholesterol, are now recognized as being very low in cholesterol. What we learned

Table 1
APPROXIMATE FAT CONTENT OF FINFISH

Less than 5% Fat

Cod	<1	Flounder	1.2	Atlantic whiting	2.2
Lemon Sole	<1	Red snapper	1.2	Pacific halibut	2.2
Black grouper	<1	Walleye pike	1.2	Yellowfin tuna	2.5
Orange roughy	<1	Sole	1.3	Brook trout	2.5
Red hake	<1	Red grouper	1.3	Skipjack tuna	2.7
Haddock	<1	Black drum	1.5	Ocean perch	2.8
Cusk	<1	Monkfish	1.5	Wolffish	2.9
Lingcod	<1	Bigeye tuna	1.6	Barracuda	3.1
Pollock	<1	Pacific whiting	1.6	Porgy, scup	3.2
Blue shark	<1	Atlantic croaker	1.7	Weakfish	3.5
Northern pike	<1	Jack mackerel	1.8	Atlantic halibut	3.6
Mahimahi	<1	Black sea bass	1.9	Striped mullet	3.7
Yellow perch	1.0	Spotted sea trout	1.9	Chum salmon	4.2
Red drum	1.0	Pacific pompano	2.0	Swordfish	4.4
Rockfish	1.0	Bass, freshwater	2.0	Channel catfish	4.4
Lake perch	1.1	Smelt	2.1	Pacific mackerel	4.8
Yellowtail flounder	1.2	Striped bass	2.2	Pink salmon	5.0
Tilefish	1.2	Crevalle jack	2.2		

5.1 – 10.0% Fat

Bonito	5.5	Coho salmon	6.6	Carp	8.5
Atlantic salmon	5.6	Sardine	6.8	Whitefish	9.0
Rainbow trout	5.8	Albacore	7.2	Lake trout	9.4
Spanish mackerel	5.9	Arctic char	7.9	Atl. pompano	9.5
Spot	6.1	Sockeye salmon	7.9	Pacific herring	9.8
Bluefin tuna	6.1	Atlantic herring	8.0		
Bluefish	6.5	Capelin	8.2		

More than 10.0% Fat

Atl. mackerel	10.7	Spiny dogfish	11.4	Sablefish	14.2
Lake sturgeon	10.8	Chub mackerel	11.5	American eel	15.8
Butterfish	11.2	Shad	12.5	Buffalo	16.6
King salmon	11.4	King mackerel	13.0		

Note: Fat content varies widely with the species, geographic location, season, analysis etc. Fat content is usually higher in the dark meat portions. Use these figures only as a guide.

Source: Nettleton, Joyce A. *Seafood Nutrition*. 1985
Osprey Books, Huntington, NY and USDA
Provisional Table HNIS/PT-103, 1986.

recently is that they contain some plant *sterols*, once mistaken for cholesterol. These plant sterols are not absorbed by us and actually interfere with the uptake of cholesterol. In fact, their presence reduces the cholesterol we get and that is a bonus.

Vitamins in Seafood

Seafood is an important source of several B vitamins we cannot live without. B vitamins assist in the processing of energy coming from the foods we eat, and are used by cells performing their biochemical tasks. Very few foods have large amounts of these nutrients. We rely on a variety of foods each supplying small amounts to make up the total we need. Because our bodies do not store these vitamins we need a fresh supply every day. Many seafoods, especially the dark fleshed species like mackerel and Atlantic bluefish,* are the richest sources of these vitamins.

Seafood is rich in pyridoxine, a B vitamin we use in metabolizing amino acids from protein. It is also one of the best sources of niacin, a B vitamin necessary for obtaining cellular energy from carbohydrates. Vitamin B_{12} is abundant in many seafoods and this cobalt-containing vitamin is required for healthy red blood cells. Vitamin B_{12} is also exceptional in that it is a water soluble vitamin that is stored in the liver.

Many seafoods have moderate amounts of other B vitamins, including riboflavin, folacin and pantothenic acid. A few milligrams here and there do not look like much, but they can make the critical difference to obtaining an adequate diet. Among such population groups as the elderly, adolescents and some children, where food habits and intakes are inconsistent and risky, the regular intake of seafood can make a critical and positive difference to nutritional welfare.

The other water soluble vitamin of importance is vitamin C or ascorbic acid. Seafoods do not have useful amounts of this vitamin. Eat green peppers and broccoli for your supply.

The remaining vitamins to consider are the fat soluble ones, A,D, E and K. As a general observation, seafood is not a good source of these nutrients. But there are exceptions.

Fish muscle, the part most of us eat, and shellfish have only small amounts of the fat soluble vitamins. This is not surprising as

---

*Note that the fish often wrongly labeled "Boston bluefish" is actually Atlantic pollock, which is a lean fish unrelated to bluefish.

most fish and all shellfish are low in fat. Even the fattier fish like salmon and mackerel do not have large amounts of these vitamins.

Fish livers, by contrast, are enormously rich in vitamins A and D. In fact, the amounts may be so great as to be toxic. Usually fish liver oil preparations, such as those readily available over the counter, contain large amounts of these vitamins. Because they are stored in the body it is easy to accumulate an overdose of these vitamins by taking fish oil supplements. It is better to get your vitamin A from carrots and dark green leafy vegetables than from bottled preparations.

Vitamin D is naturally present in large amounts in fish liver and in almost no other food. Its presence in fish liver oil is remembered, distastefully, as the way we conquered rickets in the late 1800s and early part of this century. Rickets is a serious deficiency disease where the lack of vitamin D prevents normal calcium metabolism and results in bone deformities.

Nowadays vitamin D is thought of more as a hormone than a vitamin. It is important for the calcium metabolism of bones and teeth. Too much is definitely toxic. Most of us obtain adequate vitamin D from sunshine and fortified milk.

It is easy to obtain harmful quantities of vitamins A and D by taking fish liver oil preparations. If you must take these preparations, buy one that has had the vitamin content stripped or reduced. As a guide, take no more than the *Recommended Dietary Allowance* for vitamin A which is a maximum of 1000 retinol equivalents.* The maximum vitamin D you should consume in one dose is 400 International Units. Your food will also provide some of these vitamins.

Regarding the remaining fat soluble vitamins E and K, seafood is not a useful source. Vitamin E is important in protecting some kinds of fats, especially unsaturated ones, from being oxidized or broken down. For this reason we might expect it to be important in protecting omega-3s. So far we have no indication that vitamin E metabolism is affected by the consumption of large quantities of omega-3s or that eating lots of fish raises vitamin E requirements. It is a consideration worth remembering though.

Vitamin K is important for proper blood clotting but is present

---

*Equivalent to 1 milligram (mg) of retinol or 5000 International Units in the old system of reckoning.

in fish in small amounts only. We obtain most of our supply from the bacteria in our intestinal tract.

Minerals in Abundance

Seafood is sometimes overlooked as a mineral resource except when discussing one's alleged prowess after a round at the oyster bar. Oysters aside, many seafoods have valuable amounts of iron, zinc and copper which are frequently in short supply in many people's food habits. These three minerals are needed for making healthy and numerous red blood cells. They are also part of certain enzymes or proteins that assist the body's biochemistry.

While liver, organ and red meats remain the richest source of **iron,** many fish and shellfish are a good source of this mineral. In particular bonito, mackerel, bluefish, sardines, clams, oysters and mussels have over 2 milligrams of iron in 3½ ounces. Clams, oysters and mussels are especially rich in iron. Eating a variety of seafoods on a regular basis can do a great deal to boost iron values. This is especially important for women and should be encouraged whenever possible.

Recently, people have become aware of the links between **calcium** and osteoporosis, a bone disease prevalent among elderly women. Lowfat dairy foods are the best source of this mineral but a few seafoods are also rich in calcium. Fish with small soft bones that can be readily and safely eaten have the most calcium. These fish are smelts, canned salmon and sardines. Other fish and shellfish do not have useful amounts of calcium.

Phosphorus, by contrast with calcium, is abundant in all seafoods. Most of us obtain sufficient phosphorus as it is widely used in food processing.

Magnesium, a third mineral important for bone metabolism, is abundant in certain seafoods. Anchovies, periwinkles, canned tuna and freshwater catfish head the list of rich sources of magnesium.

There is a whole host of **trace minerals** – elements needed in tiny amounts – important for a variety of body functions. Some of these minerals, for example selenium, are being intensively studied for their possible protective functions against some cancers. Many trace minerals are found in greatest abundance in seafoods, especially the molluscs we eat whole (clams, mussels and oysters). **Fluorine, iodine** and **selenium** are good examples.

13

The more dangerous trace elements like **arsenic** and **cadmium** are also most concentrated in seafoods but their presence has not been associated with any health problems. The FDA monitors the levels of these minerals in seafoods and will seize any products found to contain harmful levels.

Finally, **mercury** has received much attention as a possible health hazard in certain seafoods. There is no doubt that it caused serious disease in Japan and parts of Canada where fish from mercury contaminated waters were consumed in large amounts. Once the origin and nature of the problem were discovered, governments took steps to control the dumping of industrial wastes and prevent the consumption of fish from polluted areas. The problem also led to the development of a fisheries monitoring program to ensure that fish with dangerous levels of contaminants did not reach the food supply.

Mercury occurs in certain species of fish, occasionally in large amounts. Its presence is the result of young fish, usually bottom feeders, surviving in waters contaminated by certain kinds of industrial wastes. These small fish are eaten by larger fish, a process that concentrates the mineral upward through the food chain. That is why, for example, large, long-lived fish like swordfish may accumulate high levels of mercury.

The government now regularly tests species of fish known to concentrate mercury. Any fish with mercury in excess of one part per million of methylmercury (the major biological form of mercury) is prohibited from being sold. If fishing grounds yield large numbers of contaminated fish they may be closed to fishing.

State and federal government agencies have found no evidence of human health hazard from mercury in fish under the present system of regulation. Your safest bet is to buy your fish from a reputable dealer who obtains his fish from reliable fishermen catching fish in safe waters. Any risk of consuming mercury is reduced if you do not eat the dark red muscle portions of the flesh. Similarly, not eating fish viscera or liver oils, where most contaminants are located, protects you from possible exposure to nasty substances. Finally, eating a variety of species of fish reduces your chance of obtaining undesirable materials related to one or two species.

Bringing Seafood's Nutritional Virtues to the Table

Enjoying all the nutritional advantages of seafood depends on two approaches: preventing nutrient loss during storage and cooking and preparing seafood to enhance rather than undermine its virtues. The first of these is relatively simple. Most of the nutrients in seafood are stable and resistant to loss in normal storage and handling. Fresh seafood loses few nutrients during one or two days storage in the refrigerator. Frozen seafood tightly wrapped and kept well below freezing temperature, that is as close to 0°F. as possible, retains virtually all of its nutrients too. Frozen seafood kept longer than about three months may lose nutrients gradually but losses are more related to storage conditions and holding temperatures than to storage time.

Some B vitamins are rather fragile. They do not hold up well to heat or cooking, air, storage or processing. The best example of this instability is thiamin. As much as 80 percent of the vitamin may be lost during canning. On the other hand, home cooking is less damaging and thiamin losses seldom exceed 10 percent. Seafoods have only modest amounts of thiamin at best, so processing losses may not be a critical health issue. Where variety of foods is severely limited, however, every little bit counts.

Water soluble vitamins are usually well retained during most cooking procedures, except poaching or boiling in large amounts of liquid. With large volumes of liquid, vitamins may be leached out. Unless the liquid is consumed, as it would be in a soup, appreciable amounts of vitamins could be lost. It is always a good idea to find a way of incorporating the cooking liquid into the meal or the next day's chowder.

Baking, broiling, grilling, steaming, microwaving and stir-frying all promote the retention of vitamins because they use small volumes of liquid, if any at all, and they require short cooking times. Both features of these cooking methods preserve nutritional value because the vitamins have little opportunity to be destroyed or discarded.

Vitamins can be lost during storage if air comes in contact with the seafood. Oxygen in the air can destroy certain vitamins and promote the breakdown of other tissue components, especially the fat. For this reason, frozen seafood needs to be tightly wrapped with moisture-proof material, excluding as much air as possible. As with all frozen foods, a short storage time ensures the greatest nutrient retention.

Minerals are unlike vitamins in that they are nearly all well retained in storage and cooking. Only when they have been leached out of the flesh and discarded with the cooking liquid are their quantities diminished.

Fats are usually well preserved during freezing but some oxidation or breakdown can occur. For that reason, it is usually recommended that oilier fish be used more quickly than leaner varieties. There are species differences in keeping quality as well. Salmon freezes and holds well for months while Atlantic bluefish does less satisfactorily.

Cooking seafood presents opportunities to lose nutrients or to add ingredients not in the best interests of good health. Cooking losses occur when nutrients are destroyed or thrown away with the cooking liquid. High temperatures and long cooking times are most destructive of nutrients. With seafood, however, the best flavor, tenderness and nutrition are obtained with short cooking times. Because nutrients are well retained in seafood with usual cooking methods, you have to be rather deliberate about compromising nutrients for losses to be substantial. It is hard to go wrong.

Adding ingredients against your best health wishes is easier to do. Such goodies as butter based sauces, cream of all kinds, large amounts of cheese, salt and prepared seasoning mixes contribute saturated fat, cholesterol and sodium. These ingredients (except for salt) also add excessive calories. It is not so much that the original nutrients in seafood are in jeopardy from these additions but that the whole nutritional worth of the seafood preparation is undermined. Where seafood started out low in fat it becomes high in fat. Where unsaturated fats predominated, saturated, less healthy ones, prevail. Where cholesterol was low, it may be moderately high. Where sodium level was low it is now high. Who needs these detrimental changes?

Seafood and Health offers practical suggestions for preparing delicious seafood without these unwanted nutritional hazards. The recipes in this book are easy to prepare, are flavored with herbs, vegetables and ingredients low in sodium and use very little fat. This approach preserves the nutritional merits of seafood and all the good taste with easy preparations. And it gives you reasons for following your own good sense about seafood.

The Nutritional Virtues of Seafood

• Low in calories – many species have fewer than 150 calories for a 3 ounce cooked serving. You can safely eat larger servings without exceeding your calorie budget.

- Low in fat – most species have less than 5 percent fat. All shellfish have less than 2 percent fat. Only skinless poultry can compare with that.

- Low in saturated fat – the oil in fish is rich in polyunsaturated fatty acids, the kind that keep blood vessels healthy.

- Source of omega-3s – these are highly unsaturated fatty acids that appear to protect against heart disease and certain other health problems. Long chain omega-3s are found only in fish and shellfish.

- Low in cholesterol – most species of fish have less than 100 milligrams of cholesterol per 3½ ounces (raw). Oysters, clams, mussels and scallops are very low in cholesterol. A few shellfish, namely squid, most shrimp, abalone, octopus and razor clams are fairly high in cholesterol. So is fish roe. (See Chapter Four).

- Low in sodium – fresh, unprocessed seafood has very little sodium. Canned, smoked, salted or pickled seafood is usually very high in sodium. Shellfish have somewhat more sodium than finfish, but this modest difference is not an issue for most people.

- High in protein – fish and shellfish proteins have all the essential amino acids we need, making them top quality protein. They are easily digested because there is very little connective tissue.

- B vitamins – seafood is an important source of niacin, pyridoxine and vitamin B_{12}. It also has a good supply of riboflavin, folacin and pantothenic acid. All these nutrients are vital for processing energy.

- Minerals – many shellfish and dark fleshed fish have abundant amounts of iron. Clams, mussels and oysters are especially rich in iron. Seafood is also rich in phosphorus and magnesium. Canned salmon with its bones and canned sardines are rich in calcium.

- Trace minerals – seafood is the best source of many minerals we need in only tiny amounts: zinc, selenium, fluoride, copper and iodine.

Chapter Two

Seafood, Omega-3s and Heart Disease

Early Observations on Dietary Fat and Health

Despite decades devoted to studying the relationship between diet and heart disease, why were the effects of fish oils overlooked for so long? To answer this question, we need to look back on how our thoughts about dietary fats developed.

About 1930, G.O. Burr and M.M. Burr, who were researchers at the University of Minnesota, discovered substances in fat that were essential for normal growth and development. These substances were called *essential fatty acids**. At least two fatty acids, possibly three, are essential for proper development. The two essentials are *linoleic acid* and *arachidonic acid*. Since the body can make arachidonic acid from linoleic acid, our food need supply only linoleic acid in order to meet our needs. Linoleic acid is especially abundant in certain vegetable oils, and rather scarce in animal fats.

A third fatty acid, *linolenic*, was not considered to be essential until recently. Now there is evidence from two people living entirely on artificial feeding solutions that linolenic acid is necessary for normal nerve and muscle function. Because linolenic acid is also an omega-3 fatty acid, there is keen interest in re-examining the function of this overlooked molecule.

The discovery of essential fatty acids made it clear that not all

---

*Words printed in italics are defined in the Glossary at the end of the book. Only the first occurrence of the word is italicized.

fats were created equal. Emphasis in nutrition shifted toward ensuring an adequate supply of essential fatty acids even though it was clear that only a few grams, a small fraction of an ounce, were needed to prevent deficiency. Fortunately, essential fatty acids are abundant in our food supply and shortage is not ordinarily a problem.

The discovery of essential fatty acids also changed our understanding about the desirability of different food fats. In the 1960s, landmark studies showed that fats rich in saturated fatty acids raised blood cholesterol levels. Those rich in *polyunsaturated* fatty acids lowered cholesterol levels. Blood cholesterol level was aleady suspect in heart disease, the country's leading cause of death.

Awareness of the response of blood cholesterol to the various types of fats we eat spawned a whole series of investigations into the relationships between diet and health. Probably the best known outcome of the diet and heart research has been the idea that animal fats, those rich in saturated fats, promote heart disease by raising blood lipids while vegetable oils, those rich in unsaturated fats, lower blood lipids. With these studies came improvements in our ability to predict risk of heart disease based on measurements of blood lipids.

About the time that vegetable oils came into vogue a few observations about fish oils were reported, but these were largely overlooked. There were simply not enough observations on enough people to call attention to the powerful effects of fish oils on blood lipid levels. The differences in chemical structure between vegetable oils and fish oils were known but went unappreciated. Corn and soybean oils reigned.

Studies from the 1970s and '80s led scientists to revise their thinking about unsaturated fatty acids. The breakthrough observations about fish oils came in the late 1970s with the realization that not all polyunsaturates were created equal. Now, there is tremendous momentum in the research community to understand how the special fatty acids in fish oils are working in the body. Recognition that the polyunsaturated fatty acids in fish oil behave differently from the well known vegetable oil polyunsaturates has shattered the comfortable notion that polyunsaturates are all roughly the same.

Before continuing the story of how fish oils captured the headlines, there was one other development that took place during the

1960s and '70s that served to enshrine vegetable oils as the dietary path to lower blood lipids. This was the development and promotion of the idea of P:S ratios to express the relative amounts of polyunsaturated to saturated fatty acids in a fat.

The Push for P:S Ratios

In the period between our enchantment with polyunsaturated vegetable oils and the discovery of the healthful effects of fish oils, people were encouraged to consume vegetable oils. Between 1963 and 1980, United States Department of Agriculture figures showed that the consumption of vegetable oil in the USA rose 57.6 percent while the intake of animal fat decreased by 38.8 percent. Most health professionals would regard this change as favorable, in spite of the fact that the total amount of fat we consume has not diminished. Americans consume a whopping 40 percent of their energy from fat.

As part of the effort to persuade people to eat vegetable oils instead of animal fats, a system was devised to help people identify fats, especially margarines, rich in polyunsaturated fatty acids. This concept was the P:S ratio. The P:S ratio expresses the amount of (poly)unsaturated fatty acids (P) in a fat relative to its content of saturated fatty acids (S). Fats with equal amounts of each type would have a P:S ratio of 1. Those having predominantly polyunsaturated fats would have P:S ratios greater than one, while those with mostly saturated fatty acids would have ratios less than one. Nice simple system – just look for a P:S ratio greater than one.

Not so simple. The ratios are practically useless unless the distribution of all the fat among polyunsaturated, saturated and monounsaturated fat is considered. For example, if most of the fat is comprised of *monounsaturated* fat, as is the case in some stick margarines and olive oil, then the P:S ratio of the remaining portion may be unimportant. Olive oil, for example, has a P:S ratio of 0.6 but this accounts for only 30 percent of its fatty acid content. Furthermore, recent research suggests that olive oil probably does not have the adverse effects on blood lipids one would expect from its low P:S ratio.

A more serious drawback of focusing on P:S ratios is the assumption that all polyunsaturated fatty acids were created equal as far as health is concerned. That notion is simplistic. With the developments in omega-3 fatty acid research it is clear that vegetable polyunsaturated fatty acids have entirely different metabolic consequences from omega-3s. The P:S ratio of most fish oils is about one and this figure does not give a hint of the health advantages of omega-3s. In fact, it is misleading.

Another problem with P:S ratios is that information about the fat composition of many foods is not available. Nutrition labeling is a voluntary program that not all food manufacturers participate in. Even if a product does carry nutrition information on its label, manufacturers do not have to disclose details about the composition of the fat in the product. Usually, only very large food companies can afford to obtain these data and it is seldom in their own interests to publish information that might reflect poorly on their goods.

In their favor, however, P:S ratios can be useful in comparing similar amounts of fat where the distribution of fatty acids among saturated, mono and polyunsaturated fatty acids is known. Those fats with the highest P:S ratios have the most polyunsaturated fats. The ratio says nothing about the kind of polyunsaturated fats present.

The effect of the P:S ratio concept has been to obscure the relative importance of fish oils compared with vegetable oils. The P:S ratio for most available oils in fish comes out around one. That does not look nearly as impressive as the P:S ratio of 8 such as some safflower oil possesses. The concept of P:S ratios completely overlooks the fact that safflower oil cannot achieve the biological effects of fish oil.

But the P:S ratio concept persists. Currently the Food and Drug Administration is conducting a practical trial to see if labeling food fats with P:S ratios will make food choices easier for consumers. The question is, will it make them wiser?

The Seafood Story Unfolds

In the 1970s a group of Danish investigators began looking into the exceptional observations that had been reported about a group of Eskimos living in northwestern Greenland. These Eskimos had virtually no heart disease yet their foods were just as high in protein and fat as those of Europeans and Americans. Was there something unique about Eskimos or their way of life that protected them from the scourge of heart disease?

Among Eskimos, not only was heart and blood vessel disease extremely rare, so were a number of other diseases common in Western societies. For example, Greenland Eskimos had very little diabetes, multiple sclerosis, bronchial asthma, thyrotoxicosis, psoriasis, arthritis, kidney disease, breast cancer and peptic ulcer. On the other hand, Eskimos had more stroke and epilepsy than Danes or other Westerners. The historical record also described Eskimos as "bleeders" – people whose blood did not clot readily in wound healing, people who bruised easily. Were these observations related to their diet?

Clues From the Eskimo Diet

The Danish researchers, H. O. Bang and J. Dyerberg, analyzed the traditional Eskimo diet, took biochemical and clinical measurements and conducted feeding studies. They did their work among Danes, Greenland Eskimos and Eskimos living in Denmark. This approach gave them several kinds of data and different ways of comparing their findings. Their observations about the traditional Eskimo diet were striking.

The traditional Greenland Eskimo diet (no longer consumed by Eskimos) was based on sea mammals and fish. The Eskimo diet, like ours, was high in protein and fat and even higher in cholesterol. One of the major differences between Eskimo and Danish foods however, was that Eskimo foods had a larger share of polyunsaturated fats. More striking yet was the finding that the kind of polyunsaturated fats in the two groups was totally different. Most of the polyunsaturated fats in the Eskimo diet contained the omega-3 class of fatty acids whereas Danish polyunsaturated fats were largely of the *omega-6* type. (For more details, see the following section and the glossary).

These differences could be explained by the kinds of foods usually consumed by each group. Eskimos eat marine animals, seals, whales and fish, rich in omega-3 polyunsaturated fatty acids. Danes eat meat and dairy products with vegetables and grains being the main source of their polyunsaturated fatty acids. Close scrutiny of the customary diets of Eskimos and Danes revealed an important difference in fat composition that has had profound consequences.

To understand the nature of this difference in fat composition and how it might be important for our health we need to see how fats are made. Eventually it is up to the biochemists to figure out how such differences work to our benefit. But they have some good ideas about that now.

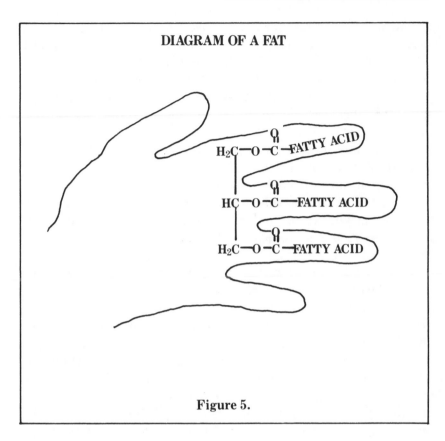

DIAGRAM OF A FAT

Figure 5.

What Are Omega-3 Fatty Acids?

Picture, if you will, a molecule of fat. You need one hand and three fingers to do so. Make a fist; then extend three fingers on one hand. Think of each finger as a chain of carbon atoms with hydrogen atoms attached all along. In a fat, each finger or carbon chain corresponds to a fatty acid. And each fat has three of these fatty acids. Just as your fingers are differ slightly from each other, so fatty acids vary. The differences in fingers (fatty acids) account for individual fats.

Now imagine the knuckle at the bottom of each finger as one carbon atom. These three knuckles correspond to the carbon skeleton of the fat. This carbon skeleton is the backbone that holds the three fatty acids together. This backbone is called *glycerol*.

Differences among fatty acids are important. If a fatty acid has all the hydrogen atoms it can carry it is called saturated. It is full (of hydrogen). Saturated fats are those with a large proportion of saturated fatty acids. They are solid at room temperature and are found abundantly in animal foods. Familiar examples are butter, lard, and the fat in beef. A few vegetable fats, notably coconut and palm oil and certain hydrogenated vegetable oils, are also rich in saturated fatty acids. Saturated fats raise blood cholesterol levels, increasing risk of heart disease.

Some fatty acids are missing hydrogen atoms. For this reason they are called unsaturated. If they miss only one pair of hydrogens they are monounsaturated. Olive oil has primarily monounsaturated fatty acids. If they miss two or more pairs of hydrogens they are called polyunsaturated. The site where a pair of hydrogens is missing is called a *double bond*. Fatty acids are often described in terms of how many double bonds they have. The more double bonds, the more unsaturated. Fats rich in polyunsaturated fatty acids tend to lower blood cholesterol levels, reducing risk of heart disease.

The essential fatty acid linoleic acid has two pairs of hydrogens missing from its carbon chain, that is, it has two double bonds. It is abundant in vegetable oils like safflower, corn, soybean and walnut.

There are two other ways fatty acids differ from each other besides number of hydrogen pairs. One is the length of the fatty acid chain or the number of carbon atoms. The other is the location of the missing hydrogen atoms. Fish fatty acids differ from vegetable fatty acids in these respects too. For a simplified diagram of the basic structure of the different kinds of fatty acids, see the Glossary.

Again look at your three fingers. Just as they differ slightly in length so do fatty acid chains. Most vegetable polyunsaturated fatty acids have eighteen carbon atoms. By contrast, however, fish oil polyunsaturates have twenty or twenty-two carbon atoms. They are longer.

Now think of the joints on each finger as possible sites for hydrogens to disappear. In most polyunsaturated vegetable fatty acids the hydrogens are missing roughly where your middle joint is. This is the six position, six carbons away from the end of the chain. In fish oils however, the first double bond (missing pair of hydrogen atoms) occurs at the joint closest to your finger nail. This is the three position, three carbons from the end.

And the name omega-3?* The omega is the distant or finger nail end of the fatty acid molecule, the end that is not acidic. Chemists call it the methyl end. The 3 corresponds to your farthest joint, the one closest to your finger nail (omega end of the molecule). The three position is the location of the first missing pair of hydrogens. This naming system gives rise to classes of polyunsaturated fatty acids, mainly omega-3 (fish) and omega-6 (plant). We have it on good authority that chemists really do count on their fingers. They also name molecules in ways only they understand.

Where Do Omega-3 Fatty Acids Come From?

Only animals that are part of the food chain from the sea have these long chain omega-3 fatty acids. That is because these substances are made in the first place by phytoplankton – the tiny aquatic plants that serve as food for small fish and produce oxygen for the atmosphere. Our bodies have the ability to make small quantities of these fatty acids too, but apparently we make very little.

Actually, a few plant oils have small amounts of linolenic acid, which is an omega-3 fatty acid. This particular omega-3 fatty acid has fewer double bonds and is shorter than the omega-3 fatty acids in fish. It does not behave metabolically in the body in the same way fish oil omega-3 fatty acids do but it can be converted to the type of omega-3s found in seafood. So, technically speaking, some omega-3 fatty acid is found in a few plants. In this book, however, the term refers exclusively to the omega-3 fatty acids found in seafood.

Heart Disease

The dietary findings about omega-3 fatty acids were supported by observations on blood and tissues of Eskimos and Danes. Omega-3 fatty acids were abundant in Eskimo tissues and virtually absent in Danes. As expected, omega-6 fatty acids were correspondingly low

*Scientists prefer the more precise nomenclature of n-3, n-6 etc. instead of the term omega-3, but n-3 and omega-3 are totally interchangeable.

in Eskimos and high among Danes. Since omega-3 fatty acids were found in tissues, it meant they could be available for metabolic and physiologic activities. The differences in diet could be translated into meaningful health consequences.

Bang, Dyerberg and their colleagues were soon able to correlate their observations about diet and omega-3s with differences in blood clotting among Eskimos and Danes. Importantly, when they compared their findings from Greenland Eskimos with those of Eskimos living in Denmark and with Danes, they found that Eskimos in Denmark resembled Danes, not their Greenland compatriots. These results meant that their observations were not due to genetic differences between Eskimos and Danes but rather to environmental factors. Diet remained high on the priority list for explaining the findings.

Bang and Dyerberg put forward the proposition that the omega-3 fatty acids abundant in Eskimo foods were responsible for the reduced blood clotting common in Eskimos. Furthermore, they reasoned that if the blood clots less readily, blockage of blood vessels leading to *heart attack* will be less likely. We now know from many additional studies that omega-3 fatty acids work in a variety of ways to discourage blood clot formation, thereby reducing one of the major conditions of heart attack. It cannot be said to be completely proven that omega-3 fatty acids are responsible for these differences, but the evidence is in favor of that interpretation. The effects of omega-3s on blood *platelet* function is one of the strongest pieces of that evidence.

How Blood Platelet Function Relates to Heart Disease

Platelets are small cells in the blood responsible for blood clotting. It is their ability to stick together or clump that forms a clot at the site of a wound. Platelets can also stick to the lining of blood vessels that have been damaged or narrowed due to *arteriosclerosis*. When the blood flow to the heart is restricted by lipid deposits and platelet clumps, a heart attack may occur. A similar process in the brain is one cause of stroke. If the flow of blood to the heart is completely blocked, the attack is fatal. Presumably, if arteries did not narrow and clots did not form we would not have heart attacks. On the other hand, if blood did not clot we might bleed to death from cuts and wounds. The ideal activity of platelets lies somewhere between harmful and helpful blood clotting.

In heart disease, the long term narrowing and deterioration of blood vessels contributes to heart attack. When the blood flow is completely blocked, a clot is formed around a clump of platelets. In order for platelets to aggregate or clump together, however, certain substances must be present. Some of these clotting factors are made by platelets from polyunsaturated fatty acids. Cells lining the blood vessel wall make other substances that interfere with the production or action of these clotting factors. The question is, do Eskimos have anything unusual about their platelets that affects platelet clumping?

To explore this question, the Danish investigators turned their attention to the behavior of Eskimo platelets. In the vein or in the test tube, Eskimo blood took much longer to clot than blood from Danes or from expatriate Greenlanders. This reduced clotting tendency was related to a decrease in the ability of the platelets to clump or aggregate. The diminished aggregation of platelets, in turn, paralleled changes in the fatty acid composition of platelets. In Eskimos there was an increase in omega-3 fatty acids and a decrease in omega-6 derived fatty acids when compared with platelets from Danes and Eskimos living in Denmark.

The connection between changes in the fatty acid composition of platelet cell membranes and reduced blood clotting becomes important in view of the metabolic activities of platelets. Scientists think that when omega-3 fatty acids are part of platelet membranes they change the kind and amount of certain products platelets make. Platelets use the fatty acids in their membranes to make a variety of compounds for the clotting process. If fewer of the materials that promote clumping are made, then clumping is less likely. Similarly, if more substances that discourage platelet aggregation are made, clumping will be deterred.

There is strong evidence to support this interpretation of events in both platelets and blood vessel cells. When omega-3 fatty acids are available, platelets produce less of the clot-promoting material, *thromboxane* A_2. If omega-3s are available to cells lining blood vessels, these cells make more substances called *prostacyclins* that discourage blood clotting. Although the effect of omega-3s in platelets is a reduction in thromboxane A_2 output and in blood vessel cells an increase in prostacyclin production, the combined effect is less platelet clumping. These two results of having omega-3 fatty acids available in cell membranes could account for the bleeding tendency of Eskimos and possibly their lack of heart disease.

Changing Cellular Traffic Patterns with Omega-3s

As the consequences unfold of having omega-3 fatty acids about the body we wonder how these remarkable substances are working. Do they do something different in every tissue where they are found? What accelerates one system and attenuates another? Are the effects in one tissue related to those of another? Is there a connection between what is happening in heart disease and the effects on the immune system? There probably is.

Polyunsaturated fatty acids are at the center of a biochemical network that makes the Los Angeles freeway system look like meandering cowpaths. The network generates families of powerful compounds that control what happens in cells and their surroundings. At the hub of this network is a polyunsaturated fatty acid called arachidonic acid. From it two families of cellular policemen are made, the *prostaglandins* and *leukotrienes*. Which products are made from arachidonic acid determines many cell and body functions.

Arachidonic acid is made from the polyunsaturated fatty acids we eat. It also comes from meats and we make it from the dietary essential, linoleic acid. It is part of our cell membranes and is in bountiful supply. As a result, arachidonic acid has a monopoly on most of the metabolic highways open to polyunsaturated fatty acids. Only when omega-3 fatty acids or drugs like aspirin are around does the relative importance of arachidonic acid change. Omega-3s and certain drugs affect the production of prostaglandins and leukotrienes from arachidonic acid.

The fate of arachidonic acid depends on the type of cell and the prevailing conditions. In platelets, for example, arachidonic acid gives rise to a group of prostaglandins called thromboxanes which promote the clumping of platelets. The activity of the thromboxanes is counteracted by the production of another group of prostaglandins in the cells lining blood vessels. These prostaglandins, known as *prostacyclins*, discourage platelet clumping.

After a person eats fish rich in omega-3 fatty acids, omega-3s become available to participate in the same metabolic pathways usually controlled by arachidonic acid. Changes in diet actually change the fatty acid composition of our cellular membranes. Competition exists between these two kinds of fatty acids with the result that less arachidonic acid and more omega-3 fatty acid rides the metabolic highways that lead to prostaglandin and leukotriene products. In some systems omega-3s may be preferred over arachidonic acid for the production of these dynamos. When omega-3s prevail, the function of many tissues governed by prostaglandins changes. These changes lead to differences in immune responses, blood clotting, blood pressure, and perhaps even tumor development.

Prostaglandins are among the most widespread and reactive substances in the body. They are much like hormones in their activities, controlling vital processes yet present in miniscule amounts. As examples of their nearly universal influence, they affect digestive functions, reproductive processes, *immune responses*, circulatory activities and certain secretory functions. They wield extraordinary power in determining what our cells will do.

Leukotrienes, the second group of regulatory substances derived from arachidonic acid, are made by a variety of white blood cells active in our immune defense system. They are responsible for a host of reactions associated with *inflammatory* and immune responses. Leukotrienes are vastly more potent than histamine, a well known inflammatory agent. When their production is moderated, many of the unpleasant symptoms of inflammatory disease are curtailed. Scientists are working on harnessing these substances for our benefit. There is more about these compounds in Chapter Three.

The effects of fish oil omega-3 fatty acids on platelet function can be summarized as follows. When we eat seafood rich in omega-3 fatty acids omega-3s become part of platelet membranes. Once there, the omega-3s compete with arachidonic acid for conversion to various prostaglandins, notably thromboxanes. In the presence of omega-3s, less thromboxane A_2 is produced, an effect that discourages platelets from clumping together. When platelets are less likely to clump they are also less likely to form blood clots that can block the flow of blood to the heart or brain.

By a similar mechanism of becoming part of cell membranes, omega-3 fatty acids encourage the production of prostacyclin by the cells lining the blood vessel walls. Increased amounts of prostacylcin inhibit platelet clumping as well, adding to the effect of omega-3s on platelets themselves. These two effects work together to make it less likely for blood clots to form in blood vessels.

What Are Blood Lipids?

Most of us are familiar with the request for a blood sample as part of a routine health check-up. Levels of various substances in blood reflect health status. Measurements in blood are also an important part of determining risk of heart disease because they provide vital information about how our body handles compounds that contribute to heart disease. Some of the most important substances related to heart disease are lipids – a group of compounds that includes cholesterol, fat, and *lipoproteins*. The more lipids in the blood the richer the supply of materials for building up harmful deposits in blood vessels.

Doctors may talk about a person's "lipid profile" meaning the pattern of several lipid substances in the blood. Because the term "lipid" includes more than just fats, as scientists define them, the term lipid is the more accurate one to use. It is less familiar to most people, though, and the word fat is often inappropriately used instead.

Patterns of blood lipids are based on the distribution of cholesterol and fat (*triglyceride*) among different lipoproteins (see Chapter Four for more discussion of lipoproteins and cholesterol). Lipoproteins are the special carriers of lipids in blood and are distinguished from one another by their density. The shorthand names of the three lipoproteins related to heart disease are *VLDL* (very low density lipoproteins), *LDL* (low density lipoproteins) and *HDL* (high density lipoproteins). All of these terms are described in the Glossary.

Certain patterns of blood lipoproteins are strongly associated with increased risk of heart disease. The most notorious of these is a pattern of very high LDL or low density lipoprotein. The most favorable pattern is one with low total cholesterol (less than 200 milligrams per deciliter) and relatively high HDL or high density lipoprotein fraction compared with the LDL fraction.

Blood lipids are affected by what we eat. The amount and kind of fat we eat, as well as the amount of cholesterol, influence the pattern of lipids in the blood. Heredity, sex, age, exercise and other factors are also important in determining the amount of lipid there is and how the different lipids are distributed. Our current beliefs about heart disease endorse the idea that each of us can improve our lipid profile and so reduce our risk of heart disease by making careful food choices. Not all health professionals share this belief, but the vast majority do.

For years the emphasis in heart health has been to lower cholesterol levels since people with low cholesterol levels are much less likely to develop heart disease. As our understanding of cholesterol metabolism becomes more sophisticated, it is clear that more than total blood cholesterol is important. The distribution of cholesterol among different lipoproteins is important too. People with high levels of cholesterol in LDL are at much greater risk of heart disease than those with moderate or low LDL cholesterol levels. Recently, the presence of relatively substantial amounts of HDL has been gaining acceptance as being protective against heart disease. It is still not clear how important are the levels of VLDL, those lipoproteins that carry fat, in the risk of heart disease. High VLDL levels, however, pose a risk of pancreatitis, a very painful disease.

The Effects of Omega-3 Fatty Acids on Blood Lipids

One of the earliest and most exciting findings associated with eating rich fish like mackerel or taking fish oil supplements was a marked reduction in blood triglyceride (fat) levels. In both healthy people and those with abnormally high triglycerides, eating rich fish led to a rapid drop in triglycerides. Even in patients with extraordinarily high levels of triglycerides, consumption of fish oil restored blood triglycerides to the near normal range. In fact, the higher the blood triglyceride level, the greater the reduction. In healthy people whose triglycerides are normally quite low, the reductions were much less.

These dramatic observations heralded a new way of helping people with lipid disorders of high blood triglycerides. Previously, there had been no useful medications for such conditions. Now, although certain drugs have become available to help lower blood triglycerides, the consumption of fish oil offers a simple and effective approach to lowering triglyceride levels in people with abnormally high levels.

What the lowering of blood triglycerides means for healthy peo-

31

ple with normal triglyceride levels is not clear. There is no reason to think that further reducing normal blood fat levels will be helpful. For those people with very high triglycerides, however, the use of fish oil and fish consumption appears very encouraging. For this reason the use of fish oil supplements is probably most important as a therapeutic agent for people with high triglycerides.

Scientists have sought explanations for how the omega-3 fatty acids in fish oil could bring about reduced triglyceride levels. The evidence so far indicates that the liver may make fewer components of the VLDL lipoprotein particles. It may be that VLDL particles are more rapidly removed from the circulating blood. More work remains before we fully understand what is happening but the primary observations on triglyceride levels have been sustained in numerous trials.

Whether omega-3 fatty acids have a consistent or predictable effect on other lipoproteins is not clear. So far the findings have been contradictory. In healthy people, omega-3 fatty acids have no consistent effect on levels of LDL, the main carrier of cholesterol. Unlike vegetable oils, fish oils do not necessarily bring about marked lowering of cholesterol levels, but neither do they elevate cholesterol. Some studies however, have shown that omega-3 fatty acids produce LDL cholesterol levels equivalent to those of vegetable fatty acids. The fact that many studies have produced conflicting results suggests that omega-3s may not be affecting cholesterol metabolism directly or have effects that are even more complicated than we have imagined. There is room for both possibilities.

The third important blood lipoprotein, HDL is believed by many to be protective against heart disease. Most would consider it helpful if HDL levels were not reduced. The feeding of omega-3 fatty acids either as fish or fish oil capsules appears to have little effect on HDL. Again, there is evidence for small HDL changes in both directions but the data are not good enough for firm conclusions. It is safe to say though, that changes in HDL levels are not prominent features of omega-3 fatty acid consumption.

It is interesting to compare the lipid patterns of Greenland Eskimos with those of Danes, who are similar to Americans. Eskimos have lower triglyceride and cholesterol levels. Unlike Danes and Americans, their blood lipid levels do not increase with age. And third, values for men and women are similar. Whereas Danish and American pre-menopausal women usually have higher HDL levels than men, among Eskimos both sexes have high HDL levels. This is especially favorable for men who, in America and Denmark, have a higher risk of heart disease than pre-menopausal women.

While the feeding studies conducted in America and Europe so far have been able to replicate many of the features observed in Eskimos, most studies have been not longer than a few months and many just a few weeks. In Eskimos, however, consuming omega-3 fatty acids has been habitual. It could well be that one of the long term consequences of regular consumption of omega-3 fatty acids by Westerners would be a more favorable blood lipid pattern.

Do Omega-3 Fatty Acids Lower Blood Cholesterol Levels?

There is no simple answer to this important question. From the studies that have been done so far the results are not clear cut. In some cases fish or fish oil consumption is accompanied by reduced cholesterol levels, while in others there have been no changes. Decreases in the total cholesterol level in healthy subjects have not been particularly large. The reductions are greater, however, the more fatty fish or fish oil people consume. It is important to note, though, that eating fish or taking fish oil supplements does not raise cholesterol levels. Some fish oil concentrates, such as most cod liver oil preparations, contain high levels of cholesterol and might be expected to have little effect in lowering blood cholesterol levels.

In people with various types of blood lipid disorders, the consumption of fatty fish or fish oil has usually been accompanied by a decrease in total cholesterol. The greatest reductions in cholesterol occurred among those having very high levels of triglycerides. There has been some favorable response among small numbers of subjects with different types of high blood lipids but we do not know enough yet to make meaningful general statements or useful predictions.

In a study published early in 1986, new information about the effects of omega-3 fatty acids on cholesterol metabolism was presented. The study was designed to see if omega-3 fatty acids from seafood could modify the rise in blood cholesterol level that usually occurs when large amounts of cholesterol are consumed. Previous studies had indicated that vegetable fatty acids could do so, but whether or not fish oils could was not known. The findings showed that consuming fish oil lowered blood cholesterol levels compared with a control diet. The addition of 750 milligrams of cholesterol to the fish oil diet increased blood cholesterol levels only a small amount – half what might have been expected. LDL cholesterol levels also showed only small increases. How the fish oil supplement was inhibiting the rise in blood and LDL cholesterol was not known.

The authors suggested that omega-3 fatty acids may be useful in diets designed to lower LDL cholesterol levels. Such diets appear to be especially useful when cholesterol intakes are substantial, as they are for most Americans.

Because of these findings, the inconsistencies among previous studies and the fact that most observations have been made on small numbers of people, it is too soon to make declarations about the usefulness of omega-3s in improving blood cholesterol levels. There is enough evidence to suggest that these fatty acids may promote healthier blood lipid patterns but we have no idea how much or how often we need to consume fish or fish oils to obtain benefits. We also know very little about possible hazards of fish oil consumption. While it is tempting to draw conclusions before the data are in, plenty of experience in medical research has shown the folly of haste.

In summary, the primary effect of omega-3 fatty acids on blood lipids is to reduce triglycerides. Cholesterol levels may decrease but the findings are uncertain. Omega-3 fatty acids may also modify the body's response to cholesterol intake in a favorable way but the data are too scarce to be conclusive. Fortunately, no harmful effects on blood lipid levels have yet been reported.

Stroke

The term stroke is used to describe the blockage of blood flow to a part of the brain. As we age, our blood vessels gradually thicken and the tube becomes narrower, thanks to the processes involved in atherosclerosis. Fat, cholesterol and cellular material build up in the lining of blood vessels, further restricting the flow of blood. If nothing interferes with this accumulation, blood flow may be completely blocked, resulting in stroke or heart attack.

Many of the underlying events of stroke are similar to those for heart attack. While there is a great deal we do not understand about the causes of heart attacks and stroke, we do know that stroke is more likely if a person has *high blood pressure*. Controlling blood pressure will decrease the likelihood of stroke and recent evidence suggest that omega-3 fatty acids may also help reduce hypertension.

Greenland Eskimos who consume substantial amounts of omega-3 fatty acids also suffer more strokes than Danes or Americans. It is not clear why this is so, but many doctors attribute it to reduced blood clotting. Eskimos develop hemorrhagic strokes, the type where blood escapes from the blood vessels. When the blood does not clot quickly enough, the brain is damaged. This event is also called a stroke. This suggests that excessive omega-3 fatty acid intake can have undesirable consequences.

High Blood Pressure or Hypertension

High blood pressure (hypertension) means that the heart has to work harder to pump blood through our tissues. This increased work load requires more oxygen. In many instances, blood pressure goes up because there is greater resistance to the flow of blood through the vessels. Resistance goes up when there are deposits lining the vessels making passageways smaller and reducing blood flow. When vessel walls becomes less elastic with age and various other conditions, blood flow requires more work. Increased blood volume, such as occurs with high sodium or salt intake, also demands greater pumping capacity. Most of these conditions develop as we age, making high blood pressure more likely the older we become.

The catch with hypertension is that we do not feel it developing. It has no warning signs and generates no discomfort. That means that it is up to us to visit a doctor and have our blood pressure measured. Adults need to do this once a year after the age of 40.

Who Gets High Blood Pressure?
Most of us develop high blood pressure as we get older. Hypertension is more common among the elderly, the overweight and blacks.

And because high blood pressure runs in families, the chances of developing the condition are greater if other members of the family have high blood pressure. Although the condition is not unknown in children it is more common among adults. As a routine part of staying healthy, checking blood pressure once a year makes good sense.

Food and Blood Pressure Connections

While many conditions work together to create hypertension, blood pressure is often sensitive to diet. One of the most important ways to lower blood pressure is to attain a desirable body weight. Achieving a healthy body weight will bring many people's blood pressure back to a safe, normal range.

Another common dietary culprit is sodium. Because sodium attracts water its abundance in tissues can lead to the accumulation of fluid. In the blood vessels this means greater blood volume and more work for the heart. Simply cutting back on the amount of sodium, most widely supplied as salt, can help blood pressure return to healthy levels. Most of us eat vastly more sodium than we need and many like a salty taste. By leaving the salt shaker off the table and limiting how much and how often we eat very salty foods like potato chips, snack foods, pickles, olives, and soy sauce, all of us can achieve a more reasonable sodium intake without sacrificing flavor.

One nutrient that may be important in achieving healthy blood pressure is calcium. We know less about the importance of calcium in discouraging high blood pressure but there is some evidence to warrant our keeping calcium in mind (and body). The importance of lifelong adequate calcium intake for maintaining strong bones and teeth is reason enough to keep lowfat dairy foods a regular habit. It certainly will not hurt.

The most recent evidence connecting nutrients with healthy blood pressure comes from studies on fish oil. Several human feeding studies have reported lower blood pressure among those eating the more oily fish or taking fish oil. There are other reports, however, of just the opposite. We think that omega-3 fatty acids may be affecting prostaglandin metabolism in such a way that hormone activity in the kidney is modified.

The kidneys are active in the control of blood pressure. They are responsible for getting rid of excess sodium and controlling the retention and removal of water. Anything that affects the sodium and water processing activities of the kidney also affects blood pressure. For example, if blood flow through the kidney becomes impaired owing to atherosclerosis in the kidney blood vessels or from other disease, both kidney damage and hypertension can result.

Some of the prostaglandins made from arachidonic acid can influence salt and water excretion and affect blood vessels. These prostaglandins will enhance the effect of the hormone epinephrine that constricts or narrows blood vessels. When omega-3 fatty acids from fish oils are present, however, the action of prostaglandins on epinephrine is diminished. This means that omega-3 fatty acids may be working indirectly by affecting other systems regulating kidney function.

The bottom line on blood pressure and diet connections has yet to be written. There is no doubt that it will include something about the remarkable omega-3 fatty acids in fish. In the meantime, eating seafood regularly may help your blood pressure as well as pleasing your palate.

Chapter Three

Omega-3 Fatty Acids, Arthritis and the Immune System

Arthritis

Arthritis has long been resistant to dietary remedies. For this reason it seems far fetched to think that seafood consumption could influence the condition. Moreover, dietary remedies for arthritis are the legerdemain of food quacks, who often extol the virtues of worthless diets as a treatment for this painful illness. Thus, it is not surprising that some skepticism greeted the suggestion that consuming seafood, with its unique omega-3 fatty acids, might have favorable effects on arthritis.

Scientists studying arthritis picked up the reports that Greenland Eskimos have a very low incidence of arthritis and other inflammatory diseases. Since omega-3 fatty acids had been identified as favorable agents in discouraging heart disease among Eskimos, inquiry about their involvement in arthritis seemed an obvious starting place. We knew already that prostaglandin metabolism was involved in generating inflammatory responses. Perhaps omega-3 fatty acids could also moderate the inflammatory responses of arthritis through changes in prostaglandin metabolism just as they apparently were doing in the activities of platelets and cells of the blood vessel wall.

This hypothesis is now supported with good evidence. Omega-3 fatty acids are able to moderate the effects of arthritis in some patients. They do not, however, prevent the disease. They influence prostaglandin metabolism in specialized cells the body uses to defend itself. How omega-3 fatty acids affect arthritis relates to the ways the immune system works. Immunology, the study of our immune system, is a young, rapidly developing science whose complexities we are just beginning to unravel. The next few paragraphs give some background information on immunology and inflammation and how they relate to omega-3 fatty acids.

The Immune System

The immune system is our body's primary defense against invaders. It protects us from the harmful effects of bacteria, viruses and particles like asbestos and pollen. The immune system consists of a network of organs, cells and molecules working together to find and destroy anything not recognized as parts of the body. Occasionally it works against its own tissues as in rheumatoid arthritis and in other autoimmune diseases like AIDS. Without the immune system we would quickly succumb to disease.

We actually have two kinds of immune systems. One is an inborn or natural immunity which resists infections. It employs several different kinds of cells which work together to disintegrate or engulf bacteria.

The second is the adaptive or specific immune system. It depends on special types of white blood cells called lymphocytes. Adaptive immunity responds to individual invaders and develops a memory system to recognize the same agents again. It produces *antibodies** – specific proteins that bind to an invading particle (*antigen*) and inactivate it. Antibodies give us protection against another invasion by the same antigen.

National Geographic published an excellent article in June 1986 describing how the immune system works. The article is illustrated with diagrams and magnificent electron micrographic pictures. Read it for more information on the working of the immune system.

The immune system is responsible for reactions that we popularly call inflammatory responses. Familiar examples of the inflammatory response are the wheezing and breathing difficulties of

---

*Words printed in italics are defined in the Glossary at the end of the book. Only the first occurrence of the word is italicized.

asthma, the red weals of hives, the sneezing and nasal response of hayfever and the pain of arthritis. These symptoms are the result of the immune system trying to cope with an insult to the body. Inflammation can occur following irritation of tissue, as a result of an injury or trauma like a burn, and from the invasion of foreign particles such as bacteria or viruses.

The distressing symptoms that we experience in an inflammatory response are actually the result of an overzealous reaction. The body is using all its forces when perhaps only the front line was needed. When we take an anti-histamine drug or an aspirin, we are trying to slow down the body's natural response to danger. The trick is to temper the reaction enough to abolish unpleasant symptoms yet not eliminate it entirely, which would leave us defenseless.

Inflammatory responses have certain characteristic symptoms – redness, swelling, warmth or fever, pain, and even loss of function. These physical responses are brought about by locally produced prostaglandins that affect blood vessels and tissues. Certain prostaglandins cause blood vessels to dilate and this action permits the flow of blood to the tissues, causing redness. These same prostaglandins also cause pain by making the skin more sensitive to other inflammatory agents such as histamine.

Prostaglandins are a group of highly reactive compounds derived from polyunsaturated fatty acids. They act as chemical signals between cells in their environment. There are several groups of prostaglandins with different functions but all share certain features: they are made from polyunsaturated fatty acids, each has 20 carbon atoms and a 5 carbon ring structure, they are produced locally, they work in the vicinity where they are made and they are very short lived.

Prostaglandins are made in cell membranes from the fatty acids that are part of the membrane itself. Diet determines which fatty acids are found in the membrane. Thus it is tempting to suggest that prostaglandin synthesis could be regulated or redirected by the fat composition of the diet. This assumption underlies many recent studies.

When we eat foods containing omega-3s, we enrich our cell membranes with these fatty acids. When the diet is not rich in omega-3s, the usual fatty acid available for making prostaglandins is arachidonic acid. The type of prostaglandin a cell makes depends on the kind of cell it is (for example, platelet, blood vessel cell or lymphocyte), the set of enzymes it has for making different types of prostaglandins, and the kind of fatty acid available for prostaglandin synthesis.

Once prostaglandins are made they are released into the part of the body immediately around them. They are not stored. They affect only cells that have receptors or a facility for interacting with the prostaglandin. They are highly potent but if not used right away they will be destroyed. Thus, prostaglandin synthesis requires repeated stimuli for continued production; the synthesis, in turn, requires renewed uptake of polyunsaturated fatty acids.

There is at least one encouraging study of people with arthritis who appeared to benefit from taking fish oil. In this study, patients who consumed a fish oil supplement and ate a diet moderate in total fat but rich in polyunsaturated fat reported a reduction in several clinical symptoms of arthritis. After 3 months the people receiving the fish oil had fewer tender joints and substantially reduced duration of morning stiffness compared with those arthritics without the fish oil, whose total dietary fat was at the same level but consisted mainly of saturated fats. The study did not measure prostaglandin metabolism but monitored the level of omega-3 fatty acid in blood plasma.

When fish oil was removed from the diet the arthritis became worse. The authors suggested that the experimental diet had been beneficial in diminishing some of the symptoms of arthritis but refrained from attributing the effects exclusively to the fish oil. If dietary fatty acids can affect particular cells so that they manufacture the kind of prostaglandins less likely to produce inflammation, we have an excellent way of treating people with arthritis.

Studies of arthritis in animals have shown that omega-3 fatty acids (albeit those from plants) along with a particular kind of prostaglandin could suppress the effects of induced arthritis. Other reports indicate otherwise. Still other studies have shown that fish oil feeding enhances the production of certain antibodies that attack foreign particles, presumably moderating the injury.

However tempting it is to speculate about the benefits of fish oil in arthritis, we do not yet have enough data to declare them positively beneficial. Scientists are actively exploring the possibility.

The Immune System and Other Diseases

Many diseases involve some disorder of the immune system. Diabetes, once thought to be mainly a malfunction of the pancreas, is now known to involve the immune system as well. Cancer, bronchial asthma, lupus erythematosus, multiple sclerosis, psoriasis, blood vessel and kidney disease all appear to have an immune system component. Even the aging process is associated with the immune system. What is striking about all of these associations is that diet can modify the strength of the immune response. The amount and kind of dietary fat is particularly important. However, the precise dietary adjustments that will be beneficial are not clear.

Omega-3 fatty acids change the fatty acid composition of the lymphocyte cell membrane, as they do in platelets. This change influences events happening on the surface of the lymphocyte and affects the flow of substances through the membrane. This change in membrane composition is important because many of the early events in an immune response, such as prostaglandin production, occur at the membrane of lymphocytes. When omega-3 fatty acids are present, they compete with arachidonic acid for enzymes making various prostaglandins, thereby reducing the amount of products being made from arachidonic acid. The products made from omega-3 fatty acids result in less pronounced immune reactions.

A few types of cells active in immune responses can make a potent group of compounds called leukotrienes. They use the same polyunsaturated fatty acids for leukotrienes as they use for making prostaglandins. Leukotrienes, however, are more powerful than prostaglandins in provoking an inflammatory response. When omega-3 fatty acids are present, different kinds of leukotrienes are produced. Some investigators think omega-3 fatty acids are preferentially used to make the kinds of prostaglandins and leukotrienes that have less pronounced immunological effects.

Leukotrienes have been implicated in producing the bronchial constriction characteristic of asthma. One type of leukotriene affects bronchial muscles and produces constriction, making breathing difficult. Although it has been shown that both asthmatics and non-asthmatics have bronchial reactions in response to this leukotriene, it is not proven that this substance is responsible for some of the symptoms of asthma.

The discovery and understanding of prostaglandins and leukotrienes that generate inflammatory responses has advanced our understanding of many diseases. Just recently it was learned that aspirin brings relief to certain types of immune responses because it blocks the formation of particular prostaglandins. It does not, however, affect the manufacture of leukotrienes. This Nobel prize winning finding by Dr. S. Moncada and Dr. John Vane helps explain why aspirin is of limited benefit in certain immune and inflammatory conditions.

The effects of omega-3 fatty acids on prostaglandin and leukotriene pathways is another advance in the study of immunology. It is truly exciting that dietary habits such as the regular consumption of seafood, especially those species rich in omega-3 fatty acids, could benefit our health in such a variety of ways.

Cancer

I can think of no word more frightening to people than the word cancer. It brings out the pessimist in each of us. Cancer has reached the lives of many of us through survival, loved ones or loss. These experiences have generated intense research efforts and progress so that there is a firm basis for optimism in many types of cancer. The news is getting better all the time.

Links Between Diet and Cancer

Over the past several years evidence has accumulated to support the idea that diet affects the likelihood of certain kinds of cancer. Since 1980 at least seven government or professional societies have published dietary recommendations for the public suggesting eating habits they think are most healthful for discouraging cancer. Some publications give specific advice about which foods to consume and restrict while others are vague. None promises protection from cancer but each attempts to translate the scientific evidence into practical advice.

Public interest in diet and cancer has brought more attention to the importance of diet in our health, growing awareness that our lavish food choices do not necessarily ensure the best health and an increased sense that some foods have benefits that others do not. A major issue remains, however. We usually understand bits and pieces about health conditions, seldom a whole picture. As more bits are added to the scene we change our mind about the relative importance of one aspect over another. That is just what is happening with polyunsaturated fats and heart disease. It once appeared that vegetable polyunsaturated fats were the most beneficial for heart health. Now omega-3s from seafood seem even more important. The final outcome will probably indicate that both are important in certain amounts.

Diet and cancer information is accumulating rapidly. We are learning more about how cancer begins, develops and spreads and how the body facilitates or blocks these stages. We also know more about the effects of diet and individual nutrients. The strongest evidence so far supports an association between the amount of fat we eat and cancer of the breast, colon, rectum, prostate, ovary and pancreas. Countries with the highest levels of fat consumption also have the highest rates of these cancers. Animal studies show that the amount and type of fat influence spontaneous and induced cancers. What is more difficult to define is the level and kind of fats that discourage cancer. Other nutrients and food components such as vitamin A, fiber and selenium have also been associated with certain cancers. This brief discussion considers only dietary fat and omega-3 fatty acids.

Type of Dietary Fat

The proportions of different fats we eat make a difference. Diets high in polyunsaturated fat may favor tumor development in animals and in cell studies compared with those high in saturated fats or low in total fat. Whether the kind of fat matters at all stages of cancer development is not known. We also do not know if the effects of different types of fat are the same at high and low fat intakes. Probably not. Now that we are beginning to appreciate that not all polyunsaturated fats are alike, the question of whether omega-3 fatty acids are helpful or harmful in cancer is an urgent one.

There is not nearly enough information relating the consumption of seafood to a lower total incidence of cancer. Among Greenland Eskimos, the incidence of all cancer is less than it is among Danes. Cancer rates are lower among native Alaskans who also eat a lot of fish but comparisons are difficult to make. And the Japanese, who eat more fish than we do, also have substantially lower rates of many cancers than Americans. The Japanese consume much less fat in total, so the importance of seafood is not clear. Interest in seafood is recent, so that some epidemiological studies have failed either to collect or to report dietary information about seafood consumption. It will take some time to back-track and obtain those data.

Omega-3 Fatty Acids and Cancer

Is there any reason to think that omega-3 fatty acids are beneficial in discouraging cancer? Yes. Omega-3s affect many systems implicated directly in some stage of cancer development. For example, omega-3 fatty acids affect immune responses, cell division, membrane structure and function and prostaglandin production, all of which contribute to the growth of malignant cells in some way. In several studies of breast cancer in animals, feeding fish oil inhibited the development of tumors. Evidence is growing that it may do so in prostate cancer as well. We can expect the list of cancers to expand as research progresses.

Intense research activity is directed towards understanding the relationships among omega-3 fatty acids, prostaglandins and leukotrienes in cancer. These compounds are involved both in immune responses and cancer. The reader will remember that prostaglandins and leukotrienes are both made from arachidonic acid, a polyunsaturated fatty acid made from linoleic acid we eat in vegetable oils and grains. Omega-3 fatty acids competitively reduce the amount of products, including prostaglandins, usually made from arachidonic acid and lead to the formation of slightly different products.

Tumors in humans and animals produce excessive amounts of certain kinds of prostaglandins. These particular prostaglandins inhibit the response of certain white cells in the immune system, and inhibit antibody production and cell destruction. Such effects may enable cancer cells to escape the body's usual defense mechanisms.

Increased thromboxane metabolism and prostaglandin production has also been associated with metastases (spread of cancer to another tissue) in patients with breast cancer. It is interesting to note that among Japanese women who do develop breast cancer, return of the disease is less likely than among American women.

Drugs given to prevent the formation of certain prostaglandins can inhibit the development of some tumors. Such drugs have been useful in treating people with such cancers as Hodgkin's disease. That these drugs are not entirely successful, however, suggests that many activities other than prostaglandin metabolism are involved.

Within the last few years scientists have discovered that omega-3 fatty acids from seafood can inhibit prostaglandin metabolism and discourage the development of tumors. These observations have been made in animal systems for a variety of cancers including breast and prostate cancer. One recent study of breast cancer in rats showed that feeding moderately high levels of menhaden oil was associated with delayed tumor development and fewer tumors. Low levels of menhaden oil had no protective effect compared with the same level of corn oil. The omega-3 fatty acids were taken up in the liver and in the tumors making it possible for them to affect prostaglandin metabolism.

We do not know how omega-3s may be affecting tumor growth. Current suggestions for which there is some evidence include effects on cell membranes, modified hormone action and interference with immune defense mechanisms. We can expect that the intense research activity in cancer, immunology and nutrition will increase our understanding of how omega-3 fatty acids can be beneficial in discouraging cancer and probably generate new controversies about diet and health. It is far too early for dietary recommendations about omega-3s and cancer but the direction is certainly a positive one.

Can Omega-3s Help Against Cancer?

Until recently, there was little reason to suspect that common dietary fatty acids could affect any of the processes in the development of cancer. Now we know that polyunsaturated fatty acids may be involved in several ways. Certain types of fatty acids are essential for normal cell growth and replication. As precursors of substances that influence cell biochemistry they are potential regulatory substances. And, as part of the food we eat, they are part of a continuously changing pool of compounds our cells use to perform their various chemical tasks.

What all cancers have in common is uncontrolled growth and spread of cells. What is it that distinguishes normal controlled growth from that out of control? Is it a question of cell regulation or defects in the basic cell machinery? Probably both processes are important. For example, damage to a cell's DNA – that part responsible for making an exact copy of a cell – results in abnormal cells. Most of these cells never survive, but those that do can develop into tumors.

Sometimes the metabolism of unsaturated fatty acids produces highly reactive substances, *peroxides* and "free radicals". Peroxides and free radicals can damage cellular DNA, perhaps starting a malignancy. Certain vitamins and minerals, notably Vitamin E and selenium, discourage the production of peroxides and protect our tissues from peroxide damage. Some fatty acids may generate these harmful products more readily than others. How vegetable fatty acids differ from fish oil fatty acids in these processes is just beginning to be studied. It may be that they are important for encouraging or discouraging the formation of stimulatory substances such as prostaglandins.

Several studies have reported that the growth of tumors, especially breast tumors, is deterred when prostaglandins are prevented from being formed. This suggests that substances that modify or reduce prostaglandin formation, such as omega-3 fatty acids, may play a part in controlling or preventing tumor growth. There have been several reports that high levels of vegetable fatty acids such as those from corn oil facilitate tumor development, whereas omega-3 fatty acids appear to counteract tumor growth. The evidence suggests that these effects may be occurring through prostaglandins, either by their formation or through the reactions they control. High levels of fat intake seem to make the situation worse.

Platelets may be involved in breast cancer through the production of a derivative of prostaglandin, thromboxane. Apparently human breast cancer cells produce more thromboxane and this facilitates the spread of the disease and the growth of the tumor. If the production of thromboxane is blocked with a drug, tumor growth is inhibited.

Related evidence of prostaglandin involvement comes from observations with prostacyclin, another prostaglandin derivative. We know that omega-3 fatty acids stimulate blood vessel *epithelial* cells to produce this anti-clotting substance. When prostacyclin is present there is evidence that the spread of the tumor is reduced. Could omega-3 fatty acids encourage breast epithelial cells to produce prostacyclin which would then inhibit tumor growth? This question and many others are at the frontier of cancer research and we can be hopeful that useful answers will emerge soon.

In the studies with Eskimos mentioned earlier it was observed that cancer occurred less frequently among the Eskimos than among Danes, although the difference between the two groups was not large. Many population studies have confirmed the observation that cancer rates are lower as fat intake decreases. In fact, a major study is just getting underway in this country to see if women at risk of breast cancer are less likely to develop the disease if they follow a low fat diet all the time. What we know so far suggests that eating less fat is protective against certain cancers.

At present, the best we can say is that omega-3 fatty acids are being actively studied for their potential benefits in discouraging the onset and development of cancer. It can do each of us no harm to think carefully about the large amount of fat we consume and how it may be quietly fostering the development of cancer. Having seafood meals regularly can provide omega-3 fatty acids and at the same time lower fat intake, thereby helping to create an environment less hospitable to the development of cancer.

Is Diet Linked to Cancer?

There is plenty of evidence that about 80 percent of all cancers are related to the way we live – our eating and drinking habits, work environment and smoking addiction.

The National Cancer Institute estimates that as many as 35 percent of all cancer deaths may be related to the way we eat. Being deliberate about the foods we choose and the way we cook can make a difference. Using seafood more often than we usually do fits in nicely with the suggestions coming from laboratory research. Here are the dietary habits that can help protect you from certain forms of cancer:

• **Eat less fat.** Nearly all of us have too much fat in our meals. The main sources are vegetable oils, margarine and butter; mayonnaise and salad dressings; all fried foods; meats, especially processed meats; dairy products (except lowfat varieties). People who eat fewer fatty foods also have less cancer. Substitute lots of vegetables and grains instead. Use lowfat dairy foods. Use fish and skinless poultry instead of red meats.

• **Eat plenty of fiber rich foods.** These are whole grain cereals, vegetables and fruits. Whole grains are the ones that still have the outer bran layer. Brown rice, bran cereals, rolled oats, whole wheat bread are examples. Plenty of fiber keeps the intestine active and speeds digestive processes so that harmful products do not accumulate or become absorbed. Just make these foods a habit.

• **Eat plenty of vegetables.** Instead of one or two vegetables at lunch and dinner, make three a minimum. This simple "rule" works to reduce the amount of meats that seems adequate, increases your fiber intake, ensures you get plenty of vitamins and minerals and shrinks fat intake. Vegetables of the cabbage family are especially healthful and may be protective against cancer. They also have vitamins A and C that may be protective against certain cancers, and helpful amounts of minerals. It is virtually impossible to overdo vegetables.

• **Use alcohol only in moderation** – no more than two drinks a day. People who consume large amounts of alcohol are more likely to develop cancer of the esophagus, mouth and pharynx. You only have one liver doing hundreds of important jobs. Alcohol undermines its activity. Heavy use of mouthwashes is also associated with cancer of the mouth and throat.

• **Avoid moldy nuts, seeds and grains.** These foods may develop aflatoxin, a natural poison produced by certain molds that is highly carcinogenic. Store these foods in dry, well-sealed containers.

• **Cook in health promoting ways.** That means use as little fat as possible in food preparation. Cook by baking, broiling, steaming, poaching, stir-frying (uses only a tiny amount of oil) and microwaving. Be cautious about charred foods. When using the grill or barbecue, avoid burning food. Scrape the racks clean to avoid picking up charred material on your food. There is some evidence that charred meats contain substances, formed during cooking, that may facilitate cancer processes. If parts become charred simply discard them at the plate or before serving. Don't eat burned or charred (blackened) food of any kind.

You might be curious about the other ways to discourage cancer, besides wise eating. Here they are:

• **Avoid ALL tobacco products.** Don't smoke, chew or snuff tobacco. Discourage your family and friends from smoking. Work to banish smoking from your work place and from public facilities. Second hand smoke is hazardous to your health too.

- **Worship the sun sensibly.** That means protect yourself against sunburn and long hours of exposure. Sunshine is most intense and most damaging from 11 a.m. to 2 p.m. Use lotions that block out most of the sun's rays and wear lightweight protective clothing.
- **Limit the X-rays you have.** A single X-ray is not harmful, but many of them over a period may increase your risk of cancer. Use X-ray shields to protect other parts of your body. Remember to count the X-rays in your dentist's office too.
- **Be cautious about hormone therapies.** Use of estrogen hormones has been linked to cancer of the uterus. Low doses and combination medications have made the use of hormones safer but caution is warranted.
- **Protect yourself from nasty things in the environment.** Such substances as asbestos in old building materials, chemical paint strippers, pesticides, weed killers, aerosol materials and the like all contain hazardous materials. If you must be near these things, wear protective clothing, gloves, eye guards and breathing masks. Special filters are available for breathing masks to make such jobs as fixing up your old house much safer.

Chapter Four

Seafood and Cholesterol

Why Cholesterol Is Important

We have become concerned about cholesterol because it is linked to heart disease. We know that the amount of cholesterol circulating in the blood is one of the features that determines our risk of having a heart attack. The more we have, the greater the risk. By lowering our blood cholesterol level we can reduce our chances of having a heart attack. Here's why.

Too much cholesterol in the blood contributes to the build up of *plaque**, the deposits that clog our blood vessels. Once these deposits form, they narrow the passageway for blood flow and invite blood clots to settle in. Eventually, the deposits and clots shut off the blood flow completely and heart attack or stroke follows. The less cholesterol there is in the blood stream, the slower and less likely this whole process of atherosclerosis becomes.

Whose cholesterol is too high? Practically speaking, just about everybody's. Risk of heart disease increases measurably once the total cholesterol level climbs over 200 milligrams per deciliter (mg/dl). Some doctors draw the risk line at 220 mg/dl. The National Heart Lung and Blood Institute says that their goal is to reduce cholesterol levels to no more than 200 mg/dl in people over 30 years old. Once you are over 40 and your cholesterol is greater than 260 mg/dl you definitely have a higher risk of heart attack. In between

---

*Words printed in italics are defined in the Glossary at the end of the book. Only the first occurrence of the word is italicized.

200 and 260, risk is greater but we cannot tell precisely who will develop a heart attack and who will not.

Because people are concerned about blood cholesterol levels many are adjusting their fat and cholesterol intakes in order to reduce blood cholesterol levels. There is sometimes confusion, however, about cholesterol and fat in foods.

It is commonly thought that cholesterol and fat are more or less part of the same thing, at least as far as food is concerned. People associate foods rich in fat, especially animal fats, with those rich in cholesterol. While some cholesterol-rich foods are also high in fat most are not. Cholesterol and fat are two entirely different kinds of substances, though they share a few chemical similarities.

Both fats (triglycerides) and cholesterol are composed mainly of carbon, hydrogen and some oxygen. In the case of fats, the atoms are arranged in long chains whereas in cholesterol, the atoms form adjoining rings with one side chain. These differences in structure make the two kinds of substances totally different from each other.

Cholesterol and fat differ in function as well. Fats are used primarily for energy, insulation and cushioning. Cholesterol is a basic building material that certain organs use for making vital compounds. Among these valuable substances are sex hormones, adrenal hormones, bile acids and derivatives of vitamin D. The outside membrane or wall of every cell has cholesterol in it as part of its structural material. In such a strategic location, cholesterol is positioned to participate in metabolic activities inside and outside the cell. Because cholesterol is distributed throughout the body in all tissues rather than being concentrated in storage sites like body fat is, it is possible to have large amounts of cholesterol without large amounts of fat.

That is the case with many cholesterol-rich foods. For example, liver, egg yolk, squid, shrimp and sweetbreads (thymus gland) are all fairly high in cholesterol yet none is especially rich in fat. By contrast, animal fats like butter and lard have some cholesterol but they are predominantly fat. When on the lookout for foods rich in cholesterol the fat content of the food is usually a poor guide.

Confusion arises because both the amount of cholesterol and the kind of fat we eat affect our blood cholesterol levels. The more cholesterol and the more saturated fat we eat, the higher our blood cholesterol level will be. By contrast, with moderate cholesterol intake and unsaturated oil instead of saturated fat, cholesterol levels are lower. Having less fat of all types also favors a lower cholesterol level. Because both fats and cholesterol in foods affect our cholesterol level we tend to lump the two together. The situation in our bodies, however, is more complicated than that.

The amount of cholesterol in food is not readily predictable. Only a few foods are fairly high in cholesterol and these are easy to learn. Cholesterol only occurs in foods of animal origin so that all vegetables and grains, including vegetable oils, are free of cholesterol. Those animal foods fairly high in cholesterol are: all organ meats, squid, fish roe, egg yolks, and shrimp. Meats, poultry and dairy products (except skim milk products) all have some cholesterol. Their ability to affect our blood cholesterol level is due more to their content of saturated fat than to their cholesterol. For this reason health professionals and agencies have urged all of us to trim our comparatively lavish consumption of these foods.

What about Good and Bad Cholesterol?

The notion that some cholesterol is good and some bad is popular. It is also confusing and misleading. Cholesterol is actually a "good" substance if we have to evaluate it in such terms. It is part of every cell membrane in the body and is the basis for many hormones including our sex hormones. An indication of its importance is the fact that its supply is beyond the whim of diet. It is made by the liver, as well as absorbed from food. Like many other useful substances though, too much of it is not so good for us. And the level at which it becomes a problem varies greatly from person to person.

The idea of good and bad cholesterol comes from the fact that cholesterol is part of different complexes of fats and proteins. These complexes are called lipoproteins. As part of lipoprotein molecules, cholesterol is able to move comfortably in blood and tissue fluids thanks to its protein partners. And because lipoproteins have parts attracting both lipid and water they can move in and out of cells and tissues.

There are several types of lipoproteins in the blood. They are grouped according to density or weight. The more protein they contain the higher their density. Their descriptive names are: very low density, low density and high density lipoproteins. These types are known more often by their first letter abbreviations: VLDL, LDL and HDL respectively. Chylomicrons are a fourth kind of lipoprotein found in blood but these are believed to have very little to do with

53

atherosclerosis. The main carriers of cholesterol are the low density and high density lipoproteins, LDL and HDL.

Different lipoproteins do different things. The VLDL carry triglycerides (fats) but very little cholesterol. Once they have surrendered their fats to tissues, VLDL can be converted to another type of lipoprotein, LDL.

LDL lipoproteins are the main carriers of cholesterol. If a person has unusually high levels of LDL cholesterol, he or she is at increased risk of heart disease. Some people have a family history of very high levels of LDL cholesterol and run an especially high risk of early heart attack. Such people often need medication to control their condition. When the level of cholesterol in the LDL lipoproteins is high, a person has the condition called Type II *hypercholesterolemia*. This means high cholesterol in the blood. LDL has earned the nickname "bad cholesterol".

By contrast, many people think of HDL as "good cholesterol". HDL carries cholesterol too, but lesser amounts than LDL. HDL helps remove cholesterol from tissues and blood. LDL takes cholesterol to the tissues, HDL takes it away. HDL helps to reduce the amount of cholesterol available to accumulate in blood vessels and tissues.

Although we have much to learn about how HDL works, there is good evidence suggesting that people whose HDL cholesterol levels are in the upper range are less likely to have heart atttacks. Unfortunately, the data are not good enough yet to be precise about the level of HDL that would indicate reduced risk of heart disease. It is also thought by many that low levels of HDL might indicate increased risk of heart disease, but again, precise levels are uncertain. Some doctors, however, consider HDL cholesterol levels below 40 mg/dl critical. The importance of HDL levels in risk of heart disease is under active investigation and we may expect clearer findings in the near future.

Since LDL and HDL function differently in blood, it is clear that measures of total blood cholesterol do not give the whole picture. In order to have a better idea of our risk of heart disease we need to know how much cholesterol is in LDL and how much is in HDL. The higher the HDL and the lower the LDL cholesterol levels, the better.

For example, two men may each have a total cholesterol of 210 milligrams/deciliter. The first has an LDL cholesterol of 175 and an

HDL cholesterol of 35; the second has an LDL cholesterol of 125 and an HDL of 65. The first man would have a greater risk of heart disease because the distribution of cholesterol is less favorable. Too much is in the LDL form and too little in HDL. The second man however, has a much more favorable distribution of cholesterol. His HDL is high and his LDL normal. When having blood cholesterol measured, ask for LDL and HDL levels as well as total cholesterol values. The detailed information will be more helpful than a total cholesterol value alone. Be sure your doctor takes the blood sample after an overnight fast or when you have not had anything to eat for at least six hours.

The most important details of your blood cholesterol picture are the total amount of cholesterol and its distribution between LDL and HDL lipoproteins. The most favorable blood cholesterol values for avoiding heart disease are:

1. **Low total cholesterol** – The best situation is total cholesterol less than 200 mg/dl.

2. **Low LDL cholesterol** – Some physicians consider LDL cholesterol values above 150 mg/dl reason to begin treatment. We know that high LDL cholesterol levels increase the risk of heart disease. In deciding whether or not to treat a patient, a doctor considers the LDL cholesterol, the HDL and total cholesterol figures along with other health information. These numbers are only an approximate guide.

3. **High HDL cholesterol** – There is no universal agreement among physicians on the upper level of HDL cholesterol that might reduce risk of heart disease. Neither do we know the level below which risk might increase. Some doctors consider a level of 40 mg/dl or less an indication of increased risk of heart disease. As a rule, the more HDL cholesterol and the less LDL cholesterol the better.

Improving Blood Cholesterol Levels

How do we achieve the most desirable cholesterol levels? The answer lies in controlling weight, eating less total fat and less saturated fat, and exercising regularly and vigorously. There are two main ways of lowering total and LDL cholesterol levels. One is by diet and lifestyle changes, the other by drugs. Diet is nearly always the first strategy. A physician will see how well a person responds to changes in food habits before recommending drugs unless the cholesterol level is very high.

Raising HDL levels is an additional approach to reducing risk of heart disease. Recommendations for increasing HDL levels focus on controlling body weight and exercising regularly. People who are overweight will lower their blood cholesterol levels and achieve a more favorable distribution of cholesterol by losing weight. Exercise is probably the most important way to increase HDL levels. People who exercise regularly and vigorously have higher HDL cholesterol and lower LDL cholesterol levels than sedentary people.

Most of us can improve our cholesterol situation by making some changes in what we eat. Four features of our eating habits are critical: amount of fat, kind of fat, amount of cholesterol and dietary fiber. Of all these, amount and type of dietary fat are probably the most important.

Amount and Type of Fat

Cholesterol levels in blood go up when we eat saturated fats. Therefore it is important to cut down as much as possible on all foods with saturated fats. These fats are most abundant in animal foods like meat, dairy products, butter, cream and in some vegetable foods like shortening, coconut oil, avocados and palm oil. Saturated fats are commonly added in making processed and convenience foods like luncheon meats, frozen meals and bakery products.

Reducing our intake of saturated fats generally lowers our consumption of all other types of fat as well. This works in our favor. Eating less fat helps control weight and helps lower all blood lipids.

Some kinds of fats are actually helpful when not consumed in excess. Generally speaking, polyunsaturated fats generate the most favorable distribution of lipids in the blood. The best known polyunsaturated fats are those in vegetables and grains: corn oil, safflower oil and soybean oil. Walnut oil is also highly polyunsaturated.

Liquid fats or oils usually have more polyunsaturated fatty acids than solid fats. With margarines it is more difficult to tell how much polyunsaturated fat there is, unless the label specifically gives you the amount. Brands that omit this information nearly always have less polyunsaturated fat than those that advertise the kind of fat they use. To find the greatest amount of polyunsaturates in a margarine, look for the brand that gives you the greatest absolute amount, not just the highest P:S ratio. It means studying the nutrition label carefully and comparing different brands.

While vegetable foods are usually richest in polyunsaturates there are notable exceptions. For example olive oil, a liquid vegetable oil, is relatively low in polyunsaturates but rich in monounsaturates. This type of fatty acid does not raise blood cholesterol levels but may not lower them as much as polyunsaturates do. Other vegetable fats, those from coconut, palm and avocado are rich in saturated fatty acids, the kind we try to limit. We would probably benefit more from substantially cutting the amount of fat we consume and worrying less about its composition, than trying to fine tune our excessive fat intake.

Food manufacturers also change the fatty acid composition of oils during processing. Shortening and margarine are made by adding hydrogen to unsaturated oils. This process increases the amount of monounsaturated fat and decreases the amount of polyunsaturated fat. It may also increase the amount of saturated fat. Such processing makes the fat easier to handle in baking and frying but not in our arteries. Because of these manufacturing habits the term "vegetable" fat on the label does not necessarily mean the product contains more polyunsaturated fat.

Better from the standpoint of heart health are the oils in fish. These too are polyunsaturated and promote a favorable distribution of lipids in blood. The best way to obtain these desirable omega-3 rich oils is to eat fish, especially the species high in oil content like sardines, mackerel, salmon and herring. The alternative, taking fish oil concentrates or capsules, is a risky business unless you are under expert medical supervision. There is a danger of taking too much, the risk of toxic levels of vitamins A and D, high cholesterol levels and the possibility of harmful pollutants. Environmental contaminants like PCBs and oxidation products are two examples of substances one would rather avoid. For more information about fish oil supplements see Chapter Six.

The fats in fish and shellfish seem to moderate the response of some cells to our customary large intake of vegetable fats. Various polyunsaturated fatty acids from foods compete with each other for involvement in certain metabolic activities. When omega-3 fatty acids from fish are present they change the kinds and amounts of products that are formed during important metabolic processes. The net result of this seems to be better health. Keeping a supply of omega-3 fatty acids available by eating seafood regularly is a con-

57

venient way of boosting our biochemistry and promoting our own good health.

Dietary Cholesterol

Cholesterol in foods is the next factor to consider when trying to reduce blood cholesterol levels. There is much debate about the importance of the amount of cholesterol we eat in determining our blood cholesterol level. Food cholesterol seems to be very important in some people and less so in others. Overall, however, we probably consume too much cholesterol – maybe twice as much as we should. Current recommendations for discouraging heart disease in healthy people are to eat no more than 300 milligrams of cholesterol a day – just a bit more than is in one egg yolk or in 12 ounces of cooked round steak.

Cholesterol is found only in foods of animal origin. It is most abundant in eggs, organ meats, meat, poultry, milk, butter and certain seafoods. There is none in vegetables, fruits, grains, dried peas and beans or nuts. Baked products like cake and cookies usually have cholesterol from eggs, butter and milk. Should we try to avoid cholesterol entirely by becoming a vegetarian, our liver would make what we need. The final balance of cholesterol in the blood is the result of complicated controls by the liver, intestinal tract and other systems. The wisest course for heart health is to keep cholesterol intake from food to an average of about 300 milligrams a day or less.

Cholesterol in Seafood

Most varieties of fish and shellfish are lower in cholesterol than meats and poultry. Look at Figure 6 for comparison. More details are given in Table 2.

All finfish and shelled molluscs have less than 100 mg cholesterol in 3½ ounces, raw.* On the other hand, some shellfish are rich in cholesterol as shown in Table 3 and 4

It is entirely possible to enjoy all varieties of seafood, even the few cholesterol-rich ones, and stay within the recommended choles-

---

*The reason for using the odd amount of 3½ ounces comes from translating scientific data from the metric system to the British system used in household measures. Tables of nutrient content express amounts of nutrients in units per 100 grams which is almost equal to 3½ ounces. Most nutrient data are for raw foods. Cooking changes the nutrient content according to how much is lost, destroyed or added during the procedure. Cholesterol is usually well retained in cooking.

Table 2
FOODS RICH IN CHOLESTEROL

Food	Cholesterol in mg/3½ oz.
Brains	2100
Chicken liver, simmered	745
Turkey liver, simmered	600
Eggs, 2 large	550
Sweetbreads	465
Liver, calf or hog, fried	440
Kidney, braised	375
Liver, beef, fried	300
Lamb most cuts	90-120
Pork most cuts	80-120
Beef most cuts	70-100
Poultry	75-90
Luncheon meats, except liver	50-70
Hot dogs	35-90
Butter, 1 tablespoon	35
Milk, whole, 3.7% fat, 1 cup	35
Yogurt, whole milk, 1 cup	30
Milk, lowfat, 1% fat, 1 cup	10

Recommended average daily cholesterol intake: no more than 300 mg.

*Data rounded to the nearest 5 mg. Cholesterol values are considered accurate ±20%. Data from USDA

terol intake for a day. Do this by saving other cholesterol rich foods for another time. When having calamari (squid), caviar or shrimp save the omelette, steak or liver for another day. Make the other main meal for that day a vegetarian one.

Minimize the effects of cholesterol on blood lipids by keeping the amount of saturated fat (mainly animal fat) in check, for these fats raise blood cholesterol levels. For example, use soft margarine instead of butter and skip cream sauces. In a restaurant ask for the sauce to be served on the side to keep the portion size small.

When eating cholesterol-rich foods, keep in mind that the more fat consumed at the same time the more readily cholesterol is absorbed. Reducing total fat intake helps reduce cholesterol absorption and gives a more favorable blood lipid pattern.

Another consideration when eating foods that are rich in cho-

Table 3
APPROXIMATE CHOLESTEROL CONTENT OF FINFISH
mg per 3½ ounces raw edible weight*

50 mg or less

Smelt	25	Yellowfin tuna	45
Pacific halibut	30	Skipjack tuna	45
Canary rockfish	35	Japanese mackerel	50
Monkfish	35	Lake trout	50
Sockeye salmon	35	Flounder/sole	50
Pacific cod	35	Striped mullet	50
Bluefin tuna	40	Sablefish	50
Swordfish	40	Grouper	50
Pike, northern	40	Pompano	50
Red snapper	40	Chub mackerel	50
Mackerel, horse	40	Sardine	50
Ocean perch	40	Spiny dogfish	50
Atlantic Cod	45		

55 to 100 mg

King mackerel	55	Drum, freshwater	65
Albacore tuna	55	Carp	65
Bonito	55	Brook trout	70
Rainbow trout	55	Pollock	70
Channel catfish	60	Chum salmon	75
Freshwater bass	60	Catfish, brown	75
Bluefish	60	Pacific herring	75
Burbot	60	Striped bass	80
Whitefish	60	Atlantic mackerel	80
Atlantic herring	60	White perch	80
Croaker	60	Walleye pike	85
Haddock	65	Yellow perch	90

*Data rounded to the nearest 5 mg. Cholesterol values are considered accurate ±20%. Data from USDA Provisional Table HNIS PT-103, 1986 and Nettleton, J. *Seafood Nutrition* 1985, Osprey Books, Huntington, NY.

lesterol, like calamari, shrimp and eggs is to keep the amounts consumed to reasonable portions. About four ounces of cooked squid or shrimp would supply as much cholesterol as recommended for one day. If you eat larger amounts of cholesterol rich foods, try the next day or so to offset the high cholesterol intake by choosing foods especially low in cholesterol. The body is flexible in adjusting to daily variations in cholesterol intake but the aim is to keep the aver-

Table 4
APPROXIMATE CHOLESTEROL CONTENT OF
SHELLFISH

Cholesterol in 3½ oz.

Molluscs	mg*	Crustaceans	mg*
Soft shell clams	25	Dungeness crab	60
Surf clams	35	King crab	60
Sea scallops	35	Lobster	70-95
Quahogs	40	Blue crab	80-100
Pacific oysters	45	Spiny lobster	95-140
Eastern oysters	45-55	Northern pink shrimp	125-135
Mussels	40-65	Gulf brown shrimp	140-160
Razor clams	105	Gulf white shrimp	140-180
Abalone	110	Tropical pink shrimp	150-160
Octopus	120		
Short fin squid	200		
Long fin squid	300		

*Data rounded to the nearest 5 mg. Cholesterol values are
considered accurate ±20%. Data from USDA Provisional Table
HNIS PT-103, 1986 and Nettleton, J. *Seafood Nutrition* 1985,
Osprey Books, Huntington, N.Y. and N.M.F.S. Gloucester, Mass.

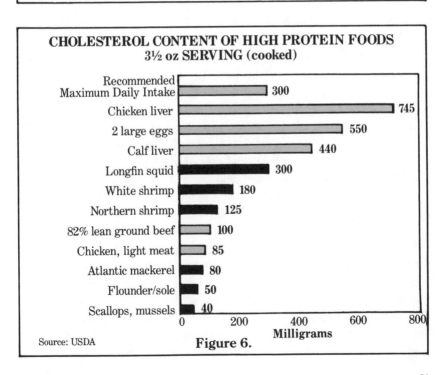

CHOLESTEROL CONTENT OF HIGH PROTEIN FOODS
3½ oz SERVING (cooked)

Food	Milligrams
Recommended Maximum Daily Intake	300
Chicken liver	745
2 large eggs	550
Calf liver	440
Longfin squid	300
White shrimp	180
Northern shrimp	125
82% lean ground beef	100
Chicken, light meat	85
Atlantic mackerel	80
Flounder/sole	50
Scallops, mussels	40

Source: USDA

Figure 6.

age cholesterol intake below 300 milligrams a day.

Recent Information About Cholesterol in Seafood

It used to be thought that all shellfish were high in cholesterol. This belief was based on data obtained with laboratory procedures that are now out of date. With refinements in laboratory analyses the quality and precision of the data has improved. One result of these improvements has particular bearing on our ideas about certain molluscs, especially clams, mussels and oysters.

Clams, mussels and oysters are filter feeders. This means they get their food by filtering the surrounding water and retaining the microscopic plants and animals it provides. Many of these tiny foodstuffs contain *sterols* of plant origin that are similar but not identical to cholesterol in structure. The old analyses counted these plant sterols as cholesterol. More than half of what we thought was cholesterol is actually plant sterol.

The good news is that these plant sterols are very poorly absorbed by the body. Instead, they interfere with the absorption of cholesterol so that what little cholesterol there is tends not to be taken up. Clams, mussels and oysters are truly heart healthy foods. Not only are they very low in cholesterol but they contain substances that discourage cholesterol uptake. Quite a bonus.

Molluscs are heart healthy for two other reasons. They are very low in fat – less than 2 percent – and have very little saturated fat. What could be better?

Most people do not have to worry about the cholesterol they eat from seafood. Very few of us eat enough shrimp, caviar or calamari often enough to make a substantial contribution to our cholesterol status. There are people, however, who are at high risk of heart disease and are particularly sensitive to the amount of cholesterol they consume. These people are usually under a doctor's supervision and have been advised to restrict their cholesterol intake to well below 300 mg a day. For them it is important to be aware of all foods rich in cholesterol. Those seafoods having more than 100 mg cholesterol per 3½ ounces are: shrimp, crayfish, spiny lobster, abalone, octopus, razor clams, conch, crayfish, squid and fish roe. The last two are very high, having more than 200 mg per 3½ ounces. People advised to keep strict limits on their cholesterol intake should consume all cholesterol rich foods only in small portions and at infrequent intervals.

Fiber

The fourth dietary consideration for lowering blood LDL cholesterol is fiber. Seafood has no dietary fiber – only plants do. Having plenty of fiber every day can help lower cholesterol. Although we are not certain how fiber achieves this effect, we think it has to do with hastening the excretion of several substances related to cholesterol metabolism. This gives cholesterol less chance to re-enter the system from the intestine. The benefits of dietary fiber come from eating lots of whole grains, fruits and vegetables every day.

In summary, all of us can improve our blood cholesterol pattern by the following:

• Achieve and maintain a desirable body weight

• Lower fat intake – to half what we are eating now if possible

• Limit saturated fats as much as possible

• Keep cholesterol intake below 300 mg each day

• Eat plenty of foods rich in fiber every day

• Exercise vigorously for 20 minutes or more at least three times a week

Chapter Five

The Many Ways Seafood Promotes Health

Adds Variety

Variety is the cornerstone of good diet. We need many different kinds of foods to give us all the nutrients we need. Some nutrients, like selenium, are found in only a few foods while others, like protein, are abundant. The wider the range of foods we eat, the more likely it is that our diet is healthful. Variety makes it more enjoyable, as well.

Variety means eating wholesome foods that supply protein, vitamins, minerals, small amounts of fat, fiber and water. All solid foods give us calories (energy) but not all furnish the essentials of life. The best diet relies on nutrient rich foods rather than on those rich in fats and sugars. Fat-rich and sugar-rich foods displace more wholesome ones, leaving us with less room for the nutritious foods which benefit our health.

The essence of variety, however, is having a number of foods from different categories. Nutritionists classify foods as dairy, fruits and vegetables, whole grains, protein-rich foods and a grab-bag of items rich in fat and sugar. Within each of these groups some choices are better than others. Emphasizing the wiser choices is a form of free health insurance. Sound eating habits help prevent many illnesses Americans develop in middle and later life. As we continue to find out, our current carefree choices may also be careless.

This book deals with a part of one food category – the importance of seafood, a group of protein-rich foods. Seafood is one of the best protein foods we have and one of the most neglected. It is also one of the best ways to increase the variety of healthful protein-rich choices we have.

Fish and shellfish come in hundreds of varieties. Large seafood markets may offer over a hundred different kinds of seafood. The Fulton Fish Market in New York, for example, has over five hundred different kinds of seafood at any time. In local markets it is not unusual to find thirty or more different types of seafood with the range expanding as distribution improves and customers become more adventurous in their tastes.

Compare this variety with meat and poultry. Beef, pork, lamb and veal are the chief meats with organ meats and processed meats adding to the variety of forms and flavors available. In poultry, chicken and turkey prevail. Greater variety is possible by using goose, duck and Cornish game hens. But nowhere near the variety of flavor, texture and form is available with these familiar mainstays as there is with seafood.

Seafood is an excellent mainstay because it is nutrient rich. It delivers not only energy, but high quality protein, a variety of B vitamins, several minerals and usually very little fat. It gives us many nutrients we need without worrisome amounts of fat and sodium.

Seafood flavors vary from mild and delicate to strong and robust. You can take it as it is or transform it with complementary flavors like tomato, cheese or curry. The form, texture and style differ widely as well. Consider cod. It is sold most often as a fillet but may be presented as dressed fish, as a steak, as smoked cod pieces or as salt cod. Each of these forms can be cooked so that the final preparation appears to be a different fish.

And seafood adds variety because it adapts to many different kinds of preparations. Routine family menus can become more interesting without being more time-consuming because seafood adapts to an immense variety of simple preparations. A few examples of this mealtime variety include seafood fettucine, fish chowder, calamari salad, spaghetti with clam sauce, seafood stir-fry, barbecued fish steaks, stuffed fish fillets, tabouli with mussels, seafood quiche and salmon burgers.

Best of all, seafood is fast to prepare, even from the frozen state. It needs less cooking time than meat or poultry, is naturally tender and can be cooked by familiar cooking techniques as well as by microwave, outdoor grill and stir-fry methods. Unlike meat and poultry, however, seafood is best when cooked for only a short time at a high temperature and served at once. It is truly fast food with all its nutritional advantages intact.

Builds Better Blood

Although blood contains a variety of cells and substances, red blood cells are vital to many of the blood's tasks. In order to have healthy, abundant red blood cells we need sufficient supplies of several nutrients. These nutrients include iron, copper, zinc, vitamin B_{12}, folic acid and certain others. Seafood has all of these nutrients, some in substantial amounts. Eating seafood regularly is one of the easiest ways to build better blood.

Iron. A major task of blood is to deliver oxygen to tissues and take away wastes and carbon dioxide. This is done by the red blood cells. The transport capacity of red cells depends on their having enough hemoglobin, an iron-containing pigment that binds oxygen. When iron is in short supply, less hemoglobin is made and fewer healthy red cells are produced. This leads eventually to anemia, which we detect in the form of fatigue, listlessness and sometimes headaches.

Muscles also need iron to make the protein myoglobin. Like hemoglobin, myoglobin binds oxygen and holds it in reserve for muscular activity. Too little iron relates to insufficient oxygen in muscles; this reduces muscular activity and the ability to perform.

Iron is the nutrient most likely to be lacking in the diets of Americans. Few foods have large amounts of iron, and many yield very little to the body. Iron is poorly absorbed and not readily available from many foods. The body most easily takes up organic iron, which is found in animal foods. This form of iron also enhances the uptake of iron from other foods where it is otherwise less readily absorbed. Seafood, because of its ready availability and positive effect on other food sources of iron, is one of the most valuable sources of iron we have.

Foods richest in iron are: liver, oysters, clams, mussels, red meats, dark fleshed fish like sardines and bluefish, and poultry. The form of iron in these foods (organic) is the kind most easily absorbed by the body.

Plant sources of iron like enriched cereals, legumes, spinach and broccoli have useful amounts of iron but its form is less easily taken up by the body. Eating a source of vitamin C at mealtime increases the amount of iron absorbed from cereals and legumes. That is another good reason for eating green vegetables or fresh fruit at mealtime.

Women are at special risk of having too little iron because of blood loss. Women eat smaller amounts of iron rich foods than men, partly because they eat less in general. Many foods that are high in iron are not well liked. Seafood, however, tastes good and is usually popular, especially among women. It also has the bonus of being lean. Using uncoated iron cookware will increase the amount of iron in food, so bring out the old iron skillet for simmering.

Copper is a second mineral important for the formation of hemoglobin and red blood cells. Its presence enhances iron metabolism. It is also required for proper collagen formation. Collagen is a part of connective tissue such as cartilage, tendon and skin. Its formation is a key to normal wound healing. Copper also affects lipid (fat and cholesterol) metabolism and nervous tissue function. While small amounts of copper are found in many foods, whole grains and shellfish are the richest sources.

Zinc, like iron, is involved in some of the body's most important activities. It acts as a helper for many enzymes which drive the body's biochemistry. It is necessary for the normal processing of protein, carbohydrate, fat and alcohol. It is involved in making DNA, the substance in cells that carries the genetic blueprint for reproduction. Zinc is important in immune reactions, taste perception, wound healing and in making the pancreas' all-important hormone, insulin.

Zinc is related to healthy red blood cells because it is part of the enzymes needed for cell production in the bone marrow. It also affects the uptake of iron from the intestine. Too much zinc reduces the absorption of iron and leads to anemia.

Interest in the nutritional properties of zinc is relatively recent. There has been concern about the shortage of zinc among some Americans, especially children, though actual deficiency is rare. Zinc is found in both animal and plant foods, but many situations conspire to keep zinc absorption low. The presence of other minerals such as calcium, copper, cadmium and phosphorus interferes with zinc absorption. The plant substances *phytate** and fiber

---

*Words printed in italics are defined in the Glossary at the end of the book. Only the first occurrence of the word is italicized.

also reduce zinc uptake.

There is one outstanding food source of zinc – oysters. These molluscs have become famous among nutritionists for their very high zinc levels. Mussels and clams are excellent sources too, as are other shellfish, fish, poultry and meats, dark green leafy vegetables and whole grains. Because seafood is such a valuable source of zinc, children, elderly persons and those eating only small amounts of food should all eat seafood regularly. In fact, all of us would benefit from having oysters, mussels or clams from time to time.

Vitamin B$_{12}$ is the chief vitamin required for red cell production. **Folic acid** (folacin) is also very important. Vitamin B$_{12}$ is a cobalt-containing vitamin needed to ensure the production of an enzyme containing folacin. The vitamins are inter-related and both are needed for successful red blood cell production in bone marrow. When either of these vitamins is in short supply, a type of anemia with large pale red blood cells develops. Supplying folic acid will correct the anemia, but will not prevent nerve damage if the anemia resulted from inadequate vitamin B$_{12}$. It is said that folic acid can mask vitamin B$_{12}$ deficiency, a rare condition. Shortage of folic acid is more common than lack of vitamin B$_{12}$ because B$_{12}$ is present in meat, and is stored in the body.

Pregnant women need more of these vitamins in order to make the additional blood necessary for the growing placenta and fetus.

Vitamin B$_{12}$ is found only in animal foods like seafood, meat and dairy products. Vegetarians need to obtain their B$_{12}$ from supplemented foods or fermented products that contain microorganisms. Vitamin B$_{12}$ is found in both fish and shellfish, but folic acid is present only in small amounts. Folic acid is abundant in vegetables.

In summary, seafood is remarkably efficient for building healthy blood because it contains useful amounts of most of the nutrients needed to make red blood cells. Some nutrients important for healthy red blood cells are difficult to obtain in sufficient amounts, especially for women. Iron is crucial for healthy red cells and frequently in short supply. Seafood, particularly oysters, mussels and clams, can make a valuable contribution in furnishing iron supplies.

Benefits from Major Minerals

Several minerals are needed in relatively large amounts and are classified as "major" minerals. Of these minerals, calcium is needed in greatest amount. Other such minerals are phosphorus, magnesium, sodium, potassium and chloride. We could count iron either way but it is usually considered a trace mineral.

Calcium is in the news because of its association with osteoporosis, a bone disease prevalent among elderly women. In this disease bones gradually lose calcium, thereby becoming weakened and prone to breaking. The strategy in trying to prevent and treat the disease is to stem the loss of calcium.

We know that many changes in aging affect the movement of calcium out of the bones. Among these are decreases in female hormones at menopause, lack of exercise and possible shortage of calcium in the diet. Diet and exercise are factors we can do something about.

Many adults abandon the milk-drinking habits of their youth without taking on any other source of calcium. This may contribute to the gradual loss of calcium from bones over the next forty years of life. One way to curb this slow calcium loss is to be sure to obtain the Recommended Dietary Allowance for calcium, 800 milligrams each day. The National Institutes of Health recommend that women and elderly men consume at least 1000 milligrams of calcium daily to help offset the age-related loss of calcium from bones.

While the best sources of calcium are lowfat milk and lowfat dairy products, there are some excellent seafood sources of calcium as well. Fish whose bones are small, soft and chewable enough to be eaten without danger of choking are good sources of calcium. Sardines, anchovies and canned salmon with its bones are the main examples. With canned salmon, simply mash up the small bones when you use the fish and help yourself to some valuable calcium. Otherwise, fish and shellfish are not rich sources of calcium. Legumes, broccoli, and tofu processed with calcium are other useful sources of this mineral.

Phosphorus is important for bone structure and for energy storage in cells. Certain substances store energy by means of "high energy phosphate bonds," a phrase that describes the form of chemical energy that most cells use.

Phosphorus is widely distributed in foods and is abundant in seafood. Usually our consumption of phosphorus exceeds our needs so there is little worry about obtaining enough of this mineral.

Magnesium, a third major mineral, is important for bone structure and like phosphorus has metabolic functions as well. It assists in a vast number of enzyme reactions including energy transfers, fatty acid breakdown and protein synthesis. It is also necessary for the communication of nerve impulses in muscle. Although magnesium is widespread in foods, it is especially abundant in seafood. Anchovies, clams, catfish and canned tuna are notable sources.

Sodium is a fourth major mineral to consider. We are more likely to consume too much sodium than too little. For this reason the best foods with respect to sodium are those with the least. Excessive sodium intake is associated with high blood pressure in many people. Sodium is discussed in greater detail in Chapter Two under "High Blood Pressure."

Potassium is important for maintaining water balance in cells. It is found mainly inside the cell where it opposes the action of sodium outside the cell. If losses of sodium become large, as can occur with diuretics, the medicines often used to control blood pressure, potassium may also be lost from cells. For that reason, people with high blood pressure who are being treated with diuretic medications are often advised to consume plenty of potassium-rich foods or are given a potassium supplement.

Potassium is crucial for maintaining normal heartbeat. In fact, under conditions of starvation or severe protein malnutrition where water and mineral loss from diarrhea occurs, heart failure may result from depletion of potassium in the heart muscle. Healthy people seldom need to think about potassium intake because the mineral is widespread in foods. Seafood is rich in potassium with mussels, scallops and many fish having generous amounts.

Chloride is a major mineral in the body. We are seldom concerned about obtaining adequate amounts. Chloride is the other mineral component of table salt and we consume abundant amounts of it through our intake of salt. Chloride is an especially important component of the acid that breaks down our food in the stomach. It is also abundant in spinal fluid.

Trace Minerals for Key Tasks

In contrast to major minerals, trace minerals are those the body needs only in small amounts. They are as vital as major minerals. Many trace elements are stored in the body so that irregular supplies from food do not compromise the body's function.

Our body depends on tiny amounts of several minerals for its metabolic activities. Trace minerals allow enzymes to operate. Without enzymes nothing happens.

Enzymes are proteins that permit chemical reactions to occur. They do not participate in the reactions directly but provide active sites to which other molecules bind.

Enzymes require a variety of minerals, including zinc, cobalt, magnesium and selenium. Insufficient amounts of trace minerals will impair the formation of certain enzymes and compromise the chemical reactions that depend on these enzymes.

Seafood is rich in many trace minerals. It is our best source of selenium and fluorine and is important for copper, zinc and iodine. Seafood is not rich in all the trace elements we need but makes an important contribution to these needs.

Iodine is naturally present in marine seafoods, most abundantly in shellfish. We need this mineral in trace amounts for the thyroid gland to make its hormones. These hormones regulate body temperature, metabolic rate and the function of most tissues. Plants derive iodine from the soil, but some growing areas are depleted of iodine. Years ago we fortified table salt with iodine to prevent goiter, which is an enlarged thyroid gland. Now iodine is abundant in foods in the USA owing largely to its use in food processing. Iodine is present in dough conditioners used in baked goods and in many animal feeds and medications. There is no need to worry about iodine deficiency in the USA but it is still a problem in many poor countries.

Sea salt is sometimes touted for the benefits of its trace minerals. Iodine is frequently mentioned as being present. In fact, iodine is lost from sea salt during the drying process. The remaining trace minerals are present in such small amounts that the overriding concern with sea salt is just the same as with table salt – excess sodium. Use sea salt with the same caution you exercise with ordinary table salt.

Fluoride makes bones and teeth strong. It can reduce development of dental caries (decay) and discourage calcium loss from bones. In many areas we obtain fluoride from drinking water. Seafood and tea are the other useful food sources. Fluoridated toothpastes also supply this mineral. If the water supply is not a reliable source of this nutrient, children may need fluoride supplements, available only by prescription.

Selenium is a mineral found mainly in marine seafoods and in plants which extract it from the soil. Selenium helps protect polyunsaturated fatty acids like those in seafood and vegetable oils from being oxidized. Selenium and vitamin E work together to prevent the formation from these fats of harmful products like peroxides. Although we are still unclear exactly how selenium prevents peroxides from being formed it probably helps protect fish omega-3 fatty acids from destruction.

Researchers are studying how selenium might be helpful in preventing some forms of cancer where disturbances of fatty acid metabolism may be involved. Selenium also offers some protection against the harmful effects of mercury. This activity may be quite important as mercury is present in small amounts in many foods, including seafood. There is much more to learn about this fascinating mineral, and it may become more widely recognized that seafood is the most dependable natural food source of selenium.

One of the key features of all essential trace minerals is that while a tiny amount is vital to health, large amounts are toxic. Trace minerals interact with each other and with other essential nutrients. When one mineral is present in great excess it can impair the absorption and metabolism of other nutrients. For example, large amounts of iron interfere with zinc absorption and too much zinc impairs the utilization of calcium. Plainly, supplements are more apt to be harmful than helpful. Mine your minerals from foods, not from supplements.

Counting Calories

The major reason people watch their diet is because they are overweight. As some 28 percent of the adult American population is overweight, this dietary challenge is important to a vast number of people. Developing eating habits for successful weight loss is a splendid opportunity for creating a repertoire of lean nutritious foods. Seafood is one of the easiest and most enjoyable mainstays of calorie-controlled eating. It is low in fat and calories yet satisfying and tasty.

There are two parts to the strategy for achieving weight loss. The first, and probably the most important, is to use up more energy than you take in. In a word, move. Regular, vigorous physical activity makes the body work more efficiently, improves heart and lung capacity, creates better muscle tone and makes you feel better. Starting a regular exercise program of brisk walking, swimming or gentle aerobics is the best way to begin a serious effort to lose weight. Besides, it creates a positive frame of mind for improving eating habits.

Exercise uses up fat and builds the efficiency of the heart and lungs. One of the best do-it-yourself guides to exercising is free from the government. Request a copy of "Exercise and Your Heart", publication number NIH 83-1677, from:

Public Inquiries and Reports Branch
Publications Department
National Heart Lung and Blood Institute
Bethesda, MD 20205

Regular vigorous exercise starts you on your way to using more energy than you eat. Keeping your energy intake in line with your energy output is the other half of the strategy for reaching a desirable weight. That simply means eating less. Of course it is easy to say and less easy to do but the combination of regular vigorous exercise with sound eating habits builds successful long term weight loss – the kind that stays off. Eating for weight loss is exactly the way to eat all the time: emphasize lean foods in appropriate amounts.

To lose weight, the body must use more energy or calories than it receives. It makes up for this imbalance by using up the stores of body fat abundant in many of us. Exercise uses up energy while eating replenishes it. In the long run, exercise helps control appetite so that overeating does not become a problem. Eating heavily before or after exercise is uncomfortable and unwise. As a result, light eating habits are easier to adopt and maintain.

The key to becoming slimmer is using the slender calories – those foods with very little fat. Calories measure the energy value of food. Because an ounce of fat has more than twice the calorie value of an ounce of either protein or carbohydrate, fat-rich foods pad your body and blood vessels instead of your health. It works this way:

Extra energy from eating is stored in the body as fat. This fat cushions and bulges tissues. Along with other substances it begins to clog the lining of blood vessels. As extra fat and weight accumulate, the heart and lungs must work harder just to keep the body going. It is rather like carrying a ten or fifteen pound sack around all day. Movement is more cumbersome and reduced activity fosters more weight gain.

Eating lean foods, those with little fat, contributes to good health. These winners are cereals, whole grains, fruits, vegetables, fish and shellfish, poultry and low fat dairy products. They cover everything we need without including the fats that often undermine health. The bonus with seafood is that most species are very lean –

less than 5 percent fat – and most are low in cholesterol. Even the oilier species, when used in place of other fat rich foods, contribute to health because of their omega-3 fatty acids. It is also useful to note that the rich species of fish have about the same amount of fat as the leanest meats.

Because seafood is low in fat, it is low in calories. We can have a larger portion on the plate and feel satisfied without over-eating. The only thing to avoid in preparing seafood is adding fat. Instead of deep fat or pan frying, cook seafood by baking, broiling, outdoor grilling, steaming, poaching, stir-frying, or oven-frying (with these last two methods add only a tiny amount of fat). Smother fish in vegetables; use wine and herbs; try zesty seasonings which complement seafood flavors. And try the recipes in this book.

The best way to take advantage of seafoods when losing weight is to use them to replace other, richer foods like cheese, processed and fresh meats and anything fried. In sandwiches and salads use low fat and calorie reduced dressings and use all dressings sparingly. Make the rest of the meal abundant in vegetables, fruits and whole grains. The carbohydrates will see you through the day. Keep spreads, sauces, dressings and packaged snack foods to a minimum.

Table 5 shows calorie values of different species of fish and shellfish.

The secret to successful weight control is mastering the combination of regular exercise and light, lowfat eating. Gradual weight loss, not crash dieting, will keep the pounds off. Establish a reasonable target weight, then promise yourself your best effort and plenty of time to achieve your goal. Use the following rule of thumb for finding the most desirable weight; then go for it.

Estimating A Desirable Weight for Yourself

Women: Allow 100 pounds for the first 5 feet of your height. Then allow 5 pounds for each additional inch. A woman 5 foot 3 inches tall should weigh about 115 pounds.

Men: Allow 106 pounds for the first 5 feet of your height. Then allow 6 pounds for each additional inch. A man 5 foot 10 inches tall should weigh about 166 pounds.

Body Frame: For a light frame subtract 10 percent of the estimated desirable body weight from the weight calculated above. For a heavy frame, add 10 percent of the estimated desirable body weight to the figure just calculated.

74

Table 5
APPROXIMATE CALORIE CONTENT OF SELECTED
FINFISH*
per 3½ ounce
raw

Less than 150 calories

Orange roughy	65	Drum (redfish)	90	Porgy (scup)	110
Red hake	70	Atlantic pollock	90	Brook trout	110
Atlantic cod	75	Mahimahi	90	Catfish	115
Sole	75-90	Black sea bass	95	Atl. halibut	115
Pacific cod	80	Striped bass	95	Striped mullet	115
Pacific pollock	80	Grouper	95	Barracuda	120
Monkfish	80	Canary rockfish	95	Swordfish	120
Rockfish	80	White sucker	95	Chum	125
Blue shark	80	Sea trout	95	Yellowfin tuna	125
Flounder	85-95	Atl. sturgeon	100	Pac. mackerel	130
Haddock	85	Smelt	100	Anchovy	130
Cusk	85	Yellowtail snapper	100	Skipjack tuna	130
Silver hake	85	Ocean catfish	100	Atlantic salmon	130
Lingcod	85	Pacific halibut	105	Pink salmon	130
Lake perch	85	Ocean perch	105	Rainbow trout	130
Northern pike	85	Weakfish	105	Span. sardine	135
Walleye pike	85	Atl. bluefish	110	Spot	135
Pacific whiting	85	Cisco	110	King mackerel	140
Tilefish	90	Red snapper	110	Span. mackerel	140
Croaker	90	Crevalle jack	110	Carp	145
Red grouper	90	Bigeye tuna	110		

150-200 calories

Atl. herring	150	Spiny dogfish	165
Atlantic bonito	150	Arctic char	165
Silver salmon	150	Albacore tuna	170
Lake whitefish	160	Lake sturgeon	170
Amberjack	160	Butterfish	175
Sockeye salmon	160	Atl. mackerel	175
Bluefin tuna	160	Inconnu	185
Pacific bonito	160	Sablefish	185
Pacific herring	160	King salmon	185
Calif. pilchard	165	Shad	185
Atl. pompano	165		

More than 200 calories

Buffalo	215	Eel	225

* Calorie values have been rounded to the nearest 5 calories.
Source: Nettleton, J. *Seafood Nutrition,* 1985. Osprey Books.

Lowering Blood Cholesterol

The evidence is clear – the higher your blood cholesterol level, the more likely you are to have a heart attack. You do not even have to have a very high cholesterol level to be at risk of heart attack. Half the people who get heart attacks have cholesterol levels below 250 mg/dl. Above 260 mg, consider yourself at high risk. You need your cholesterol below 200 mg to be at a much lower risk of heart disease.

There are a number of ways to lower blood cholesterol levels. The more of them you do, the better your chances of lowering your blood cholesterol as much as possible.

• Reach your most desirable body weight. Overweight people have higher cholesterol levels.

• Exercise vigorously at least three times a week. People who are physically fit have lower cholesterol levels.

• Limit your intake of saturated fats. These include animal fats from red meats and processed meats; dairy products, especially butter; hydrogenated vegetable fats like margarine, shortening and non-dairy creamers; and the coconut oil and palm oil used often in commercially baked foods. The oils in seafood have very little saturated fat.

• Eat plenty of fiber rich foods. Whole grains, bran rich cereals, brown rice and vegetables help to lower cholesterol levels. No one knows why they are helpful, only that they work.

• Eat only low fat dairy products. Forget cream, sour cream, butter, whole milk, cream cheese and soft ripened cheeses. Use other cheeses in small amounts for they are high in both total fat and saturated fat. Non dairy creamers are also high in saturated fat.

• Keep your cholesterol intake to no more than 300 mg per day. Cholesterol is found only in animal foods. Be lavish with fruits, vegetables and grains and niggardly with meats. Richest sources of cholesterol are egg yolks, liver, other organ meats, squid and fish roe. These foods are otherwise very nutritious, so instead of eliminating them altogether, use them infrequently and in moderate portions.

• Do not eat fried foods. Trim meats before cooking and eating. Skip gravies and cream sauces. Use salad dressings and oils sparingly. And forget frying.

Seafood — A Food for the Times

Seafood is a major part of wise eating for the eighties and nineties. It fits in with all the current dietary recommendations as a nutrient-rich, lean food. It is part of wise eating to discourage heart disease, cancer and other types of chronic diseases.

Seafood carries with it none of the dietary components we know are associated with major diseases in America. In addition, regular consumption of seafood outfits your cells with omega-3 fatty acids to discourage heart disease. Having these fatty acids in cells permits the body to respond more temperately to a wide range of conditions that bring us distress. In particular, conditions such as arthritis, bronchial asthma, diabetes, migraine, high blood pressure and possibly even some cancers may be less likely to develop or may be less severe if omega-3s are part of the body's cellular equipment. Medical research in the coming decades should give us the information and understanding we need to be able to give more concrete advice.

Seafood fits in with our fast-paced lifestyles where kitchen time is minimal. Without sacrificing taste, wholesomeness or precious time, seafood can make it to the table in ten minutes or less. It takes longer to chop the vegetables or make a salad than to cook seafood in a tasty way. Seafood cooks well by conventional methods of baking or broiling and by cuisine techniques of steaming, poaching in wine, cooking on the outdoor grill, stir-frying or microwaving. The trick in successful seafood cookery is to undercook the seafood slightly so that it remains tender and moist. Very high temperatures with short cooking times ensure quick, fail-proof cookery.

Enjoying seafood is part of a healthful lifestyle where wholesome food, quickly and easily prepared, contributes to well-being. The good taste comes free.

Chapter Six

Fish Oil Supplements

In the light of our understanding of omega-3 fatty acids and the benefits of the oils in fish it is easy to congratulate our parents and grandparents for feeding us cod liver oil. We thought we were taking liquid sunshine but we were probably establishing heart health as well. Is it time to restore this distasteful custom or is fish oil the snake oil of the '80s?

The answer is both yes and no. Fish oil supplements may be useful for people with certain types of blood lipid disorders. In particular, people with high blood triglycerides would be expected to respond favorably to regular fish oil consumption. A doctor can identify individuals with high triglycerides (Type V and Type IIb *hyperlipidemia**) by requesting the appropriate blood tests. Certain people with other blood lipid disorders might benefit from these preparations but there is no way, save by trying, to know whether or not omega-3 fatty acids could be helpful for a particular individual. On the other hand, healthy people may show no response to fish oil supplements.

There have been several studies among patients with various lipid disorders but the results are based on such a small number of patients that no general predictions can be made yet. People with high triglycerides are more likely to respond than those with other types of lipid disorders. If a member of your family has a lipid disorder, ask your physician about the possible use of fish oil to improve

---

*Words printed in italics are defined in the Glossary at the end of the book. Only the first occurrence of the word is italicized.

his blood lipid pattern.

Other medical conditions such as arthritis and bronchial asthma might respond to long term consumption of fish oil but the evidence we have is so preliminary that no recommendation can be made. Fish oil supplements are not benign products. Their indiscriminate use could make an unfortunate situation worse. Arthritis in particular has been the target of many worthless diet remedies and to raise false hopes with yet another bottled preparation smacks of snake oil remedies. Arthritis sufferers are strongly urged to consult experienced rheumatologists and to ask about the possible usefulness of long term fish oil supplementation. Perhaps the physician is interested in conducting a study among his patients to test the usefulness of omega-3 fatty acids in treating arthritis. Be aware, however, that it is likely to take months before any effects might be detected. We are just at the beginning of exploring the possibilities of omega-3 fatty acids in immune and inflammatory conditions.

Fish oil supplements may be useful as a cautionary measure in slowing down the progress of atherosclerosis. We do not know if small amounts of fish oil taken regularly can halt the development of blood vessel blockages or lower the risk of heart disease in healthy or in high risk people. These are pressing questions facing medical researchers and are being actively explored.

What about healthy folk who are interested in safeguarding good health? The best answer is to eat more fish – lots more fish. Eat as many different varieties of fish and shellfish as you can find and prepare them without adding more than one or two teaspoons of oil per serving. All the studies we have so far among people who regularly eat fish indicate that seafood eaters have less heart disease, cancer, arthritis, asthma and other chronic diseases.

Even people with serious heart disease who kept to a low fat diet eating fish three times a week lived more than four years longer than those who paid no attention to their diet. That means it is never too late to improve your heart health with seafood.

Are There Risks in Taking Fish Oil Supplements?

Taking fish oil supplements, like consuming any other kind of supplement, is a form of self medication. The *hazards* have to do with excess amounts of substances in the supplement and how well the body deals with the surplus. Most people take supplements in the hope that somehow they will benefit. It is usually taken for granted that the supplement will not be harmful, an assumption that is seldom warranted.

With fish oil supplements the quality of the product as well as the kind and amount of substances that may be present vary widely among different preparations. The label usually does not have enough information to permit you to judge quality. The oils themselves vary with the species of fish, sex, season, environment and so on. The composition of the oil differs according to whether it comes from the liver or the flesh: liver oils are much richer in vitamins, metals, organic compounds and cholesterol than oils from the flesh. Fatty acid composition, especially the omega-3 fatty acid content, varies with the species and source of the oil. Processing may affect the easily-damaged omega-3 fatty acids.

Shelf life and storage conditions affect final quality. Fish oils spoil readily, especially at warm temperatures. Light can have harmful effects too, promoting oxidation or breakdown of the fat. Dark glass bottles and opaque packaging offer protection against light. Very few stores protect their fish oil with refrigeration.

Air promotes the oxidation and destruction of the omega-3 fatty acids in fish oils. Some manufacturers have found that the fish oil is better protected from air when the oil is packaged in capsules. Antioxidants are usually added to protect the polyunsaturated fatty acids from oxidation. Vitamin E (tocopherol) is a naturally occurring antioxidant sometimes added to margarine. This vitamin is not particularly abundant in fish oil, however, and there is some question about how effective it is in protecting omega-3 fatty acids. An anti-oxidant called TBHQ (tertiary butyhydroquinone) or other anti-oxidants may be added to fish oil to protect the omega-3 fatty acids.

The wary buyer should be on the lookout for the levels of several potentially harmful substances in fish oils. Among such substances are the fat soluble vitamins A and D. These vitamins are naturally present in some fish oils in amounts that are toxic to people. Some manufacturers "strip" the oil of these vitamins leaving only small amounts behind. The label should tell the amount of both vitamins A and D contained in the product. Do not take preparations or doses of fish oil in excess of the *US RDA* for these vitamins. The US RDA for vitamin A is 5000 International Units and for vitamin D is 400 International Units.

The reason these vitamins are potentially harmful is that they are stored in the body. Excess from supplements and food accumulates in the liver and over time can produce illness. The amount required to bring on symptoms varies widely among individuals but there are documented cases of people becoming ill with intakes just a few times greater than the US RDA. A daily dose of several spoonfuls or capsules a day of fish oil, each containing just the US RDA, may seem safe. But you can easily accumulate dangerous amounts of these vitamins from such dosage.

Vitamin E is another vitamin whose metabolism is closely linked to polyunsaturated fatty acids. This vitamin is an anti-oxidant, which means that it offers itself for oxidation in order to protect other valuable substances, like polyunsaturated fatty acids, from being broken down. We need it to protect polyunsaturated fatty acids in the body. We know that our need for vitamin E increases as we consume more polyunsaturated fats. Our need for vitamin E is usually taken care of by the same foods furnishing polyunsaturated fats. Fish oils, however, have relatively little vitamin E. Taking large amounts of fish oils might increase the need for vitamin E. So far, there is no evidence that people consuming fish oil capsules have increased vitamin E requirements, but most feeding studies have been of short duration. From what we know presently, one's vitamin E requirement does not appear to be a problem, but it is a consideration worth remembering.

The cholesterol content of fish oil is another potential disadvantage. Fish liver oil preparations that have not had the cholesterol removed may have substantial amounts of cholesterol. The U.S. Department of Agriculture recently published a value of 80 milligrams of cholesterol per tablespoon of cod liver oil, with herring oil having over 100 milligrams. Obviously, taking more than one tablespoon a day adds a considerable amount of cholesterol. Just two tablespoons provides 160 milligrams of cholesterol – half the maximum amount recommended per day for heart healthy eating.

What other potentially harmful substances may be present? Liver oils may have concentrated levels of environmental contaminants, for the liver is responsible for processing metals and organic compounds such as polychlorinated biphenols (PCBs). Unless the oils have been refined to remove heavy metals and organic substances the buyer has no way of knowing whether or not the product contains dangerous amounts of undesirable compounds. While this

81

concern is especially great for fish liver oils it also applies to oils prepared from fish flesh and by-products. The only way to find out if purification has been adequate is to read the label. More often than not, however, the label has no information about heavy metal or organic residue content. Knowing these possibilities, what can you assume about a silent label? No news is not necessarily good news.

There are responsible manufacturers of fish oil concentrates who purify their products and take precautions to protect the omega-3 fatty acid content from destruction during refining. Such producers reduce the high levels of vitamins and cholesterol and remove metal and organic contaminants. When manufacturers undertake these extensive procedures they are happy to tell the consumer about it by showing the analysis of the product. Look for this information on the label if you are considering buying a fish oil product.

The refining process may create other difficulties with the fish oil. One of these is the formation of peroxides, breakdown products of fatty acids. Peroxides are potent and potentially dangerous substances the body takes great care to eliminate. Their formation has been associated with the production of highly reactive compounds that have been linked with cancer. Taking supplements that may have peroxides could be a risk. We know very little about the level of peroxides present in fish oil products beyond our understanding that they can be formed quite readily. Careful manufacturers will screen their products to be sure the peroxide level is very low. The question is, how readily do peroxides form during storage and usual handling conditions, whatever those may be?

Another consideration of fish oils is calories. Fish oil is a high calorie product – about 120 calories per tablespoon. That may not seem like much and it is not on a once-in-a-while basis. But accumulated over time, 120 extra calories a day will soon add up to weight gain. If you take an oil supplement, another source of calories has to go. Most of us are familiar with the difficulty of eating less.

While it is obvious, it is worth pointing out that fish oil supplements will increase your total fat intake unless you reduce consumption of other fat rich foods. All evidence indicates that we already consume too much fat and taking more is a step in the wrong direction. By contrast, using fatty fish instead of other forms of food fats – from meats, oils, salad dressings, dairy foods – is likely to be helpful because it provides omega-3 fatty acids no other foods have. Only when used as a substitute for other kinds of fat will a fish oil supplement not increase total fat and calorie intake.

The decision to take fish oil supplements without medical supervision or advice may pose other risks. We know, for example, that people who have consumed large amounts of fish oil capsules develop an increased bleeding tendency just like traditional Eskimos. How much fish oil it takes to delay blood clotting to an undesirable extent is not known. Certainly the amount having such an effect will vary, some people developing slower clotting more readily than others. In some tests, taking large amounts of fish oil reduced the number of platelets in the blood, a result that would diminish blood clotting. The main point is that we do not know how much fish oil or omega-3 fatty acids it takes to bring about favorable changes in blood clotting in different people without compromising wound healing. Most of the studies so far have used rather large amounts of fish oil. We are just beginning to find out what happens with modest intakes of omega-3s.

Although fish oil supplements might appear to be a simple way to obtain omega-3 fatty acids, we do not know how much fish oil it takes to benefit healthy people. Further, we do not know what is the most favorable balance of different kinds of food fats. Saturated fats are useful for energy but promote high blood cholesterol levels: we want to limit the amount of saturates we eat. Polyunsaturates from vegetables and grains help reduce blood cholesterol levels but favor what some consider an excess prostaglandin production. Omega-3 fatty acids from seafood modify prostaglandin production in a favorable way and promote a variety of healthy responses in tissues. But we really do not know how helpful omega-3s may be when our intake of other types of fats is high. When total fat intake is low, however, the relative amounts of different fats is probably less critical. In low fat eating, small amounts of omega-3s may be especially valuable. Right now we are at the pioneer stage of omega-3 fatty acid research in seeking answers to these complicated issues.

In summary, here are the cautions about unprescribed fish oil supplements:

• They may have potentially toxic levels of vitamins A and D
• They may have a large amount of cholesterol

- They may contain undesirable levels of metal and organic contaminants from the environment
- They may have undesirable amounts of peroxides
- They may increase vitamin E requirements
- Excessive intake may interfere with blood clotting
- Prolonged use may increase fat and calorie intake leading to weight gain
- We do not know how much is either desirable or harmful to consume
- The label seldom gives you information about the source or analysis of the contents
- Packaging, storage and handling may not foster long term stability

Fish or Pills?

I have often been asked if fish oil supplements are fine for people who do not like to eat fish. My reply is that it seems amazing that someone who does not care for fish would like capsules. They are much less palatable.

The question of taste is important. Many people do not like fish because they have not had it well prepared. Frequently fish is overcooked, so dry and flavorless. Childhood memories of unhappy seafood suppers or lack of familiarity with how to prepare seafood prevent many people from cooking fish at home. To help you overcome these experiences, *Seafood and Health* includes some zesty, easy recipes to encourage the enjoyment of simple, delicious seafood.

Capsules cannot compete with seafood in either variety or flavor. If you do not care for one fish, try another. You can keep on trying distinct varieties, a new one every week, for well over a year before beginning again. The odds are that even the most resistant seafood sampler will find some species he enjoys. The immense variety of species, form and preparation is one of seafood's greatest attractions.

Supplements are a quick fix. Insurance in a swallow, we can toss back everything we "need" and get on with our daily pursuits.

Or so it seems. The difficulty is, no one has been able to encapsulate prevention. No array of pills and potions has improved on food. Even with supplements we still eat. The need for suitable food choices remains. Good food can be quickly fixed. For those not wishing to spend much time in the kitchen, nothing is faster than seafood to prepare. Time-saving kitchen equipment and top quality, fresh foods are available to make it easy and fast to eat nutritiously.

Fish oil supplements do not have the nutritional advantages of seafood either. They lack the B vitamins and minerals, and have no protein. They add fat to meals that already have excessive fat. And supplements, by their nature, imply that we cannot obtain an optimum diet from foods. That notion is completely false. A capsule of this and a tablet of that swallowed with essence of rose hip cannot compensate for indiscriminate food habits. No one has yet bottled good health.

Sometimes the charge of high cost is levied against seafood. This is unquestionably true of fish oil capsules. It is true that some forms of seafood are costly, and some regions of the country seldom have fresh seafood bargains. But the seafood marketplace is changing. The demand for seafood is expanding, the distribution system improving, retailers are handling seafood more carefully and consumers are becoming more discriminating. Better quality seafood is becoming more widely available throughout the country. Farm-raised fish makes it possible to have high quality fish all year round, everywhere in the country. While it is unlikely that seafood will ever be as economical as poultry, it is a high value product with no nutritional liabilities and almost no waste.

Less familiar species of fish like cusk, smelts, mackerel, hake or whiting, are usually cheaper than the more popular varieties like cod, sole, snapper and salmon. Cost also depends on the season, weather and abundance of the fish stock. Harvesting fish from the wild is a difficult and costly business with remarkable job specifications.

Inexpensive seafood is available in both canned and frozen forms. These offer excellent nutrition and variety. Canned tuna and mackerel offer some of the cheapest protein foods available. Frozen fish is also often an economical buy. The high cost of fresh red snapper or swordfish does not mean you have to do without the benefits of eating fish.

Finally, people's tastes change. It was not long ago that broccoli was a rather obscure vegetable. Now it is commonplace. People are finding seafood more widely available in restaurants, seeing attractive fish counters in supermarkets, discovering the many ways seafood is available. Trying seafood for the first time is more likely to be a pleasant experience than it used to be because better recipes are available. Health conscious consumers are demanding quality seafood and this makes it more available to everyone. Seafood consumption has been gradually increasing over the past twenty years and has surged recently. We expect this trend to continue.

What Are the Best Sources of Omega-3s?

The answer is simple: seafood. All varieties of fish and shellfish have some omega-3s but the fattier fish have the most. Lean varieties like cod, sole and shellfish have the least amounts. Rich fish, especially salmon, sardines, herring, mackerel, rainbow trout, lake trout, lake whitefish, bluefish, tuna, anchovy, spiny dogfish and sablefish all have more than one gram per 3½ ounces of raw flesh. Table 6 shows approximate omega-3 fatty acid content of some fish. Data for many species are not available.

It is frequently stated but it is not true that cold water, ocean fish have the largest amount of omega-3 fatty acids. Cold water fish like cod and pollock have very little omega-3s. The species listed in the table live at various temperatures, though none is tropical. Florida pompano have as much omega-3 fatty acid as pollock and more than cod, though much less than one might expect for its fat content. The best guide to the amount of omega-3s in a species is its total fat content.

Both freshwater species like trout and marine species like haddock have omega-3s. Fattier species from both environments have the most omega-3s.

Fish raised on farms or in ocean pens depend on their formula diets for their omega-3 fatty acids. Unless the feeds contain fish products with omega-3s, the farm raised fish will have low levels of omega-3s. Lower levels of omega-3s have been found in farm-raised catfish compared with wild samples. It is known that trout require omega-3 fatty acids for successful development and farmed trout receive omega-3s in their ration. In fact, trout is an excellent source of omega-3s. Providing omega-3s in aquaculture for the well-being of both the fish and the people who dine on them is an important consideration in today's fish technology.

Table 6
OMEGA-3 FATTY ACID CONTENT OF FINFISH
gm per 3½ ounces raw fillet

Less than 0.5 gm

Sole	0.1	Swordfish	0.2	Silver hake	0.4
Northern pike	0.1	Red snapper	0.2	Pacific halibut	0.4
Pacific cod	0.2	Grouper	0.3	Skipjack tuna	0.4
Haddock	0.2	Atlantic cod	0.3	Rockfish	0.5
Yellowtail	0.2	Yellow perch	0.3	Atl. pollock	0.5
Ocean perch	0.2	Brook trout	0.4	Sea trout	0.5
Flounder	0.2	Catfish	0.4		

0.6 – 1.0 gm

Yellowfin tuna	0.6	Wolffish	0.7
Turbot	0.6	Striped bass	0.8
Chum salmon	0.6		

More than 1.0 gm

Capelin	1.1	Lake whitefish	1.3	Spiny dogfish	1.9
Pacific mackerel	1.1	Albacore tuna	1.3	King salmon	1.9
Rainbow trout	1.1	Sablefish	1.4	Atl. mackerel	2.5
Atl. bluefish	1.2	Lake trout	1.4	Sockeye salmon	2.7
Sardines	1.2	Anchovy	1.4	Norwegian	
American eel	1.2	Bluefin tuna	1.5	sardines	
Atl. salmon	1.2	Atl. herring	1.6	(in sild oil)	5.1
Atl. halibut	1.3	Pacific herring	1.7		

Sources: Nettleton, J.A. *Seafood Nutrition* 1985, Osprey Books, Huntington, N.Y. and USDA Provisional Table HNIS PT-103 1986.

A major advantage of obtaining omega-3s by eating fish rather than supplements is the opportunity for adjusting the amount of fat we eat from land animals (saturated fats) and plants (vegetable oils). By substituting fish for meat, poultry and dairy mainstays we can reduce the amount of saturated fats we eat, increase the amount of omega-3 type polyunsaturates and moderate the amount of vegetable (omega-6) type fats we consume. This change in variety of fat is likely to benefit most of us. The advantage of using fish often is offset, however, by preparations that add saturated fat (cream, butter, shortening) or substantial amounts of vegetable oils. Keep the nutritional advantage of seafood by avoiding the addition of extra fats.

Quite reasonably, people want to know how much fish or seafood we should eat in order to improve health. Is it only people with extreme intakes of seafood who are healthier than we? So far there is reasonable evidence that people with modern lifestyles who eat seafood on a regular basis are better off than those who do not eat fish. When we try to calculate how much fish to eat or how often to eat it in order to improve our lot, it gets more complicated. There simply are not enough data to do the arithmetic. There are other conditions besides seafood consumption that affect health. Family background, exercise, age and smoking habits are some of the other influences.

To sort out the importance of eating fish from all other issues is a gigantic task. We need purified omega-3 fatty acids and careful feeding studies before we can collect the needed information. In the meantime, from looking at the customs of those who have benefitted from eating seafood, it appears that eating fish about three times a week is distinctly helpful. Current suggestions from those close to the fish research scene are for us to use fish in place of meat, poultry and dairy mainstays at least two to three times a week. We know that this level is safe, possible and delicious. More frequent consumption of seafood is fine too and will not be a risk so long as we choose several varieties of seafood.

As the bumper sticker in Massachusetts says, "If health is your wish, eat more fish!"

Chapter Seven

Nasty Substances in Seafood

Because of the complexity of our environment and our limited understanding of what constitutes harm, the answer to this question will probably never be complete. But we do know that some substances have been found in unsafe levels in seafood and we are on the lookout for others. The question is made more difficult to answer because we know that a little of a substance may be tolerable or even essential, but in excess it becomes hazardous. Vitamins and minerals are splendid examples of this.

The best known environmental contaminants are heavy metals such as mercury, cadmium and arsenic and organic residues from agricultural and industrial chemicals such as PCBs, dioxin and DDT. Regular monitoring programs test both the waters and the fish for the presence of these and many other substances. The U.S. Food and Drug Administration (FDA), has set action levels for these and other harmful substances and works with individual states to ensure that fish harvested for commercial sale are safe from environmental contaminants. When contaminated fish are discovered, they are prohibited from sale and fishing grounds may be closed to commercial and recreational fishermen.

Strict regulations are in force to monitor the quality of all seafood at risk of environmental contamination. Many species of fish are inspected for mercury, PCBs and other potentially dangerous substances. Imported seafood is monitored for safety.

There are laws prohibiting the dumping of industrial wastes into the waterways. The federal government has made available funds to build sewage treatment plants, although we still have a long way to go on this score. Laws restrict the use of harmful pesticides but it takes many years to obtain the evidence necessary to ban the use of noxious chemicals our agricultural system depends upon. We know more about the substances to look for, and the species most likely to carry them.

What Harmful Contaminants Might Be In Seafood

While it is encouraging to know that some progress has been made in cleaning up the environment and establishing monitoring systems, the question remains in the minds of many consumers, just how safe is it to eat fish three times a week? The answer, of course, is a nice comfortable "it all depends..."

Like us, fish are what they eat. If their food supply has harmful substances in it, or if they cannot excrete harmful materials, fish will accumulate chemicals in their bodies. The muscle (flesh) will have the least amount of these substances. Most harmful substances are concentrated in the liver and viscera of fish, parts we usually discard. Some substances like organic residues dissolve in fat and are concentrated in liver and fat tissues. Discarding the fattiest portions – the belly flaps, skin, fatty strip along the lateral line and red muscle – greatly reduces the amount of contaminants we might consume.

We can imagine a situation where someone could consume large amounts of certain species of fish that happened to come from contaminated waters. The fatty species, the ones now recommended as especially healthful for their omega-3s, sometimes concentrate nasty substances in their fat. Eel from the Great Lakes is an example. So if you ate generous servings of these eels a few times a week over several weeks you might accumulate a fair amount of undesirable substances in your own liver and tissues. Of course, most of us do not do that. We eat a variety of species and we eat seafoods only once in a while. Annual seafood consumption is only about 14 pounds per person – most of us do not eat much seafood at all.

The point is that you have to go a long way out of your way to risk measurable harm from eating seafood. Extremes of anything are risky. While we never encourage people to eat any fish with dangerous levels of harmful substances, market supplies of seafood are safe for people to enjoy liberally. Of course, if you usually buy your fish from the back of a truck, or harvest your own clams from untested waters, or obtain fish from waters known to carry contaminants, good luck – you'll probably need it.

You will be safe from environmental contaminants if you:

• eat a variety of species, both lean and rich fleshed

• eat reasonable portions

• avoid eating the viscera of fish – that is where contaminants are concentrated; organic residues settle in the fat, so avoid the fatty portions, skin and red muscle sections of fish harvested from waters known to have harbored chemical wastes

• buy your fish only from reputable stores

• harvest your own shellfish only from inspected and approved waters

• observe fishing restrictions when catching your own fish

• avoid fish liver oils

Other Hazardous Substances in Seafood

Besides chemicals from the environment, seafood may have substances "naturally" present that may be unpleasant or dangerous. Seafood can also acquire bacterial contamination through poor handling and distribution. The following sections describe the major reasons why someone might become ill after eating seafood.

Bacterial Dangers

Like everything else, seafood is a natural host to all sorts of bacteria. Bacteria of many types are always present on every surface, including our food and our food preparation areas. It is not feasible to remove all bacteria. Neither is it necessary. What is important is to stop bacteria multiplying to harmful levels. Most species of bacteria reproduce in warm, moist conditions. To minimize the increase in the numbers of bacteria, scrupulous care must be given to the handling of fish after it is caught. Seafood can pick up bacteria from the surfaces it touches, from gut contents during cleaning and from seafood handlers. Icy temperatures and sanitary handling procedures are the best safeguards against bacterial activity. Preserving or consuming the fish as quickly as possible after harvest reduces the spread and activity of bacteria.

Like other foods, fish can be a source of food poisoning if it has not been cooked or handled properly. The organism most widely responsible for food spoilage is Salmonella. Its occasional presence in seafood reflects poor food handling.

Two other kinds of bacteria can be a problem with seafood. One produces the botulinus *toxin** that causes the sometimes fatal disease botulism. Problems with botulinus toxin can occur with canned or vacuum packed seafood because they offer the appropriate conditions for the toxin to develop. To grow, the botulinus organism requires low acid conditions deprived of oxygen and a temperature of at least 38°F. When seafood is canned, processors follow strict procedures specifying time, temperature and pressure that will destroy the organism. If canned fish is found contaminated with botulinus, it is nearly always because the organism entered the can through a leak after processing.

If using vacuum packed fresh, smoked or prepared seafood, always store it in the coldest part of the refrigerator and use it within the time period suggested on the package.

The other main disease caused by bacterial activity is scombroid or saurine poisoning. It is confined to a limited number of species, mainly mackerels, bonito, various tunas, swordfish and mahi-mahi. These fish are not normally poisonous. The danger develops only under poor handling conditions. When these fish are kept at warm temperatures for a few hours after they are caught, certain bacteria normally present on the fish will convert the amino acid histidine into saurine. This substance is not destroyed by heat. Because saurine is similar to the histamine produced in some allergic responses, taking anti histamine drugs may be helpful. The distressing symptoms of headache, nausea, gastric upset and skin reactions usually go away in 12 or so hours but severe cases can be fatal. If the fish smells bad it probably is, so don't eat it.

Potential Problems with Shellfish: Red Tide, Hepatitis and Others

This category of unpleasantries comes from two main sources: sew-

---

*Words printed in italics are defined in the Glossary at the end of the book. Only the first occurrence of the word is italicized.

age and phytoplankton – the otherwise good creatures who bring us omega-3 fatty acids. The most famous shellfish *poison* comes from "red tide," the profuse growth of plankton whose periodic abundance can turn the sea red. Molluscs, particularly clams and mussels, eat and accumulate this plankton without themselves suffering harm. If we eat these shellfish during a red tide outbreak we are exposed to a toxin produced by the phytoplankton. This toxin results in paralytic shellfish poisoning, a disease characterized by numbness and respiratory distress. If the amount of toxin consumed is not excessive you will recover, but the toxin can be lethal. There are no helpful medications.

Since the toxin is not destroyed by heat, the only way to avoid it is not to eat the affected shellfish. Under a long-standing Federal program to ensure the safety of shellfish, state health departments monitor coastal waters for levels of the red tide organisms and prohibit gathering shellfish when concentrations are hazardous. The hazard exists if you harvest your own mussels or clams unaware of the presence of red tide organisms, though restricted areas are posted.

Oysters, mussels and clams may also be responsible for illness if they have been gathered from sewage-contaminated water. Such shellfish may contain viruses causing hepatitis, and bacteria causing severe gastrointestinal disease and cholera. Most of these harmful organisms are destroyed by heat so the problem is mainly associated with eating raw shellfish. Gathering shellfish on your own without checking into the safety of local waters with the local wildlife service or health department is inviting problems.

Shellfish harvested for commercial purposes must carry a tag certifying that they came from clean, inspected water. Your retailer must have this tag with his shipment of molluscs although he does not display it at the sales counter. Buying from itinerant dealers is no assurance of safety.

Tropical Fish: Ciguatera

Those living or vacationing in Florida and the Gulf, the West Indies or Hawaii may encounter varieties of fish caught in reef or shore areas which have ciguatera toxin. Species that may be affected include barracuda, jacks, snappers, sharks, groupers, sea bass, trigger fish, surgeon fish, parrot fish, eels and wrasses. The larger the fish, the more likely it is to have toxic amounts of the poison.

There is no way to identify an affected fish. The poison is resistant to heat while the flesh may be quite tasty. Most of the poison is confined to the liver and viscera with very little in the flesh. Consumption of affected fish can produce symptoms that may last for months but are seldom fatal. The symptoms include tingling, numbness, nausea, cramps, muscular pain and fever among others.

The toxin is believed to come originally from phytoplankton consumed by very small fish. When these fish are eaten by larger ones, the toxic substance becomes concentrated in the larger fish. Scientists believe that is why young fish of the species mentioned above seldom give problems, while large ones may be highly toxic.

The only way to avoid ciguatera entirely is to shun all of these otherwise fine fish. Until procedures are developed for testing the raw fish for the toxin, ciguatera remains a hidden danger. Although we do not have reliable figures on the incidence of this poisoning, it is believed to be a major health problem in some tropical areas.

Poisonous Fish

A much rarer source of illness from seafood comes from eating fish that make their own poisons. Such disease is rare in America but occurs in Japan and China where some of the most toxic fish are also the most prized. The best known example is pufferfish (blowfish or fugu). Some Japanese chefs are highly trained to identify and handle pufferfish. If the poisonous liver and viscera can be removed without contaminating the flesh, the white meat may be safe to eat. Pufferfish poison is deadly and causes many fatalities in Japan and China. Although we know its chemical structure there is no treatment for its victims. Heating does not completely destroy its toxicity. Importing pufferfish into the USA is prohibited. The domestic puffer, caught off the mid-Atlantic coast, is much less poisonous than the Japanese. Usually sold as sea squab, it is tasty but nevertheless best avoided.

Seafood Parasites

Perhaps nothing is more repelling to the seafood customer than finding "worms" in fresh fish destined for dinner. Although these parasites are nearly always harmless, very few people would consider eating infested fish. Removing the worms or cutting away the affected portions leaves a perfectly edible remainder. Fish parasites do not produce poisons.

Parasites too small to see may be present and these are completely destroyed by cooking. Parasites will also be ruined by freezing for at least 72 hours and by hot smoking. They may survive other procedures like brining, pickling, cold smoking and marinating.

It is not possible to list the species that get parasites and those that do not because their occurrence depends on biological cycles. They are found in cod from time to time and are rather common in freshwater fish like walleye pike and perch. Virtually any species can be a host if the environmental conditions are right. The likelihood of encountering a seafood parasite is greatly enhanced by eating raw seafood.

While nearly all seafood parasites are harmless there are a few exceptions. One is anisakiasis that may be present in herring and mackerel. Its association with severe intestinal pain was first noted in the Netherlands where people consume innumerable cured herrings.

To avoid all risk from parasites, enjoy your seafod cooked.

Allergies to Seafood

The notion of *food allergy* is enriched with many myths. Whereas many people claim to have food allergies, many of the discomforts they experience have nothing to do with an *allergic response*. A true food allergy provokes an immune response. The term "food sensitivity" is also used to describe an immune response to a food. Immune responses reveal themselves in a variety of ways, frequently by intestinal upset, hives, skin disorders, and rhinitis. True food allergies are relatively rare in adults although they are fairly common among children.

The foods most often producing an allergic response are cow's milk, wheat, eggs and nuts. Seafood allergies are well known but much less prevalent. They occur more frequently among people who work with fish. Fish allergens, those substances causing an allergic response, are proteins. The proteins are changed by cooking, freezing and processing but they seldom lose their ability to cause distress. An allergic response can develop in a sensitive individual from eating the fish, from breathing cooking vapors and from inhaling dust from processing wastes or even fish glue.

Shellfish are particularly notorious for producing adverse reactions in some people. A person may be sensitive to only one species or several related ones. The only way to find out is to try a little of the food. If more than one exposure to the food produces the same result, and sensitivity to other foods present at the same time can be ruled out, then one has a good basis for suspecting a particular food. Confirmation of a food allergy can only be made through several tests carried out by a reputable allergist. Much health quackery focuses on food allergy. "Cytotoxic" tests or "food drops" are worthless. The only treatment is to avoid the food entirely.

People with confirmed allergies to seafood need to pay careful attention to food labels. Ingredients statements must tell what is in a product. Derived seafood products such as imitation crab salad are made largely from finfish but may contain small amounts of real crabmeat, shrimp or other shellfish. Prepared seafood salads, dinners, soups etc. may have small amounts of the offending seafood whose presence is not clear from the description of the item. Foods available in restaurants, delicatessens, salad bars and friends' homes may be difficult to identify properly. The safest bet is to go for the potato salad instead.

Consumer Safeguards

Virtually all seafood served in restaurants and sold in retail outlets presents no health risk to the consumer. Remember that most hazardous substances are stored in the liver and viscera of the fish. Very little reaches the flesh, the part most of us eat. Because some substances are found in the oil portion, a person can further reduce possible exposure to any questionable substances by not eating the skin, the fatty deposit just below the lateral line, the belly flaps or the dark red muscle sections. These parts have the highest fat content. The safest way is to eat just the muscle or "meat" portion.

Another good practice is to eat a variety of seafood species. Relatively few species of fish have contaminants in them and trying different species regularly ensures that your chance of accumulating harmful substances is virtually zero.

Look for open dating on the seafood packages you buy. Use the fish within the time recommended and keep it as cold as possible until use.

Seafood is the cause of human illness only when:
• it comes from contaminated waters and you eat it raw

• you eat it raw and it has spoiled owing to improper handling

• it spoils because it has not been handled properly either by the fisherman, the dealer, the restaurant or you at home

• it spoils because there is damage to the package and bacteria have entered

• the species of fish or shellfish contains toxins produced by or found naturally in that fish

• you are unlucky enough to be allergic to a species of fish or shellfish and you eat or inhale fumes from that species of seafood raw or cooked; food poisoning is often mistaken for food allergy

• it contains certain parasites that have not been destroyed because the fish is served raw or lightly cured

What About Raw Fish and Shellfish?

Perhaps the greatest hazard of illness from eating seafood comes from eating raw or undercooked shellfish. These animals are highly perishable and keep well only for very short periods of time. They need to be kept just above freezing temperatures after harvest and served quickly. Eating raw shellfish, no matter how tasty, is an invitation to illness.

Raw shellfish, particularly clams, mussels and oysters, can harbor viruses and bacteria that would otherwise be destroyed by cooking. Eating raw shellfish obtained from back-of-the-truck dealers or harvested locally from waters whose safety you do not know is enormously risky. Buy only from reputable markets even if it costs more. Hepatitis is no joy.

Japanese style sushi and sashimi have become very popular. The chefs in restaurants serving raw seafood are highly trained both in preparation technique and the recognition of seafood quality. Obviously it is in the interest of the restaurant that its patrons do not get sick following a meal and much care is taken to be sure this does not happen. But you can get sick and raw seafood is as ideal a vehicle for food related illness as can be devised. If you fancy these foods go to an establishment with trained and experienced chefs. Preparing raw seafood at home is risky.

Chapter Eight

Things to Know about Fresh, Frozen, Canned, Smoked and Prepared Seafood

What is "Fresh" Fish?

The word fresh applied to seafood has two meanings: one is "not frozen," while the other means "top quality." In this book, the word means "not frozen." This and the following Chapter Nine tell you how to find and maintain the highest quality seafood products, both fresh and frozen. Chapter Nine gives purchasing and handling information about seafood while this Chapter explains what happens to a product before it reaches the sales counter.

Fresh, that is never frozen, seafood can offer the diner the best in seafood eating if it has been handled with:

• Care – the fish has been handled properly after being taken from the water

• Cold – it has been carefully maintained at near-freezing temperatures during all stages of its handling, transportation and retail

• Speed – it has been rushed to the retail counter as quickly as possible after harvest

• White gloves – it has been carefully handled by the retailer to ensure cleanliness, cold and adequate moisture

That list is a tall order. That is why the distribution system for fresh fish is a difficult one to maintain.

As a purchaser, you have no way of knowing how long it has been since the fresh fish you are buying was taken from the water. For the most part it does not matter because if it has been handled properly at sea and thereafter, the fish you buy is still very fresh. Fishing boats may stay at sea just for the day or as long as ten days. Large fishing vessels which remain at sea for weeks may process and freeze their catch on board.

The point is that properly handled fish several days out of the water are likely to be better eating than slovenly handled fish one or two days old.

The sooner you eat fish after purchasing it the better it will taste. You may safely store it in the refrigerator for a day or two, keeping it very cold and moist, but fish does not improve with age.

Is Fresh Fish Treated?

In most instances the answer is no. On some fishing boats, certain species of fish are stored in refrigerated seawater or brine. Use of brine or sea water increases the sodium content of the flesh but enhances the keeping quality. There is no way to tell at the retail level whether or not any fish has been so handled. It would be difficult for the retailer to find out too, because fish is bought from many different companies and fishing vessels whose practices vary widely. This practice should not worry the consumer.

Sometimes, fresh fish may be dipped in a phosphate solution to keep it white. Sometimes fish destined for the freezer will be dipped in phosphates to retain moisture and later sold thawed with the tag "previously frozen." There is no way to know if the fish has been dipped.

Polyphosphate solutions are not necessarily "bad" if used in moderation. They add sodium and phosphorus to the fish, but if used properly, they enhance the appearance of the fish and help it stay succulent. Very glossy, slippery or slimy looking pieces of fish imply excessive dipping. These products should be passed by.

Occasionally seafood processors may use solutions containing small amounts of antioxidants or antibacterial agents such as benzoate or sorbate. These chemicals retard natural spoilage processes and discourage bacterial growth, helping to prevent harmful changes. It is difficult to estimate how widespread this practice is and there is virtually no way for the consumer to know. It is believed not to be a common habit.

Rinse fresh fish under very cold running water. Then dry it with a paper towel before preparing it for cooking. Rinsing removes both debris from filleting and surface bacteria. Rinsing also removes odors accumulated in the package. If you plan to keep the fish overnight before cooking it, rinse and rewrap it in plastic film for storage in the refrigerator.

Fresh Shellfish – Molluscs

The term shellfish includes both molluscs and crustaceans. The most familiar molluscs are scallops, clams, mussels and oysters. The last three are often sold alive, in the shell. **Scallops** are seldom sold in the shell in the USA – we only see the meat. Live scallops are highly perishable and distribution is not practicable. Other molluscs include abalone, conch, periwinkles and whelks. Except for periwinkles they are usually sold without the shell.

Some molluscs, namely **squid, octopus** and **cuttlefish,** have no shell. What used to be a shell has evolved into a crude type of bone made of cartilage. In squid this structure is called the "pen" or "quill" while cuttlefish "bones" are used as a source of calcium for parakeets.

Vitality is a sure sign of freshness and any shellfish intended to be live at the time of sale should generally still be alive when you start to cook it. Check that the shellfish is alive by tapping it or by putting it in fresh water and watching that it tightly closes its shell. Any that fail to close should be discarded. Also discard any with cracks through the shell. **Clams, mussels** and **oysters** are all marine shellfish and cannot survive in fresh water. Therefore they protect themselves from fresh water by closing their shells tightly.

Sometimes molluscs are sold already shucked, and may be pasteurized. If not pasteurized, they should be cooked or frozen immediately. Oyster meats are often sold this way. Cooked, shelled molluscs may be available and these have better keeping qualities than their raw counterparts. The snail (scungili) from the North East is usually sold as cooked meat.

While many molluscs are harvested directly from the wild, commercial farming of molluscs is expanding. Oysters, mussels and hard shell clams are successfully cultivated. The farming of soft shell clams and scallops is still experimental. We owe the growing popularity of mussels largely to successful cultivation techniques. Farming techniques are responsible for another consumer convenience – mussels with very little beard to remove.

Clams, mussels and oysters may contain sand inside the shell. This can be removed by rinsing the cooked meats in the cooking liquor, or very lightly under tapwater. It will not be removed by soaking the animals in water before cooking as the animals shun fresh water. Achieving the necessary salt water conditions to purge the animals is nearly impossible at home. It is a myth that adding cornmeal to the soak water will cleanse the animals.

Molluscs should be very well scrubbed before they are cooked. This reduces the chances of grit entering the mollusc once its shell opens in cooking.

Fresh Shellfish – Crustaceans

These shellfish are the ones with an outer skeleton or "shell" and legs. They include shrimp, lobster, crabs, langostinos, crayfish and spiny lobster.

American lobsters are strictly a North Atlantic animal. Attempts to resettle them on the Pacific have so far been unsuccessful. For food safety, they must be kept alive until cooking time. Lobsters are sold live from saltwater tanks or as fresh cooked meat with or without the shell. Cooking your own live lobster is definitely the way to achieve the very best results.

You will read numerous prohibitions against cooking and eating a dead lobster. The reason for this is that once a lobster dies, its digestive system starts to digest its own body, producing by-products that are unpleasant and may even be toxic. The process starts as soon as the lobster dies. However, if you know that a lobster was alive a couple of hours earlier – for example, you bought it alive and kicking at 5 p.m. and want to eat it at 6 p.m. – it is perfectly safe to cook and eat it. It is NOT safe to use a dead lobster unless you know without any doubt that it died less than a couple of hours earlier. It is also important that the lobster has been kept cold.

Of course, some lobster recipes request that you kill the creature before cooking it. I have yet to find such a recipe that cannot be prepared after the lobster has been briefly steamed.

Spiny lobsters or rock lobsters are commonly sold frozen as "lobster tails." Most of these animals come from Florida or are imported from many parts of the world. They are tasty but quite different from the true northern lobster.

Freshwater crayfish are being farmed in the South and sold whole either live, or cooked and frozen. The tailmeat is the part you eat. Just the tail meats may be sold, usually in cooked frozen form.

Shrimp is the most popular crustacean in this country. There are many different species of shrimp, some caught in American waters and others imported. Shrimp fall into two main types, northern and tropical. Northern shrimp are generally small, sweet and sold as cooked, peeled meats. Tropical shrimp available retail are usually sold as shell-on tails, though more are now being offered cooked in the shell. There are also freshwater shrimp, sometimes called prawns. These are invariably imported product. The term prawn has no specific meaning as far as the legal description of shrimp is concerned.

Shrimp is nearly always sold frozen either cooked or raw. It may be sold whole with the head and shell, as shell-on tails, or peeled and possibly deveined. Approximately two thirds of the body is head, so check your quantities carefully if you buy whole shrimp. Except in local markets where shrimp are "right off the boat," shrimp that appears fresh at the retail counter was previously frozen. It should have a label saying "previously frozen." Fresh, raw tropical shrimp, that has never been frozen, is seldom available away from the Gulf coast where most of it is caught.

Once shrimp (and some other crustaceans) have been taken from the water they have a tendency to turn black. The spots formed are unattractive but not harmful. To prevent this natural event, shrimp are treated with sulphite, a substance with a long history of safe use for most people. For use in shrimp, the Food and Drug Administration (FDA) has established maximum amounts of sulphite considered consistent with good manufacturing practice. The amount remaining in the shrimp, either held fresh on ice or frozen, is always considerably less. When high levels are found in shrimp it is the result of excess used in processing. FDA will impound imported shrimp containing sulphite in excess of 100 parts per million (ppm).

People have become concerned about the safety of sulphite

because of the highly publicized cases of illness and death among asthmatics who have consumed sulphite treated foods. Only a tiny percentage of the population is at risk of illness from sulphites. These people are a small fraction of those who suffer from severe asthma. Dried fruit (except dark raisins and prunes), bottled lemon and lime juice, salad bar lettuce, wine, molasses and sauerkraut contain the greatest levels of sulphites – 100 parts per million (ppm) or more. Shrimp can be expected to have less than 100 ppm and usually less than 50 ppm.

Among seafoods, sulphites are used mainly with shrimp. Very small amounts may be present in dried cod.

Crabs may be sold live. They are frequently sold cooked in the shell, frozen cooked or as pasteurized, shelled meat. The meat may also be canned. Crabs are highly perishable and taste best when they can be cooked live.

Frozen Fish and Shellfish

Frozen fish used to win little respect because its quality was highly variable. Nowadays, frozen fish is often premium quality, being preserved shortly after harvest from the sea. The idea that frozen fish is of inferior quality is, in most cases, wrong. The quality of frozen fish depends on how carefully it has been handled after being taken from the sea, how long it is held before freezing, and how quickly it is frozen. Modern factory trawlers that freeze the fish while still at sea can produce top quality product. Flavor and freshness are well retained.

Of course, there is some poor quality frozen fish around. Look out for and avoid retail packages of fresh fish that were tossed into the freezer on the last day for sale. Such fish is usually far below ideal quality and has almost never been washed and rewrapped for freezing. This practice, all too common in some supermarkets, may work satisfactorily for some meats but is nearly fatal for fish. Fish frozen properly by a seafood processor will be better than fish frozen by the retailer.

Fish destined for the freezer may be dipped in a solution usually containing polyphosphate and sometimes other salts as explained at the beginning of this Chapter. These solutions help to retain moisture in the fish and reduce the amount of water lost when the fish is thawed. Not all processors use such dips and there is no way of telling if they have been used. There should be no major nutritional consequences of this practice except increases in the levels of phosphorus and sodium. It is not possible to estimate how much phosphorus or sodium may be taken up because the initial mineral level is usually quite variable and the amount remaining in the final product is also difficult to estimate. It is thought to be nothing to worry about. When dips are used, the ingredients are supposed to be stated on the package label.

Frozen fish should be tightly wrapped with good quality waterproof material. There should be virtually no air spaces in the package to permit drying or the development of freezer burn. Tightness and quality of the wrap also have a direct effect on the loss of moisture from frozen fish. Exclusion of air slows the rate of chemical breakdown. These features apply equally to fish you freeze yourself.

The frozen fish package should be very solid and hard, with no punctures or rips. Avoid soft or spongy packages. Look for open dating on the label. Frozen fish that was top quality to begin with and has been kept well below freezing will retain its quality for many months. If it has been allowed to thaw partially, or if holding temperatures have fluctuated widely, keeping time is substantially reduced.

One feature of supermarket freezing cases is that they have automatic cycles for defrosting. The temperature can vary widely during these cycles and this may compromise the keeping quality of frozen seafood. It is not only seafood that is adversely affected by these temperature swings, but seafood is more susceptible than some other products.

Home freezers and refrigerator freezing sections are less satisfactory than commercial ones because they are not as cold. That means that the fish you freeze yourself will not freeze as quickly as it does under commercial conditions, nor will it be held at as protective a temperature. The net result is that your own frozen product is likely to be fine but not the finest. Date the package and use it as quickly as possible. If you are considering freezing fresh fish that you could not use up soon enough, cook it instead and use it in a salad or soup. Freezing fish that is less than top quality is a waste of time.

The nature of home freezers and freezing compartments means that the frozen fish you bring home is also best used within a fairly short period of time. It is impossible to be exact about how long is long enough; use the date on the package as a guide. Fish can be stored safely in the freezer for many months. Texture changes are more pronounced with long term storage.

Some fish keep better in the frozen state than others. Those are the lean fish and shellfish. Fattier fish like tuna, mackerel, herring, eel and bluefish lose their quality and flavor more quickly. In fact, because their fats continue to break down (that is, turn rancid) during frozen storage, they may develop off flavors. It is crucial that these species be of optimum quality at the time they are frozen. Fat fish are safe to eat when stored for longer than a couple of months or so, but their quality declines noticeably. Be fussy about these and enjoy them early.

As a rough guide, lean fish keep better than oilier fish. Note that frozen salmon, though oily, can be kept for exceptionally long periods if properly frozen, handled and glazed. Because of the great many variations possible in the fish, the freezing time, packaging and temperature fluctuations, it is just not possible to give realistic advice on how long fish may be stored before it should be eaten. If it smells fine before cooking and tastes good, it is perfectly good. Expect a deterioration in texture during storage. Oily fish may begin to show signs of rancidity anywhere from one to three months after freezing. But most fish will be perfectly safe to eat long after that.

Frozen fish that has been thawed is best cooked and used. If you cannot use it all, cook it and then freeze the cooked fish for later use in salads, soups or quiches. A few species can be refrozen with little loss of quality if they have been kept cold and clean in the meantime. Squid, the prime example, can be refrozen a number of times with no noticeable loss of taste or texture. If you should need to re-freeze, make sure that the fish has been kept cold and well wrapped while thawed. Otherwise, there may be far too many bacteria thriving on it. Not all bacteria are killed in the freezer, and some will be ready and eager to start breeding as soon as they are again warmed up to 40°F. Refrozen fish will normally be less firm than once-frozen fish: use it up quickly.

Canned Seafood

Canning is undoubtedly the safest method of preserving seafood. The contents keep for years as long as the can itself retains its integrity. Because seafood canned in oil or water is low in acid there is

105

nothing to erode the lining of the can. Seafood canned in tomato or spicy sauces however, has greater acidity which facilitates the breakdown of the lining of a conventional can. Containers with bonded or enameled linings are much more resistant to acidity. Seafoods are normally processed in cans with a special lining called C-enamel.

Dented cans make it easier for the contents to react with the can itself. Bonded cans are more resistant to damage from dents but there is no certainty damage may not have occurred. Damage to the contents is more likely if a dent affects the lid or the seam. Never buy any canned product in a bulging can.

Besides safety and convenience, another advantage of canning is that it makes the bones soft and digestible. It is a good idea to eat these with the fish for they are a rich source of calcium. Otherwise seafood is low in calcium.

The canning liquid may be water, bouillon, oil or sauce. Only in diet pack seafood is the water added without salt and seasonings. Oil-packed seafood is usually made with vegetable oil. It is not fish oil unless the label expressly says so. (Some sardines are packed in sild oil, which is sardine oil). You can remove much of the oil by lightly rinsing the fish under cold water. The oil will float to the top and wash away. Besides adding many calories the packing oil may leach out some (but not all) of the more desirable fish oils, substances you do not want to lose. For calorie and fat considerations, drain off the vegetable oil in canned fish.

Canned salmon is one of the few fish to which water is not added. The liquid in the can comes from the fish as a result of the canning process. It also includes some of the fish oil and omega-3s. Keep this liquid and mix it with the salmon.

All product is cooked during the canning process. The combination of heat and pressure destroys most of the thiamin that might have been present. Vitamin B_{12} losses may be substantial as well. Most other vitamins are fairly well retained. Minerals and other nutrients are very well retained. There may even be some increase in certain elements owing to the slow migration of minerals (mainly zinc) from the can to its contents. There is no danger from the process so far as we know. The gain in minerals from the can is considerably greater in seafood packed in acidic sauces. The widespread use of bonded linings in cans virtually eliminates any potential hazard from the can itself. Cans packed overseas, however, are less likely to have enameled linings.

Once a canned product is opened it is safe to store any unused portions in the original can if the can has been enameled and the enamel on the inside of the seam is still intact. Cover and store the leftovers in the refrigerator. If you have any doubt whether the can has a bonded lining, or whether the lining is intact, transfer the leftovers to another container.

The major nutritional concern with canned fish is the high level of sodium. Processors usually add substantial amounts of salt to the product and this makes it difficult for people who are trying to restrict their sodium intake. If you rinse the product gently under cold water you can remove a great deal of the sodium.

Canned (and frozen) seafood is often scorned as being of inferior quality. I do not endorse this prejudice and find such preserved seafoods extraordinarily useful. They are nutritious and nearly always economical.

Canned seafood products provide great convenience, excellent nutrition and economy. Canned mackerel, sardines and herring are among the least expensive sources of omega-3s in the marketplace. With a can of clams or mussels on hand you can always make an acceptable linguini sauce or quick salad. Storage is easy and not dependent on continued power supply. Overall, canned fish are important and useful products.

Smoked Seafood

Smoked seafood is becoming increasingly popular and more widely available, partly because of improvements in technology and marketing. With small, simple smoking kilns, some restaurants may even prepare their own smoked seafood on the premises. You can find smoked seafood at retail counters fresh, vacuum packed, frozen or canned.

Be aware of two aspects of smoked seafood: safety and nutrition.

Smoking used to be a major method of fish preservation when it was combined with large amounts of salt, heat and drying. Nowadays it is primarily a flavoring process, not a means of long term preservation. That means that smoked fish needs to be respected as a perishable item. Keep it no longer than 4 or 5 days in the refrigerator. For a longer holding period, freeze it. In fact, think of it as you would think of fresh fish.

Smoked fish may be vacuum packed to preserve freshness. Once it has been opened, however, be sure it is kept under refrigeration. Low acid foods like smoked fish kept under conditions of little oxygen are a perfect home for botulinus bacteria whose activity will make the food lethal. Guard smoked seafood carefully.

Vacuum packed seafoods can safely be frozen. In fact, if you are not going to use them for a few days, that is the preferable way to store them. Once you take them from the freezer, thaw and open the package and treat the product like fresh seafood. It is perishable.

Vacuum packaging deserves some additional comments. The use of vacuum packs or "skins" is expanding as the technology of the equipment and the films improves. Vacuum packs have been shown to extend the shelf life of top quality seafood, both fresh and smoked. The difficulty for the consumer, however, is that it is not clear just how long a product will maintain its freshness in the vacuum pack. There may be no changes in color or odor to alert you to changes in the product, until you open the package. Even then, certain bacteria may thrive without leaving telltale signs.

Vacuum packaging does not sterilize food. It limits or excludes oxygen which is largely but not entirely responsible for spoilage. Certain films used with smoked fish actually allow the passage of oxygen into the package to prevent the activity of the deadly bacterium, *Clostridium botulinum*. Whether these films are entirely successful is not yet known. There are no guarantees and at present only the use of nitrites will eliminate the danger of botulism. See Chapter Seven for more on this topic.

The health aspects of smoked seafood center around the use of nitrites and salt and the formation of complex organic substances during the smoking process itself. The use of nitrites destroys most bacteria and greatly reduces the likelihood that botulinus bacteria will thrive. Nitrites have the potential for conversion into nitrosamines, which are carcinogenic substances. The presence of sugar may facilitate such a conversion. The extent to which nitrosamines may form in the body after we eat smoked seafood is unknown. Note that the body itself forms nitrosamines from many other foods that have never been treated with nitrites, so we do not avoid nitrosamines entirely.

The dilemma is whether to leave out nitrites and risk bacterial spoilage or use small amounts and enhance safety, possibly increasing the risk of nitrosamine formation. It is a difficult question for a manufacturer to decide. He goes out of business if botulism develops in his product but he does not want to be in the position of using hazardous chemicals either. Perhaps the issue is one of safe amounts, but how much is necessary to ensure safety yet provide "negligible" risk we do not know. Maximum amounts of nitrite are regulated by the Federal Government through the Food and Drug Administration.

Some processors use nitrites to enhance flavor and color. Top quality smoked seafood can be and is produced without the use of nitrites. It is safe and delicious provided the product is handled properly throughout its preparation, packaging and subsequent use.

Read the label on the package to see if nitrite has been used. If it is present it must appear on the label. Intense orange-red color is sometimes an indication that nitrites (or artificial colors) have been used.

The National Cancer Institute and other health agencies have expressed concern about the safety of smoked foods. Their worry comes from studies about the tars that form during the smoking process. Smoke is a complex mixture of substances whose composition varies enormously with the food, fat, fuel and conditions of smoke production. Temperature, together with the condensation of volatile substances on to the food during smoking, has a lot to do with the nature of what remains in the food. Similar concerns are related to char-broiling and "blackening" processes as well. There is a whole family of compounds formed under different conditions of smoking and char-cooking. Separating the safe from the risky is no simple task. We need to know much more about these problems and how they affect seafoods. Meanwhile, the safest course is to avoid eating all charred or burned parts.

Smoking requires two separate operations. First the fish must be salted or brined. Sometimes, flavors are added at this stage. Then, the product is smoked. Salting is necessary to remove some moisture from the flesh. Modern tastes are moving towards less salty flavors, and processors are adjusting curing recipes to suit. However, there is no way to tell how much salt is in the product except by tasting it. Lightly salted and smoked products are available. If you find a brand that you like, stay with it. Nearly all smoked seafood can be described as salty or very salty – it is not for sodium restricted diets. Some of the salt can be removed by soaking the smoked product, but that impairs texture and flavor.

The safest advice regarding smoked seafood is to select the most lightly smoked products and use them only occasionally. Try to avoid those containing nitrites as the choice is available. Keep smoked seafood frozen or under refrigeration at all times. Avoid them if you are on a sodium restricted diet.

Pickled Seafood

Pickling is another traditional preservation method and one capable of adding a great variety of flavors to fish. Like smoked fish, it is not for those on a sodium-restricted diet as the first stage in most pickling procedures is salting or brining. Most pickled seafoods keep for extended periods. They should be kept cool and dark. The refrigerator is ideal.

Pickled herring products are widely available, in sour cream, wine sauces, mustard and tomato sauces and many others. Herrings were a European staple food in past centuries. The seasonal fish were salted in barrels, then vinegars and spices added for palatability before the fish were eaten. These products are now gourmet foods and offer a good variety of interesting flavors, with great convenience – all you have to do is open the jar. Pickled rockfish, eel, mussels and many other species are also available from some specialty stores.

Surimi-based Products

The word surimi is unfamiliar to shoppers because it seldom appears on a package label or supermarket flyer. It is the term used most often in the fish business though and as surimi products proliferate, we can expect it to become more common. Surimi is actually the raw material from which a number of increasingly familiar products are made.

Surimi is a Japanese word for boneless, minced, washed fish flesh. Preparing a fish mince was how the Japanese used to preserve their excess catch in the days before refrigeration. The minced fish flesh is washed, removing soluble proteins. The result is a block of high-protein, tasteless, odorless product, which can be manufactured into many different products, depending on how the surimi is further processed and cooked. Surimi is a raw material for producing not just fish products but also imitation meat items such as sausages or hot dogs. Because surimi has no taste or texture of its own, it can be blended with shellfish and other foods and manufactured into many forms.

Alaska pollock is, for the time being, the fish most often used to make surimi. Japan and Korea are the major suppliers. US producers are now entering the business and some are experimenting with other cheap and abundant species such as Gulf croaker and Atlantic red hake.

Surimi is currently used most commonly to make imitation crab, scallop and shrimp products. The surimi is sometimes blended with small amounts of genuine crab or shrimp. Many other ingredients may be added: sugar, salt, spices, flavorings, color, binding agents, vegetables and fats to name the most common. Surimi based products are sold frozen or thawed at the retail counter. Some US producers are offering fresh products, which have the advantage that they need far less sugar than the products transported frozen from long distances.

Among the products widely available are imitation crab leg meat, which are cylinders with red-colored layers on the outside, white in the middle; imitation crab meat, salad style, which has flakes or chunks of material that looks very much like snow or king crab meat; imitation scallops, both breaded and unbreaded; and imitation shrimp, usually breaded. Seafood salad sold loose or in bulk in supermarkets and delis is nearly always made from surimi, though it seldom says so on the label. Such salads are widely used in restaurants, too.

The flavor and acceptability of these products varies widely between manufacturers, because of the great variety of ingredients that may be added to the basic surimi. They are remarkably inexpensive, compared with the real products that they emulate. The problem is that too often they are not honestly labeled. Deli counters and restaurants may call the material "crab salad" when actually it is made from surimi. This is fraud, of course. It is also a health risk. Because some people are allergic to fish and others to shellfish, it is most important that everyone should know what they are eating. If someone allergic to fish orders crab and instead is given fish-based surimi, the results could be unpleasant.

From a nutritionist's viewpoint, surimi has the advantage of being a moderately priced source of high quality protein without a significant amount of fat or cholesterol. It is usually lower in protein, niacin, other vitamins and some minerals than the fish it is made from or the shellfish it imitates but these are not serious defects. Its nutritional faults are the high sodium levels found in many brands and the presence of sugar (something we have in abundance already).

Of concern is the potential for the erosion of nutritional quality owing to the addition of fat, especially animal fat, water and sugar. At present there is no official standard of identity for surimi and brands differ substantially in their composition. These seafood products are convenient, tasty and versatile. We can hope they retain their nutritional merits as they expand in the marketplace.

Note that fresh surimi normally contains less sugar than frozen. When frozen surimi is thawed, it loses moisture, which collects in the display pan. The absence or presence of such dripwater is the best indicator of whether the product was previously frozen. This is by no means a foolproof test, however. The safest way to buy surimi products is to stick with a brand name that you like and avoid generic labels.

Frozen Prepared Seafood

If you survey the expanding array of prepared frozen snacks and meals in a supermarket you appreciate that convenient, tasty preparations are very much in demand. Seafood items are among the most popular and sometimes creative offerings. Many, unfortunately, fail to retain the nutritional advantages they begin with.

The two main citicisms of the nutritional worth of frozen prepared seafood items are:

• very high sodium levels and

• abundance of fat, frequently saturated fat.

These two features contradict the natural nutritional merits of seafood – low fat, low saturated fat and low sodium. When you select frozen, prepared seafood, read the ingredient listing and the nutrition panel usually on the package. See how much fat and sodium is present and look for the kind of fat used in preparation. For nutritional superiority you are likely better off starting with the plain fish and baking it in a hot oven.

Strong criticism can be made of prepared fish items that

depend on large amounts of coatings and fat for their taste appeal. These foods give far less nutritional worth than you might expect. That is because up to half the weight of the food may be coating and fat. Worse yet is the fact that the fat used is usually highly saturated – either animal fat or coconut or palm oil. Excessive sodium and maybe a dab of ketchup add insult to injury.

All is not lost however, as savvy manufacturers have developed lighter lines of seafood dishes that have less coating and less fat. Best of all, some may have no added fat which gives you the bake, broil or microwave option of retaining the nutritional treasures of seafood. You can distinguish them from the others by reading the ingredients listing and comparing the quantity of fat among different products.

Prepared foods offer considerable advantages. Branded products are consistent, and because brands are expensive to develop, the manufacturer takes pains to ensure that his product is good. They are convenient. Most can be cooked from the frozen state with no preparation time. And there are many more available now which are nutritionally good.

Restaurant Fare

More people choose to eat their seafood in restaurants than at home. There are many reasons for this – the skill of chefs, the idea that seafood is one of the healthiest choices on the menu and the worry about preparing seafood at home. But is seafood a wiser choice when eating out?

Fast food places serve more seafood than any other type of restaurant. When you compare the nutrients in a fish sandwich or platter with those in a chicken or beef one, the fish serving has the most calories and the most fat. This unhappy finding is a result of the breading and frying of the fish, not of the fish itself. Coatings increase the amount of fat soaked up. Many fast food purveyors generally use cooking fats rich in saturates, the least desirable kind of fat. The final product is one greatly compromised in nutritional virtue.

White tablecloth restaurants may do the same thing in a fancy way. They serve generous sauces made from heavy cream and butter which give you more fat, saturated fat and even some cholesterol besides. Many broiled and baked items come swimming in a sea of oil or butter.

There are ways around this situation and restaurants are paying attention to the criticisms. First of all, choose items that are not fried. If your preference is not offered in a bake or broil preparation, ask if it can be prepared that way. Surprisingly often, it can be done. In any case, your request will alert the management that people do want healthier alternatives.

Second, ask for sauces to be served on the side. That way you can sample a little without having to forage for your entree.

Third, choose menu items that are baked with vegetables or wine, grilled, stir-fried, poached or steamed. You can ask to have your selection prepared that way if they do not offer the species of your choice in the style you would like. Fish is nearly always cooked to order and many restaurants are happy to handle such requests.

Fourth, when you have a well prepared seafood meal that is not loaded with fat, compliment the chef. That way the good choices will stay on the menu.

Chapter Nine

How to Buy, Store and Prepare Fish and Shellfish

The expression "fresh seafood" in this book means seafood that has not been frozen. It also means it is not stale. There is no question that fresh, unfrozen seafood at peak quality is unmatched. Whenever possible, cook it the day you buy it. On the other hand, a premium frozen fish is preferable to a questionable fresh one.

Charlotte Walker, in her book *Fish and Shellfish*, says you should be flexible when you shop for fish and buy the best quality available that day rather than making up your mind ahead of time which species you want. That is exactly the right spirit to bring to the market and dinner table when it comes to seafood. Many different fish are adaptable to the same manner of preparation. The recipes in this book are simple, fast and designed to be used with as many different species as possible.

Buying Fresh Seafood

At the fresh fish counter you will find fish presented in several different forms. For example you may see **dressed** rainbow trout, halibut **steaks**, **pan-dressed** whiting, sole **fillets**, and salmon **roasts** (see below for definitions of these terms). The variety of forms depends on the species available where you live, the season, and the fish itself. Coastal cities may offer more variety of prepared forms and usually will have more dressed and pan dressed fish available than inland markets. Variety depends on the fish dealer too.

There are several reasons for the different forms. One is that some fish can only be cleaned and cut up in one or two ways; local custom determines the way certain species are preferred; and size or fish structure may limit the way you can handle the fish. These variations are also true when it comes to the presence of skin. Some fish fillets like bluefish will fall apart when cooked if the skin is removed first, others, like cod and haddock fillets, may be offered with the skin on or off. Still others, like orange roughy and monk-fish, are never sold with the skin on.

The basic descriptions of the ways fish are cut up for serving are given below. Details may vary from region to region and with different fish.

Whole: just as they come from the water with head, guts and everything; they need to be cleaned before cooking. Most fish are not sold this way because fish spoils much faster if the viscera and gills are left in. Smelts and similar very small fish are occasionally sold whole.

Dressed or drawn: fish have the viscera and gills removed but the head, fins and scales are still remaining. It is rapidly becoming undressed. Examples are trout, mackerel and butterfish.

Pan-dressed: these fish have the viscera, head, tail, gills, fins and scales removed. They look like the body without its moving parts. Examples are whiting, croaker and catfish.

Fillets: lengthwise cuts of fish where the whole side of the fish is removed from the backbone; they are not necessarily boneless. Examples are cod, sole and bluefish. Note that the fish trade distinguishes between fillets and boneless fillets. If you must have fillets without bones, specify this. The dealer will cut away the center strip of the fillet where there is usually a row of small pinbones. You will pay extra for fillets prepared in this way.

Steaks: crosswise sections of fish having skin and bones. Examples are salmon and cod. Portions of such slices are also called steaks: halibut, for example, sometimes weigh several hundred pounds and a single slice would be far too large. U.S. Department of Commerce definitions of steaks include a minimum weight of 2½ ounces for salmon steaks and 2 ounces for halibut steaks.

Chunks or roasts: crosswise sections 4 inches or more long. Salmon is the most frequent example.

Having a Good Eye in the Shop

Top quality is impossible without freshness. The most important aspect of keeping fish fresh is temperature. The second most vital factor is moisture. Fresh fish should be held in pans on ice or in refrigerated cabinets where the temperature is held as close to freezing as possible. 31°F. is the ideal temperature.

Fish requires moisture and cold to maintain freshness. For this reason, holding fish in layers of flaked ice is perfect. If ice is used however, it must be changed frequently to keep it clean and to keep it in contact with the fish. Cut fish kept on ice should be separated from the ice by plastic wrap, otherwise the melting ice will draw moisture from the cut surfaces of the fish.

Fresh fish on ice should not be displayed near cooked or smoked fish. Most of the bacteria on raw fish are much more energetic than those on cooked fish. Contamination of cooked product from the drip from raw fish can lead to major problems. Melting ice must also be kept away from live shellfish since the fresh water may kill them. They are seawater creatures and not able to live in fresh water. Other foods used to garnish the iced display can be a germ hazard. It is costly and laborious for the retailer to hold fish on ice. A well-run iced fish operation is pricey, a mediocre one is hazardous.

A second good alternative is holding fish in trays on ice or in very cold refrigerated cabinets. Many retailers package fish in moistureproof trays right after it has been cut. Prepackaged fish is not at risk of contamination from further handling or contact with other fish and prospective purchasers. It also remains moist.

A point to note about cut fish held in trays is that fish juices accumulate in the pans. This is unavoidable as cut fish loses moisture immediately. Too much juice in the pan indicates that the pans have not been changed frequently or that too much fish was cut at once. These juices will support bacterial activity but they help keep the surface of the fish moist. Pan juices should not be murky.

Tray packed fish usually contains some absorbent material to retain the juices. If the trays contain a lot of juice the fish was probably cut a long time ago and its quality may have started a downward slide.

About Odor

Fish kept in an open counter has air circulating around it so that

117

odors do not build up. Packaged fish does not have this advantage and odors usually accumulate. Therefore, when you open a package of fish which has been sealed in plastic wrap, it is normal for it to smell fairly strong. After you open the package, rinse the fish under gently running cold water, pat it dry with paper towels and then sniff it. The odor after rinsing should be free of sour or sharp essences and have a fresh, sea-like quality. There is always some smell but it should not be offensive.

The odor at the fish counter is a general indicator of the quality of the seafood being offered. Scrupulous sanitation procedures are necessary to maintain a clean and safe fish outlet. The smell of bleach is a good sign that the management pays attention to detail. Although a fish shop that is cleaning fish has to contend with the disposal of highly perishable wastes that readily reveal themselves to the nose, the odor of fish should not be overpowering. Observe the care being taken by the staff as they handle fish. It is a good clue.

Examining Cut Fish

Most of us buy fish after it has been cut into fillets, steaks, chunks or roasts. Having the fish dealer prepare the fish makes it ready to use instantly. Look at the fillet or steak carefully for its color and transparency. The color should be bright, even for dark fleshed fish like bluefish and bluefin tuna, and the flesh should be almost translucent. It should not look creamy or milky even if it is a snowy white fish like orange roughy. There should be no discoloration. The flesh and skin, if present, should be shining and moist.

Test the firmness and elasticity of the flesh. Poke the package gently and see if the flesh springs back easily. It must. Do not touch unwrapped fish even if the fishmonger allows you – it is a question of hygiene. The fish should look freshly cut. The edges should be clean and smooth, not ragged and separated.

Look to see if the flesh is clean, free of blood spots and debris. Check the edges to see that they have not dried out or changed color. In certain species the flesh begins to separate into sections when the fish ages. It is a telltale sign. Other fish like Atlantic bluefish have so little connective tissue that the muscle separates very easily and this is not then an indicator of age.

Supermarket fish counters usually display an open dating label on the package. This date, commonly a "sell by" date, tells how long the fish will retain its quality for sale. If you buy fish on the expiry date be prepared to cook it that day.

Take your fish home quickly. Never leave it in a hot car. Keep it in the refrigerator or an ice chest.

Inspecting Fresh Cut Fish

Look for this:	Avoid this:
• firm, elastic flesh	• soft, flabby flesh
• translucent color	• milky color
• moist, fresh-cut appearance	• any signs of drying
• clean, fresh odor	• sharp, nasty or ammonia smell
• open dating for freshness	• expired dates

Examining Whole and Dressed Fish

Dressed fish keeps better than cut fish, retains more flavor in cooking, has choice morsels not available in cut fish and offers another way to vary your fish preparations. It is ideal for the outdoor grill too.

Certain changes occur in fish out of water even under the best conditions. One of these is loss of color. The bright blues and yellows of mahi-mahi fade, the brilliance of mackerel pales and the glitter of smelts diminishes.

If you are buying whole or dressed fish, there are some additional signs of freshness. With whole fish the eyes have it. They must be bright and shining, clear and not sunken. The gills are usually removed, but if they are still present, they should be bright red, not pale or grey. The gills are among the first tissues to spoil. There must be no slime on the skin. This protects the living fish but deteriorates very quickly after the fish is landed.

The skin on truly fresh fish is glistening, tight and elastic. The flesh is firm and springy, not spongy or flabby.

As with cut fish, whole and dressed fish have a clean fresh smell, reminiscent of the sea. They do not smell fishy. Check the smell after the fish has been eviscerated and rinsed, for spoilage begins in the gut cavity. Traces of blood or viscera can be washed away, and with them go, usually, any off odors.

Live fish, which are occasionally available, are obviously going to be "fresh." Eels and trout are the most likely species to be offered live. Ask the dealer to kill them for you right away. If they are kept out of water, struggling, they use up glycogen and the flesh will quickly become less sweet and tougher.

Color, Flavor and Texture

The flavor of fish is partly due to its fat content. The more fat in the fish, the richer, moister and stronger the flavor. The more fat, however, the more perishable, for the oils in fish become rancid readily. This property underlies the difficulty in obtaining truly fresh species such as mackerel, herring, capelin and sablefish. These species are worth seeking and trying though, because they are not only delicious, they are the richest in omega-3s.

Rich fleshed fish are usually cooked with the skin on. Broiling, baking or outdoor barbecuing is the preferred way of cooking oilier fish. Recipes for such fish often call for strong accompanying flavors such as mustard or horseradish. The notion is that it "cuts the oil" but in fact, it complements the flavor. See the recipe section for many good ideas.

Fish differ in the fineness or coarseness of the flesh. Flatfish like sole and flounder have soft, almost fragile flesh. Cod, grouper and perch are moderately firm. Tuna, monkfish and swordfish are firm, dense fish. These differences affect how you cook the fish. Delicate fish are best baked, broiled or steamed, while firmer fish can be barbecued, stir-fried, poached, baked or broiled.

The color of the raw fish gives no indication of the color of the fish after it has been cooked. Except for snow white flesh, most fish becomes much lighter after cooking. Usually a fillet with a grayish or pinkish cast when raw will be white when cooked. Others like bluefish have a dark grayish-blue flesh when raw but become nearly completely white after cooking. The same is true for mackerel. Fresh tuna is another example. Bluefin tuna is a deep red color raw but turns a soft peach color after cooking. The dark red muscle sections in swordfish and others remain dark after cooking.

Shellfish

Molluscs

Shellfish may be sold live, cooked or fresh shucked. The form depends on availability and the animal itself. Shellfish most often sold live are clams, mussels, oysters, periwinkles, crabs, lobsters and crayfish. Because of their extremely high perishability, scallops are seldom sold live.

There is no need to avoid oysters or other shellfish in the months without an "R" as the old wives' tale cautioned. This notion developed partly to protect the breeding oyster, partly because oysters with roe are generally less palatable and partly because before the days of refrigerated distribution, keeping them alive in the hot weather was not so easy.

Shellfish harvesting is monitored by the Federal Government's Shellfish Sanitation Program. This inspection program requires that all shellfish being sold carry a tag certifying that they came from clean waters. While these tags are not displayed at the sales counter, your fish dealer must have the tags from his shipment. This program has done a great deal to reduce the risk of shellfish-borne disease, especially since many people eat shellfish raw. (For more detail, see Chapter Seven). Shellfish taken illegally from restricted waters can enter the market, bringing the risk of hepatitis and other diseases. Protect yourself by patronizing only reputable dealers.

Live molluscs must show their vital signs. Mussels, oysters and clams will open their shells when held on ice or in a tray pack. If you plunge them into a sink or basin of cold water they shun the fresh water immediately. Discard those that do not "clam up." They are dead or dying. Shellfish with chipped, cracked or damaged shells die quickly and if they do not respond to a water bath, throw them out. Be prepared to find a few questionable or expired shellfish in the lot as some animals are less vigorous than others.

Clams. East Coast steamers, also called soft-shell clams, and West Coast geoducks, have oversize necks (siphons) that do not permit the shells to close tightly. Out of water this makes them easy prey to bacteria and water from melting ice. Both can kill the clam. If you touch the siphon or neck it will retract and this indicates that the animal is alive. It is well to cook or process these clams as quickly as possible. Their life out of seawater is short. By contrast, large quahogs – hard-shell clams – can survive long periods out of water without harm.

Oysters may be sold in the shell or as fresh shucked meats. Pasteurized oyster meats are also available. Live oysters should have tightly shut shells or should close quite quickly when disturbed.

When buying shucked meats, check that the liquor around the

oyster is clear, not cloudy. Meats should be plump and creamy. The flavor of oysters varies with the species, its native habitat and the season. Those taken prior to the summer spawning season taste quite different from those harvested after spawning. Oysters build up fat reserves which are used in the spawning process. Oysters about to spawn are very fat, too fat for many tastes. This is one reason for oysters not being eaten in the summer months. To avoid this problem, some enterprising breeders have developed hybrid oysters that never spawn, so making them marketable all year around. These "triploid" oysters cannot be distinguished externally from the regular, breeding oysters – a problem which will probably limit their marketability as it is not possible to tell which sort you have until you open each one.

Calamari (Squid). Like many seafoods, the appeal of squid is greatly enhanced by giving it a more elegant name. In this case, the name is calamari. The Italians have also conferred upon this creature some of the best cuisine. If you have not yet tried it, do so (see recipe section).

There are three main species of squid sold in the USA, and many more available from all over the world. The East Coast has short finned and long finned species. The latter are preferred. The California squid, which is in some years very abundant in Monterey and San Pedro, is also highly palatable and generally inexpensive. Sometimes the long finned squid are sold as loligo from their Latin name. The long-finned California squid is slightly different from its Atlantic cousin. Technically, squid belong to the mollusc family. Instead of an outside shell however, they have developed an interior skeletal structure called the pen or quill. The body of the squid is called the mantle or tube. This and the tentacles are eaten. The ink may also be used as cooking liquid and sauce.

Squid are sold fresh and frozen and are available whole or cleaned. Frozen cleaned squid may be in the form of tubes alone, or the tubes may be packed with the tentacles. Before using fresh squid, remove the head, viscera, ink sac and pen. This is not difficult to do but it is time-consuming, unless you have a lot of experience. The skin may be peeled off under running water, or left on. It is perfectly edible, but detracts from the clean, white appearance of the meat. The variations in the color of squids' skins are not significant of quality or freshness. While alive, the animal has the ability to change color to merge with its surroundings. The pigments which achieve such camouflage gradually emerge into the outer skin of the animal after it is caught, where they are visible, natural and in no way unpalatable. Cleaned squid is usually available and if you are in a hurry, it is worth paying the difference.

Squid can be "bleached" or whitened by soaking it in iced water before using or before freezing. This makes the flesh more appealing after it is cooked too. Otherwise the cooked flesh has a slightly peachy color.

Squid keeps very well when kept cold. Freshness is indicated mainly by a clean sweet smell and the absence of off-odors. It should look shiny and firm.

Crustaceans

Lobsters are supreme when purchased live and cooked at home. Their liveliness is apparent immediately they are removed from the holding tank. Lobsters are also fine bought cooked, if the cooking was recent and the holding cabinets properly chilled. Dead, raw lobsters should not be bought. See Chapter Eight.

Lobsters grow by shedding their outer shell and growing into a newer, larger one. When the new shell is first formed it is soft. The lobster takes on water to fill in some of the space. In this stage it is known as a soft-shell lobster. The meat of such animals is less tasty and less firm than their hard shell elders but is still edible. Go for the hardest shell if you have the choice. The heaviest lobster for its size is likely to be the meatiest. A shell covered in barnacles indicates that the lobster has not moulted for quite a long time, so again it should be meatier.

Some people express preferences for male lobsters or for female lobsters. Unless you dislike the red coral or roe of the female, which is very tasty, there is really no point in making the distinction.

Crayfish are freshwater relatives of the lobster, harvested and farmed mainly in Louisiana and elsewhere in the South. The edible part is the tail. The meat is very mild. These animals may be sold live but usually escape the South in the form of cooked and frozen meats.

Crabs are one of the finer delicacies, but do not find their way around the country very easily, due to their perishability when live. Canned or frozen meat is available for you to become hooked on the taste. Frozen, cooked whole crabs are increasingly available.

Live crabs may appear sluggish from having been held at cold

temperatures whereas they prefer temperatures closer to 40°F.
Warmer conditions increase perishability however, so you are better
off finding a sleepy cold crab. As with lobsters, do not use dead
crabs.

Crabs are distinctly regional. The largest industry is in the
Chesapeake and the Southeast where blue crabs thrive. Blue crabs
are at their table best in the soft-shell stage, just a few hours after
they have moulted. Increasing quantities of soft-shell blue crabs are
frozen, so they are becoming widely available and well known. Blue
crab meat, pasteurized, is also widely available. Another way to
make their acquaintance is through William Warner's fine book,
Beautiful Swimmers.

Many species of hard shell crab are available as frozen legs and
claws or as meat, which may be pasteurized or frozen.

Dungeness crab is one of the West Coast glories and is nearly
always sold cooked. Frozen, whole cooked crabs are distributed
through retail markets. Frozen, cooked meat is also available.

King crab, once the prize of the Northwest, has suffered big
declines in catches over recent years, but is still available in expensive restaurants. The legs and claws, cooked in the shell, are the
prime part. Body meat is used for salads. King crab is almost never
available unfrozen.

Snow or tanner crab comes from the East Coast of Canada and
from the North Pacific. The Pacific species generally are larger and
have better flavor. At its best, Alaskan snow crab is one of the finest
crabs to eat, tastier than the much more expensive king crab. Like
king crab, it is hardly ever available unfrozen. Legs and claws, in
the shell, are the most popular form. Salad meat from the bodies in
retail packs may also be available from the grocer's freezer.

Jonah and rock crabs may be held live in tanks as lobsters are.
They are East Coast species and again, because of perishability,
seldom find their way very far inland. The industry has not developed sufficiently to make picked meat profitable but it is delicious.
They are sometimes sold cooked.

Stone crabs are a Florida delicacy, though only the large
crusher claws are eaten. Fishermen are required to remove the claw
and return the rest of the crab to the sea, where there is a very slender chance that it may regenerate another claw. Stone crab claws
are shipped around the country frozen, both cooked and raw. It is
better if they are cooked before being frozen. The meat in raw, fro-

zen crab claws tends to stick firmly to the shell and is difficult to remove.

Shrimp is seldom available fresh. Almost all the shrimp sold in retail markets around the country has been frozen. For information on shrimp, see the following section on frozen product.

Smoked Fish

Smoked fish is increasingly popular. The health aspects have been discussed earlier. Lox is a lightly smoked and usually very salty form of salmon. Smoked salmon, as well as lox, is widely available throughout the country. Gravlax is appearing in more markets, both fresh and frozen. This is a Scandinavian delicacy made by marinating raw salmon in salt, sugar and herbs. It tastes like a very delicate smoked salmon, but is actually marinated, not smoked.

What To Do When the Fish Comes Home

If you are planning to use your fresh fish that day, keep it in the coldest part of the refrigerator in its original wrap. Sometimes the package leaks so put the fish on a plate to protect other food.

If you plan to hold the fish one or two days, remove the fish from the package, rinse it well under gently running cold water, pat it dry with paper towels and re-wrap it. You can use plastic wrap or heavy waxed paper. If you use paper, an outer wrap of aluminum foil helps retain moisture.

The best treatment you can give your fish in the refrigerator is to pack it in a layer of crushed ice. This keeps it as cold as possible in a moist environment.

Inspect pan dressed fish to see that all traces of viscera have been removed. Sometimes in gutted fish there is a long line of dark red tissue (the kidney) right along the backbone. This should have been removed during cleaning. If it is still there, wash it away immediately using your fingers, a brush or a small knife and cold running water. If the cavity materials have already begun to deteriorate, the rest of the fish may still be fine, but rinse very carefully and sniff. Progressive spoilage is unmistakable whereas residual visceral material, when promptly removed, will not be a problem.

If you have purchased frozen seafood that you plan to store, put it into the coldest part of your freezer (away from the door) as soon as possible.

Try to use live shellfish the same day. Store them in the refrigerator until just before cooking time. Be sure that live animals have some air circulation. The packages should be amply perforated if not already in mesh bags. Keep lobsters in waxed paper bags not too tightly closed to avoid suffocating them. Do not put any live shellfish in plastic bags – they will die.

Hard shell clams, oysters and mussels should be put in a cold water bath before cooking. This helps you to identify and discard any dead animals. Throw out any that do not close their shells in the water. This method does not work with steamers (soft shell clams) since they do not close tightly. The necks of soft shell clams and geoducks should retract when touched. The meats should smell mild and somewhat briny from the sea.

Scrub and de-beard mussels before steaming them. Scrubbing gets rid of dirt on the shells, makes the broth cleaner and means less sand mixes with the meats.

Frozen Seafood

Top quality fish handled carefully and frozen quickly is flavorful and of high quality. Its only disadvantage is small changes in texture and the time it takes to thaw it sufficiently to separate. Even this last step is not always necessary; unless it is very thick, frozen fish can be cooked directly from the frozen state. Top quality frozen fish is certainly preferable to questionably fresh unfrozen fish.

Modern freezing techniques are responsible for the availability of many species year round and beyond the local harvest region. Most of us would not know shrimp or orange roughy otherwise.

Most of the fish used in the USA is sold in frozen form. Frozen fish supplies the needs of many food service customers and is the basis for fast food fish servings. For these purposes, fillets are processed into blocks that are usually skinless and virtually boneless. These blocks are then cut or formed into portions, sticks, breaded and battered products, and many other prepared items that are a mainstay of the grocer's frozen display and restaurant menus.

The equivalent of frozen fish blocks for individual consumers is frozen, boneless fillets. The species most commonly available in this form are cod, haddock, pollock, flounder, sole,turbot and sometimes whiting. They are excellent value and there is no waste at all.

The keys to producing top quality frozen fish are careful handling aboard ship, minimum holding time before freezing, rapid freezing, and storage temperatures well below 0°F. The ideal storage temperature is about -20°F, quite beyond the reach of home freezers. Flavor and texture are best retained when the fish is frozen quickly to minimize the damage to the cell structure of the fish. When the temperature fluctuates during storage, damage to cell structure is greater and this reveals itself by changes in texture, usually softening or mushiness of the flesh.

Modern supermarket freezers vary in their ability to maintain satisfactory freezing temperatures. Because they need to offer shoppers convenient access to the products, grocery store freezers have variable holding temperatures, caused by constant opening of doors, removal and replenishing of contents and so on. Defrost cycles cause further variations in temperature. Nevertheless, grocers' freezers are usually colder and better than domestic freezers. What this means is that you should select packages with the longest storage times on the open dating label, and look for very solid, undamaged packages.

What to Look For in Frozen Fish Packages

• solid, firm packages with no soft spots
• heavy moisture proof wrapping with no tears or holes
• as little air space as possible around the item; tray packs taken directly from the fresh fish counter without being individually rewrapped will not keep well
• no sign of discoloration or darkening of the flesh
• no freezer burn which is a white or yellow cottony appearance caused by evaporation of moisture and drying out of the flesh
• if the fish is visible through the packaging material it should have a firm, glossy appearance with no signs of drying about the edges. It is worth noting that in Japan, where fish is eaten on a much larger scale than it is in the US and where quality is a paramount concern to the fish consumer, packages that do not show the contents either entirely or through a substantial window are virtually

Table 7			
SHRIMP SIZES AND NAMES			
Descriptive Name	Count Per Pound (with shell)	No Fewer Than Per Pound	No More Than Per Pound
Colossal	10/15	10	15
Extra Jumbo	16/20	15	20
Jumbo	21/25	20	25
Extra Large	26/30	25	30
Large	31/35	30	35
Medium Large	36/42	35	42
Medium	43/50	42	50
Small	51/60	50	60
Tiny	Over 70	70	–

Source: Code of Federal Regulations

unsaleable.

• no thick layer of frost on the inside of the wrapper; frost indicates temperature fluctuations during storage

Shrimp

The most common form of frozen shrimp is raw tails with the shell on. Some shrimp is frozen whole, either raw or cooked. Headless shrimp retain their quality better than whole shrimp. The most expensive form is cooked, peeled and deveined shrimp. This shrimp has no waste though, as it is ready to use.

In buying shrimp you need to decide not only what form to select, that is, with or without head, shell or vein but also whether it should be raw, cooked or breaded. You also need to consider size.

Shrimp are sold according to count – the number of shrimp per pound. Word descriptions like large and jumbo may also be used. There is a Federal legal definition for such descriptive names according to the size range of the shrimp and the number of shrimp per pound (count). However, some retailers are not above inventing their own descriptive terms like "cocktail size." The most common terms are defined in Table 7.

The appearance and color of shrimp vary with the species and whether or not it has been cooked. All shrimp turn pink or red when cooked. The color of a raw shrimp is not much of a guide to the cooked color. Shrimp that are grey or brownish when raw cook to pleasing colors.

Major Varieties of Shrimp

There are two main types of saltwater shrimp, northern and tropical. Northern shrimp are mainly of one species and come from Alaska, the Northwest and Maine. They may also be imported from Canada and Scandinavia. These are relatively small shrimp and almost always sold cooked and peeled. They are a delicate pink color and somewhat narrower and more elongated than tropical varieties. Their flavor is distinctly sweet and differs from tropical species. They are ideal for salads as they are ready to use and thaw very quickly.

Most tropical shrimp is classified as white, pink or brown. White shrimp usually costs a little more than pink or brown. Brown shrimp have, perhaps, a better flavor. Species of all three colors are harvested throughout the Gulf of Mexico. US production is nowhere near adequate to supply the market. The US is the second largest importer of shrimp in the world, after Japan. Mexico is traditionally our largest supplier, followed by Ecuador. Other countries in South America also supply large quantities. Many Asian countries also sell a lot of shrimp to the USA.

There are numerous different types of shrimp. Tiger shrimp are becoming popular. So-called freshwater prawns, from the brackish estuaries of the huge rivers of Southern Asia, are widely used, especially for baked, stuffed shrimp in restaurants, which value their large size. However, the word prawn should not be used as it has no definite meaning either legally or in the seafood business. It is sometimes used to mean "large shrimp" but this meaning is as unclear as any other. Avoid the word.

"Scampi" is another term sometimes applied to shrimp. Strictly, scampi is a species of langoustine sometimes called Dublin Bay prawn or Norway lobster or lobsterette. The word scampi is the Italian for this species, which was first harvested from the Adriatic. It was traditionally prepared with butter and garlic. The name of the species has now been associated with this form of preparation, with the result that you get the nonsensical menu description of "shrimp scampi" applied to shrimp sautéed in butter with garlic. It tastes good but sounds very peculiar.

Most shrimp offered retail has been thawed. This fact should be noted on the product sign or label, but seldom is. Fresh shrimp is very rare away from the Gulf and Florida coasts where it is caught. Assume that your market's fresh shrimp is in fact previously frozen. Shrimp tails are traditionally packed in blocks of about 5 pounds, which take time to thaw. Current trends among retailers are to buy individually quick frozen (I.Q.F.) shrimp instead, which are very fast and easy to defrost. This should improve the quality available to consumers.

Shrimp grown in aquaculture operations are increasingly available, mainly from South America. These shrimp are the same species as those normally caught in the wild.

Scallops

Scallops are members of the mollusc family but in the marketplace bear no resemblance to their cousins. That is because we eat only the adductor muscle from the scallop and discard the body, whereas we eat the whole clam, mussel and oyster. Gourmets like eating scallop roe along with the muscle but you need to seek out this treat in a specialty shop.

Although scallops generally appear on the fish counter fresh, they are also sold frozen or thawed. If they have been previously frozen they should be so labeled. Previously frozen scallops may have been dipped in polyphosphate solution just as cut fish sometimes is. The purpose of the dip is to control the loss of moisture from the scallop especially during the thawing phase. Dips may give the scallop a whiter appearance than the never frozen animal. The label should have the word polyphosphate if a dip was used but some tray packed seafood has little label information.

There is a myth that fake scallops abound – allegedly cut from skate wings. Such a product would be much more costly to produce and very unlike the true animal. The structure of scallop muscle consists of parallel fibers of uniform consistency. Verify this for yourself the next time you enjoy a scallop. No fish was ever built quite that way.

There are three types of scallops most commonly found on the market and all come from the Atlantic. Small quantities of other species are imported and there are small landings on the Pacific Coast from time to time.

Sea scallops are the largest ones. Most of these come from

Georges Bank, where they are harvested by American and Canadian fishermen. Other sea scallops are found off the West Coast, where quantities are small and only erratically available. Imported scallops from South America, Asia, New Zealand and other places complete the market.

Bay scallops are small and very highly prized. These are the sweetest, most delicious scallops of all. Most of them come from Cape Cod, Rhode Island and Long Island. They are, most years, scarce and expensive. The season opens around September and few scallops are available past the turn of the year. Most are sold fresh, though in abundant years some dealers will freeze them for later sale. Many frozen imported substitutes, from England, Ireland, Iceland and the Far East are offered. European queen scallops are excellent, very similar to bays. Some warm-water alternatives are horrible.

Calico scallops, which are cheaper and much inferior to bays, are also frequently illegally labeled as bay scallops. Calicos are small. They are whiter than the creamy bays and a little taller, but the two types are difficult to distinguish unless you can see them side by side. Calicos come from the Carolinas and Florida. All scallops are easy to overcook. Gentle and very brief cooking is mandatory for good results.

Crab

Frozen crab is sold as picked meat, legs and claws in the shell, and occasionally as whole eviscerated crabs. Frozen cleaned soft shell crab is finding its way into restaurants and specialty shops outside the Chesapeake and it is truly a treat.

Crabs are cooked immediately after harvest so that the meat can be separated from the shell. Often supplies are not great enough to permit the sale of crabs outside the local harvesting region. That means that Easterners have to go to San Francisco for Dungeness crab.

Major West Coast species are (Alaska) king, Dungeness and snow crab. Eastern varieties are blue (soft-shell), rock, stone and red crab.

Crabs vary greatly in flavor and texture of the meat. It also depends what part of the crab you are eating. In some, like the stone crabs of Florida, only the claws are eaten. Others, like the scarce king crab, are prized for the leg meat. Crabmeat is noted for its delicate sweet flavor. As flavor and texture may be better preserved in some species by pasteurization and refrigeration rather than by freezing, some crab meat will be sold that way in the seafood market.

Like other types of seafood, careful handling after harvesting, good packaging and rapid freezing are crucial to retaining premium quality. Since crab commands premium price, you should be fussy about quality.

Frozen Prepared Seafood

The most convenient seafood of all is that already prepared for you. All you have to do is heat and eat it. Carefully prepared entrees and dinners that have been kept well frozen can be tasty so long as you do not overcook them when applying heat. Increasingly sophisticated seafood meals are being offered with seafood combinations, interesting sauces and delicious seasonings. From a nutritionist's point of view, however, these meals still have some major drawbacks. One is the excessive use of sodium. If you read the nutrition label on the package you will often find that the sodium content of the meal is in excess of one gram (1000 milligrams) and sometimes closer to two grams. Manufacturers rely too heavily on salt for preserving and flavoring effects.

Another worry is the amount and kind of fat used. Seafood starts out being very low in fat but in many meals, rich sauces account for several grams of fat. That may not sound like much, but it contributes most of the calories. The fat used in sauces and coatings is often of the least desirable type, rich in saturated fatty acids. Look out for this on the package by reading the nutrition panel and the list of ingredients. There are 9 calories for every gram of fat and that soon adds up.

Heavily battered, fried seafood used to be the most popular way to eat fish. Deep frying is inadvisable, not because it doesn't taste good (it does) but because it gives you much too much fat, usually of the wrong kind. Breading and batter increase the amount of fat the food absorbs. This gives you far too many calories and can raise your blood cholesterol level as well as your weight.

Breaded seafood products may contain up to 50 percent breading or more. That means half the food is coating. The coating may or may not contain fat but usually does. The only way to be certain is to read the list of ingredients. If fat is not added you can select the product with more comfort. Just heat it without adding oil, butter, margarine or shortening.

There is good news in coated seafood products though. Many processors know that people want to cut calories and fat and want more healthful products. They have responded by offering seafood with light coatings, some as little as 14 percent of the finished product. Prepared seafood does not have to be fried to heat or cook it. You can bake it in a hot oven (450°F.) or broil it.

Pay for convenience, but not with your well-being. Fish is fast and easy to prepare yourself, one of the original unadulterated fast foods.

Freezing Seafood At Home

Recognizing that you cannot do as good a job at home as commercial seafood processors can, you can still preserve good seafood in your own freezer. If the product is to be acceptable afterward, you need to start with good quality material. Fish that is on its way out is far better cooked and used cold in salad or used in fish cakes and soup.

To freeze fish, clean it under cold water and pat it dry. Wrap it tightly in heavy plastic wrap, excluding as much air as possible. Heavy freezer paper overwrapped with foil is also satisfactory. Plastic materials specially designed for freezer use protect the fish better. They are much less permeable to moisture and air. Using an outer wrap of foil protects the package from puncture or damage in the freezer. Take care that the packages are well sealed (use freezer tape) to prevent loss of moisture, oxidation and the development of freezer burn. Label each package with the contents, amount and date.

Put the packages in the coldest part of your freezer where air can circulate around them, freezing them as quickly as possible. If you can, turn down the thermostat ahead of time so that they will freeze more rapidly. Hold frozen seafood as close to -20°F. as possible.

If you expect to hold fish longer than about two months you can give the fish extra protection from drying out and slow breakdown with a solid ice glaze. While this is a time-consuming nuisance, it pays off in the end by giving you better quality fish. An ice glaze is a complete coating of ice around the fish. Be sure the fish is frozen solid first. First freeze the fish unwrapped on a sheet of waxed paper until it is hard. Then remove it from the freezer and dip it in an ice-water bath. Immediately a thin coating of ice will form around the fish. Return the fish to the freezer for 15-20 minutes and then repeat the glazing process. Repeat the glazing and freezing steps until the fish has a coating of ice at least ¹⁄₁₆ inch thick. Make sure that you hold the fish in a different place each time you coat it, so that you avoid leaving a thumbprint without glaze. When the glaze is complete, seal the fish carefully in plastic wrap and avoid cracking the glaze. Label and date the package and store as close to -20°F, as possible. Ice glazing is often used for salmon and other dressed fish.

Thawing Frozen Seafood

Seafood is one type of food that does not necessarily need to be thawed before it is cooked. Whether or not to thaw fish before cooking depends on the recipe you plan to use, how much time you have and how easy it may be to separate the portions. Certainly one pound blocks of frozen fish fillets are easily cooked directly from the frozen state. You just need to double the cooking time. Wherever possible cook frozen fish directly from the freezer without thawing. This keeps the fish moist and tender and reduces weight losses.

Usually the least amount of thawing necessary to separate the servings or handle the fish is the most you should do. Complete thawing is seldom necessary and promotes tissue breakdown and excessive loss of moisture.

Thaw frozen fish by putting it in a sink of cold water or else under cold running water. **Never** use warm or hot water. You will ruin the flesh.

A second and much better way to thaw fish is to leave it overnight in the refrigerator. This takes longer, and you have to remember to do it the night before (or first thing in the morning) but it works better than any other method.

The third way to thaw fish is in the microwave oven. Follow the manufacturer's instructions for thawing and plan for only partial thawing. Let the fish stand a few minutes after partial thawing and you should be able to separate the pieces and begin cooking. Watch out that you do not start cooking the fish in the microwave.

Thawing at room temperature is undesirable for several reasons. One is that the edges and surfaces thaw first and can begin to spoil, while the center remains frozen. Another reason is that moisture loss can be excessive. Use the cold water method if speed is

Table 8
HOW MUCH SEAFOOD TO BUY

Seafood Item	Amount per Person
Fish:	
Whole fish, eg. rainbow trout	¾ to 1lb.
Dressed and pan-dressed eg. flounder	½lb.
Fish steaks with bones, eg. halibut	½lb.
Fish steaks without bones, eg. shark	⅓lb.
Fish fillets, eg. sole, cod	¼ to ½lb.
Molluscs:	
Oysters, hard-shell clams (live)	6
Mussels and soft-shell clams (steamers)	12 to 18
Shucked oysters, clams, mussels	⅓ to ½ pint
Scallops	¼ to ⅓lb.
Squid, whole	⅔lb.
Squid, cleaned	⅓lb.
Crustaceans:	
Lobster, crabs, live	1 to 1½lb.
Lobster, crab meat only	¼ to ⅓lb.
Shrimp, whole	1lb.
Shrimp, headless with shell	⅓ to ½lb.
Shrimp, headless, peeled & deveined	¼ to ⅓lb.

essential. But it is generally better to cook the fish from the frozen state, without thawing.

Determining How Much Fish To Buy

Figuring out how much fish to buy for the number of people you are serving depends on the form of the fish, the appetites of your companions and how many other foods you are serving. Because of bones and skin you need to allow more for whole or dressed fish and steaks than for fillets. It also depends somewhat on the kind of seafood being considered. Some, like oysters, mussels and salmon are more filling than others. But then, oyster lovers can put back an astonishing number of oysters given half a chance.

When recommending amounts of foods, especially seafoods which I love, I have a small discussion with my selves. The nutritionist part of me says that a three ounce cooked portion will be just fine for meeting most people's nutritional needs. It is also plenty if

I am stretching an expensive bit of seafood among many mouths. In fact I have been known to slip to two ounces and get away with it. On the other hand, the fish fancier self says that a three ounce portion on a plate is rather stingy fare. The amounts suggested below are based on moderate, plate-happy portions rather than minimalist conditions. That is how most of us eat. In the recipes, however, portions are designed to yield 4-6 ounces on a cooked weight basis. This is more than nutritional adequacy but less than restaurant practice.

What do restaurants do? One famous Boston seafood establishment serves 5-8 ounce portions at lunch and 8-12 ounce (or more) portions at dinner. These portions are measured raw, so the final serving is probably an ounce or two less. These are generous servings.

What this means is that in many homes seafood portions are likely to be in excess of those recommended by nutritionists thinking about nutritional needs. You can nearly always "get away" with larger servings of seafood at no greater calorie cost because seafood is leaner than nearly all of its mainstay rivals. Figuring your total amount based on the suggestions that follow will cover the servings you require.

Chapter Ten

Basic Seafood Cookery

The Well Equipped Cook

The best results with seafood do not require special tools or gadgets but if your basic equipment is good your results will be better. Simply delicious seafood can happen with the things you have right now.

When you try more adventuresome preparations like steaming or poaching whole fish, shucking your own oysters and cooking your own lobsters, then tools like a fish poacher, oyster knife and lobster crackers become highly desirable, even essential to doing the job most easily.

The equipment I consider indispensable is described below. There are not many items.

Tools

Heavy baking dish made from enameled iron, glass, stoneware or porcelain. These hold the heat better than lightweight metal pans and do not react with the acids often used to flavor seafood. Enameled iron and some glass products have the additional advantage that they can be used on top of the stove as well as in the oven. An oval shape is well suited to the shape of fish and fish fillets; it keeps the most marinade in contact with the fish.

Heavy cast iron skillet or wok for stir-frying and steaming.

Food processor or blender is useful for mincing garlic, chop-

137

ping parsley, nuts and vegetables; makes both smooth and chunky soups. You can do all these tasks by hand but it takes longer.

Garlic press if you do not have a food processor. The back of a French knife will do, too.

Vegetable steamer, the flexible kind that fits into any covered saucepan. This is a three dollar item that permits you to serve thirty dollar entrees. Bamboo baskets work well, too.

French knife made of heavy carborundum steel to hold a very sharp edge; this is indispensable not only for fish but for vegetables to go along with seafood; one good knife serves a lifetime; get a sharpening stone at the same time. People cut themselves on dull knives (because they slip), not sharp ones.

Paring knife with a sharp point for delicate cleaning jobs and trimming.

Wire whisk is a most efficient and effective tool for blending a simple sauce and makes it easy to prepare small quantities.

Outdoor gas grill is my favorite cooking utensil for fish. This device permits the equivalent of baking, broiling and steaming. The flavor imparted is without equal, there is no mess, and all the odors stay outside. It is not an essential tool, but I think it well worth the investment. Its advantage over the simple hibachi or other grills is the time saved in heating the coals and the ease of adjusting the cooking temperature; otherwise, any outdoor grill will do. The covered kettle types are the best. They permit gentler cooking of the fish, without the scorching often caused by regular barbecues.

Well Stocked Pantry

If you always keep these on hand you will NEVER be caught short for preparing any variety of seafood in a delicious way.

- good quality dijon mustard – baseball mustard won't do
- fresh lemon, lime
- whole black peppercorns
- fresh garlic bulbs
- fresh ginger root
- fresh herbs: parsley, dill, others when available
- dried leaf herbs: dill, oregano, thyme, rosemary, basil, bay leaves, tarragon

- "hot" seasoning – any one of Tabasco sauce, cayenne pepper, crushed chilies
- olive oil or other vegetable oil
- sesame oil
- dry white wine. It keeps well for a long time in the refrigerator. Red wine is an asset, too.
- teriyaki and/or tamari sauce (optional)
- light or low sodium soy sauce
- canned whole tomatoes
- tomato paste, preferably in tubes – try a specialty food store or Italian market; this highly convenient form of tomato paste is imported from Europe.
- plain yogurt
- reduced-calorie mayonnaise
- bottled lemon and lime juice – with these on hand you are never stuck but the fresh is definitely more flavorful and gives rind as well.
- good quality vinegars – a variety of flavors gives you much flexibility at minimal cost and they double for tastier salads too; start with white wine, red wine and balsamic vinegars, adding cider and herb flavors if you like. It is easy and inexpensive to make your own herb and flavored vinegars from white vinegar and fresh herbs.

I count on having green peppers, green onions, celery, cooking onions, fresh garlic, carrots, grated parmesan cheese and some other natural cheese on hand and at least one package of frozen chopped spinach as a lifesaver. Your own preferred back-ups might include blue cheese, dried onions, garlic powder, pizza sauce, barbecue sauce and commercially prepared marinades and salad dressings. I prefer my own last-minute variety. Use what works best for you.

So that I can always make a fish soup or chowder in a hurry I am sure to have canned shrimp and/or clams, frozen pollock or other white fish, frozen mussels, skim milk powder, frozen green peas and lean, fat-trimmed bacon (frozen in ¼ pound packets). Canned or frozen corn is also useful.

Some Make-Ahead Ideas that Save Preparation Time

Tomato paste is often available only in quantities greater than you need. Open a small can and freeze two-tablespoon portions in ice cube trays. You can package the tomato cubes in plastic wrap for later use as needed.

Fresh herbs. When parsley and dill are available fresh from your garden or the market, freeze small quantities in ice cube trays. Wilting the herbs over steam enables you to pack them tightly. Store frozen cubes in plastic wrap for later use. These are perfect for soups too.

Sauces. Fish becomes elegant and more flavorful with a simple sauce. Although the ideas in this book are quick to fix you may want to store leftovers or make quantities to freeze. Remember to label your containers.

Stock. Making a fish stock may seem like work but it is easy to do. Ask your fish dealer to give you heads and trimmings from lean fish and boil them all together with seasonings, white wine and vegetables (onion, carrots, celery, bay leaf, peppercorns). You can also use the scraps (bones, trimmings, skin) from your own fish preparations. Reduce the stock so that it is concentrated and freeze it in one cup containers for later use. Freeze some in ice cube trays for "flavor cubes" to use in sauces.

Basic Cooking Techniques

The Canadian Cooking Rule
This is a fool-proof way to cook fish to avoid overcooking and to keep the fish tender and moist. It applies to baking, broiling, steaming, poaching and barbecuing. It does not apply to microwave cookery. It does not apply to shellfish.

1. Preheat the oven to 450°F. or turn on the broiler.
2. Measure the fish at its thickest part as it sits in its cooking dish or broiler pan. Fold thin parts under to make the fish as evenly thick as possible.
3. Cook thawed or fresh fish for 10 minutes per inch of thickness.

Cook frozen fish for 20 minutes per inch of thickness. If steaming or poaching, begin timing when the cooking liquid returns to the boil after the fish has been added.

4. Fish is cooked when it has just turned opaque when separated with a fork. It is better to serve fish just slightly underdone than slightly overcooked, for that way it will still be tender and juicy.

The methods used in this book are:

Grilling or Barbecuing. Cooking on an open rack over a heat source. The heat may come from gas, electricity, hardwood or charcoal. Grills vary from the simple open brazier with no vents or lid to the elaborate covered grill with adjustable heat controls. Grilling fish is ideal because it cooks quickly, offers the possibility of both steaming and grilling and keeps all the odors outdoors. There are no cooking pans to wash either. Because of the aromatics and smoke from the grill the flavor of grilled fish has no equivalent in baking or broiling.

Baking. Cooking in an oven without the addition of liquid. Often liquids form during fish cooking so that part of the cooking may also be accomplished by steaming. Fish is best baked in a hot oven – 450°F. for as short a time as possible, based on the 10 minutes per inch rule.

Broiling. Fish is cooked at very high temperatures just below a heat source. Thick cuts of fish may be turned once. Broiling sometimes dries out the surface of the fish forming a crusty coating. You can avoid this by covering the fish in vegetables or sauce during cooking.

Poaching. Seafood is cooked in simmering liquid just below the boiling point. It can be done in the oven or on top of the stove. The dish may or may not be covered. If the liquid covers the fish, as it does in a chowder or soup, the cooking is achieved by simmering.

Steaming. This method cooks seafood over boiling liquid, not in it. The fish is held out of the liquid on a rack or a simple vegetable steamer. The cooking vessel should have a tight fitting lid or be covered in aluminum foil. Fish cooked in a covered outdoor grill also partially steams because the vapors are trapped and help to cook the upper surface of the fish. The method is ideal with whole fish like sea trout (weakfish).

A variation of both poaching and steaming is to cook fish in individual sealed packets made of parchment paper or foil. The fish actually cooks from a combination of poaching and steaming as the fish juices are retained as well as the steam.

Stir-frying. Joyce Chen, the person who has done more than anyone else to bring the essence of Chinese cooking to American households, calls stir-frying "quick stirring." That is a more descriptive phrase, for the cooking process is just that. Put a tiny amount of oil into a large skillet or wok over high heat. Have vegetables prepared and fish ready at hand for the final few minutes of cooking. First add the dry vegetables to the oil and quickly stir until they are bright but still crisp. Take them from the pan with a slotted spoon and then add the fish to the pan. Take care that the fish is not very wet or else the oil will splatter. Quickly stir the fish pieces until they are just opaque and starting to flake. Return the vegetables to the pan, add any marinade or liquid in which a small amount of cornstarch has been dissolved, stir to combine flavors and thicken, then serve at once.

Not all seafood will stand up to stir-frying but many do. Virtually all molluscs and crustaceans are fine. Firm fleshed fish like swordfish, tuna, shark and monkfish are ideal. Some moderately firm fish like snapper and grouper will work well if you treat them gently. Tender fish like sole and flounder simply disintegrate.

Oven-frying. The answer to those wanting crispy-coated fish, oven fried fish is coated in crumbs, flour or other topping, dribbled sparingly with oil and baked in a hot oven (450°F.). The result is a nicely browned crunchy topping with a juicy interior. With oven-frying you can achieve all the advantages of crispy coatings and moist interiors without the liability of fat.

Marinating fish. While not cooking in the conventional sense, some kinds of seafood can be marinated in acid, either vinegar or citrus juice, for several hours or overnight without the use of heat. The acid accomplishes what heat usually does, altering or denaturing the protein. This procedure will not kill all microorganisms so that if contaminated seafood is used there may be health risks.

Microwave Cooking

This is especially suited to the high temperature, short time requirement for cooking fish and shellfish. Microwave cooking is a version of oven steaming although the source of energy for cooking is different from conventional ovens. Cooking is accomplished when food absorbs energy from the microwaves which are a type of electromagnetic energy similar to radio and TV waves. The microwaves cause the molecules of water and other substances in the food to vibrate rapidly and this process generates heat.

Thicker foods cook more slowly than thinner foods because the microwave energy is used up mainly in the outer portion. It then takes longer for the heat generated at the outside to travel to the center. It is important that foods be as uniformly thick as possible so that cooking is even. For example, fish fillets should have any thin ends folded under so that the whole portion is even.

If fish cannot be folded to make the whole portion evenly thick, arrange fish so that the thinner portions are at the center and the thicker parts are toward the outside of the baking dish.

Frozen fish should be thawed completely before microwave cooking to ensure even cooking. Ice absorbs microwave energy more slowly than water so frozen parts will cook more slowly than the thawed edges. The microwave is useful for thawing fish - just check your oven manufacturer's instructions carefully.

In the microwave, fish is usually covered loosely with plastic wrap or waxed paper to prevent moisture loss and spattering. Leave the edges of the the wrap loose or turn back the corners so that some steam can escape. Properly microwaved seafood is always tender and juicy.

Cooking time is very short. In most microwave ovens a pound of fish will cook at high power in 3-5 minutes. It is not possible to give exact cooking times for microwaving fish, however, because the power of different microwaves varies with the make and model. Unlike conventional ovens, increasing the amount of fish being cooked increases the cooking times. Doubling the quantity does not necessarily double the cooking time. Check the cooking instructions with your oven. Sometimes it may be faster to cook two small batches or servings of fish separately than to cook both at once. Try out your oven to see.

When checking the cooking times for fish, check for doneness after the shortest cooking time recommended. Fish will cook for 3-5 minutes after it has been taken from the microwave so that removing it for serving just before it is completely cooked will ensure perfect cookery. There is a certain amount of trial and error in discovering the exact cooking times for fish in your own microwave but the results are worth careful checking.

Another advantage of microwave fish cookery is that the microwave oven helps to contain fishy odors from spreading throughout the house. To remove any fish odor from the microwave, put 1 cup water in a 2 cup glass measuring cup with 2 tablespoons of lemon juice. Boil 2-3 minutes.

The recipes in this book were developed for conventional cooking methods. Because of the large variations among microwave ovens, adaptations for microwave cookery have not been included.

A Word About the Recipes

There are two ideas behind the recipes: simplicity and savor. A third, nutrition, is implicit. They are designed to be easy to do with ingredients you are likely to have on hand. Each one tastes wonderful, not just okay, but really flavorful. Many were tried out on people who "don't like fish" and who do not like cooking. These recipes passed the test.

Most of the recipes were "invented" when I began supper at six o'clock with a package of fish and the question, "what should I do with this?" Many ideas were inspired by the accomplishments of well known chefs but modified to save time. Since I like cleaning as little as anyone I know, the preparations use a minimum of dishes.

Most recipes can be used with almost any fish. Try them on different species and see how they work out.

Since I am foremost a nutritionist, not a chef, all recipes and serving suggestions have nutrition in mind. Good nutrition complements good taste. All recipes use a minimum of fat and most do not need any salt. The ingredients do not require special stores or out-of-the-way shopping trips. Some foods like sesame oil, tamari or low sodium soy sauce may be difficult to find in small communities, but one shopping trip to an ethnic market or large supermarket will give you a supply that can last over a year and costs less than ten dollars. Everything I used in these recipes came from a large local supermarket.

Nutrition information for the major nutrients is given at the bottom of each recipe. I have made allowances for changes in nutrient content after cooking, and sometimes this entails "guesstimates". That is the state of the art in nutrient calculations. These figures demonstrate the fact that I have tried to keep fat and sodium to a minimum. Happily, calories are reduced with the fat.

When ingredients are listed, I sometimes include alternatives that I have tried and found suitable. Try them yourself if your pantry is low or if you would like a change. I am not a purist about such things as olive oil and pasta. I am about cream however: I don't use it. I really do not need the saturated fat and cholesterol and have found excellent alternatives. The occasional listing of butter or cream remains as a courtesy to the contributor of the recipe.

Mayonnaise is a food that divides connoisseurs, brand loyalists and all others into at least three camps. Since mayonnaise is mainly oil, I have opted for the reduced calorie variety and relied on other flavorings and ingredients for the character of the dish. Its main value in these recipes is to enhance smoothness and body. Its color is important too. If you use your own or commercial varieties, know that the fat and calorie value of the recipe goes up.

I strongly prefer fresh herbs over dried ones, because the flavor is so much better. But I have never used fresh oregano or thyme because of its scarcity (and the lack of sun in my garden) and have become used to the dried variety.

For me, wine is an essential ingredient in many dishes I cook. I keep both red and dry white table wine on hand so that a tablespoon here and there is simple. If this is not your habit, try using cooking wine instead. Vinegar, juice or stock is sometimes suggested as an alternate but I think it is a poor substitute. With few exceptions, sweet wines like cream sherry do not serve well.

About the fish itself. My first assumption is that most readers will buy their fish ready for the pan dressed, filleted or steaked. This book is not for the person wishing to learn how to fillet a fish. To learn about filleting and dressing fish, read *McClane's Encyclopedia of Fish Cookery* or the new Time-Life book, *Fresh Ways With Fish and Shellfish*. Or get your fish dealer to prepare the fish for you.

The Recipes

For the recipes, fish can be grouped as lean fish, rich fish and shellfish. Recipes are as interchangeable as possible for species within each of the groups. That means that if a recipe suggests cod, it will also be appropriate for orange roughy, haddock, tilefish and many others. A list of suggested alternatives is included with many of the recipes.

Certain preparations limit which species can be used. For example, stuffed, rolled fillets require thin fillets like sole, while stir-fry preparations need firm-fleshed fish or shellfish that will not fall apart.

Nutrition Information in the Recipes

We provide estimates of five nutritional characteristics of each recipe as a guide to nutritional merit. In general the recipes add few ingredients rich in fat and sodium and very little salt is suggested. Ingredients rich in saturated fats are used in small amounts. Low fat dairy products are specified wherever possible. Where salt is suggested as optional it has been omitted from the estimate of the sodium content of the recipe.

These recipes have more generous portions than necessary for nutritional needs. 3 ounce cooked portions of meat or fish are commonly used in meal planning. The fish servings here range from 4 to 8 ounces, amounts we are more likely to serve.

The recipes are designed to make it easy to prepare meals that provide no more than 30 percent of their calories from fat. A few recipes exceed that guideline, mainly because the fattier species of fish have more than 30 pecent of their calories from fat. The average of 30 percent of calories from fat for the entire meal, however, can be achieved by including plenty of vegetables with the fish dinner.

For us to keep our fat intake within the 30 percent calories from fat guideline, all foods, meals and snacks must be considered. Individual items may have more or less than 30 percent calories from fat, but the goal is to average no more fat than this amount. For example, rich fish are balanced by having plenty of lean vegetables. A breakfast of cereal and low fat milk will counterbalance a dinner of meat, vegetables and salad with dressing.

To make "30 percent calories from fat" meaningful we need to know how much fat that is for most people. A sedentary man might consume 2,000 calories a day. 30 percent of these, a maximum of 600 calories, should come from fat. At 9 calories per gram, the 600 calories translates to about 65 grams of fat daily. Women, whose energy intake is closer to 1,500 calories a day, should consume about 50 grams of fat. That gives a range of fat intake of 50 to 65 grams total for a day, or 20 grams per meal.

The estimates of the nutrient content of the recipes were based on data from the following sources: USDA's revised tables of food composition entitled, *Composition of Foods*; Pennington and Church's, *Food Values of Portions Commonly Used* 14th edition; data from manufacturers; USDA's *Provisional Table on the Fatty Acid and Cholesterol Content of Food*, 1986; and Nettleton, J. *Seafood Nutrition*.

Values above 100 for calories, sodium and cholesterol were rounded to the nearest 10 calories or milligrams respectively. Values below 100 for these nutrients were rounded to the nearest 5 units. Protein and fat values were rounded to the nearest gram.

The lack of nutritional data is indicated by N/A, meaning not available. Where nutritionally negligible amounts of a substance are present, the level is indicated by a "less than" symbol (<). Minimum estimates of sodium are indicated by the symbol > (greater than).

Where the type of fish is not mentioned in the title of the recipe, in the lean fish section the data used for the nutrition information was based on cod. Under rich fish, data were based on Atlantic bluefish.

Recipes

Chunky Seafood Spread

Ingredients:

¼ lb. frozen peeled and deveined shrimp OR 1 6 oz. can shrimp OR the equivalent of the seafoods listed below

1 tablespoon finely chopped red pepper OR canned pimiento

2 tablespoons finely chopped pinenuts OR walnuts

1 teaspoon freshly grated ginger root

¼ cup reduced calorie mayonnaise

1 tablespoon freshly squeezed lime juice

Other fish you can use with this recipe:

shrimp, crabmeat, lobster, cooked mussels, chopped clams, plain or smoked oysters and cooked scallops

Yield: About 1 cup, 4 servings

1. Cook frozen shrimp by plunging in boiling water for ½-1 minute. Drain and rinse canned shrimp OR coarsely chop other seafood

2. Combine all ingredients by hand or in a food processor.

Serve with crackers, raw vegetables or wedges of pita bread

Approximate Nutrition Information per Serving:

Calories: 60	Fat: 2g	Sodium: N/A
Protein: 9g	Cholesterol: 65mg	

Old World Herring Platter

Prepare this attractive platter several hours or the night before serving. Allowing the ingredients to mellow produces a delicious flavor. If you've never tried herring before, here's the place to start.

Ingredients:

2 8 oz. jars of herring pieces, marinated in vinegar, not sour cream

2 large Granny Smith apples, cored and thinly sliced

½ cup onion, chopped

¼ cup chopped garlic dill pickle

½ cup reduced calorie mayonnaise

½ cup plain lowfat yogurt

1 tablespoon lemon juice

dash white pepper

12 small potatoes, pared and left whole; OR 4 large ones cut into 1½ inch chunks. There should be about 4 cups

½ cup chopped fresh parsley

Yield: 6 servings

1. Drain the herring and cut the pieces into bite-sized morsels if necessary.

2. Combine the apple, onion, pickle, yogurt, mayonnaise, lemon juice and pepper with the herring and mix well. Refrigerate for at least six hours and preferably overnight.

3. About 15 minutes before serving, cook potatoes until just tender but not mealy.

4. To serve, pile herring mixture in the center of a large platter and surround with the potatoes. Sprinkle the potatoes with the parsley.

Note: The potatoes may be served hot with the cold herring mixture, California style, or cold. Red-skinned potatoes in their jackets are also attractive. If desired, toss the potatoes in additional yogurt-mayonnaise mixture to which some chopped parsley has been added.

Approximate Nutrition Information per Serving:

Calories: 370   Fat: 15g   Sodium: >100mg
Protein: 31g   Cholesterol: 80mg

Salmon Mousse

My good friend Robin Orr gave me this recipe with a note saying "I especially like this as you can do it so far ahead". It is always a winner.

Ingredients:

1 15 oz. can red (sockeye)
    salmon (see Note)
juice from salmon brought up to
    ½ cup with water
1 envelope unflavored gelatin
grated rind from half a lemon
2 tablespoons freshly squeezed
    lemon juice

½ cup reduced calorie
    mayonnaise
1 teaspoon paprika
1 tablespoon chopped fresh dill
    OR 1 teaspoon dried dill weed
1 cup plain lowfat yogurt

Yield: 4 cups – 8 appetizer servings

1. 6 hours to 3 days ahead of serving time, drain salmon liquid into a measuring cup and add water to make ½ cup. Heat the liquid.

2. Remove any skin from salmon but keep the bones. Mash the bones with a fork.

3. In a food processor or blender, add gelatin, lemon juice and hot salmon liquid. Blend until gelatin is dissolved.

4. Add salmon and remaining ingredients and blend until smooth.

5. Pour mixture into a 4 cup fish shaped or ring mold and refrigerate at least 6 hours before serving. To unmold, dip mold in lukewarm water until loosened. Run a knife tip around the edge before turning out on serving platter.

6. Garnish with sliced ripe olives, thin slices of unpeeled cucumber overlapped like scales or simply with sprigs of fresh dill weed. Serve with Scandinavian flat bread and crackers.

You can use canned pink salmon but the mousse will be much paler in color. Increasing the amount of paprika helps give the mousse a more robust color.

Approximate Nutrition Information per Serving:

Calories: 130   Fat: 6g   Sodium: 260mg
Protein: 13g   Cholesterol: 20mg

Tapenade – a Fish Spread

Here's an elegant and easy way to use some overlooked seafoods. Make the spread up to 3 days before needed and serve with Scandinavian thin crackers, sliced pita bread or vegetables. It is tasty in sandwiches with tomatoes, cucumbers, sprouts and lettuce.

Ingredients:

1 6-7 ounce can sardines
1 large clove garlic
2 green onions, finely chopped
3 tablespoons freshly squeezed
  lemon juice
grated rind from half a lemon
1 tablespoon olive oil
¼ cup ripe olives (see Note)

2 tablespoons cognac, brandy
  or red wine
2 tablespoons capers (see Note)
2 teaspoons dijon mustard
½ teaspoon black pepper
pinch each of ground cloves,
  nutmeg and ginger

Other fish you can use with this recipe:
light tuna, mackerel and pilchard

Yield: 1½ cups, 6 servings

1. Drain and rinse packing liquid from fish. If using sardines or mackerel packed in tomato or mustard sauce, include the sauce with the remaining ingredients.

2. In a food processor or blender, mince the garlic. Add all the remaining ingredients and blend until smooth. Chill well.

3. Serve spread on crackers, cherry tomato halves, cucumber shells, pita bread slices or celery and carrot sticks. Garnish with finely minced red onion, minced red pepper or grated lemon rind for color contrast.

Note: The olives and capers make this spread somewhat salty. You can omit these and substitute 1 tablespoon of tomato paste.

Approximate Nutrition Information per Serving:
Calories: 130   Fat: 8g   Sodium: >600mg
Protein: 10g   Cholesterol: 10mg

Mussel Pick-ups

Steamed mussels served in their handsome black shells with a dab of sauce make a simple, enticing appetizer. Choose the sauce you like – salsa, salsa verde, barbecue, mustard, or cucumber. Serve six mussels for an appetizer.

Ingredients:

1 quart or about 2 lb. live
  mussels in the shell
  (about 24)
1 clove garlic, quartered
1 medium onion, sliced
6 sprigs fresh parsley

2 bay leaves
1 teaspoon dried thyme leaves
½ cup dry white wine
1 recipe of any of the sauces
  given later.

Other fish you can use with this recipe:

littleneck clams

Yield: About 24 mussels – Serves 4

1. Early in the day or up to an hour before serving, in a sink of cold water scrub the mussels with a brush and remove the beards. Discard any mussels that do not close. Put the cleaned mussels in a large pot.

2. Add the garlic, onion, parsley, seasonings and wine. Cover and cook over high heat just until the mussels open, about 3-5 minutes. Overcooking makes the mussels tough.

3. Remove the cooked mussels from the broth. If you wish, filter the broth through an old towel or layers of cheesecloth and save it for soup.

4. Pluck the mussel meats from the shells reserving a half shell from each for serving. Set each mussel in a shell and top with a teaspoonful of the sauce of your choice.

Approximate Nutrition Information per Serving, without sauce:

Calories: 60   Fat: 1g   Sodium: 170mg
Protein: 8g   Cholesterol: 40mg

Soused Herrings

Ingredients:

6 or more herrings, scaled, cleaned and split along the bellies

1 teaspoon salt

1 teaspoon black pepper

2 bay leaves

6 peppercorns

3-4 whole allspice berries

2 onions, thinly sliced

1½ cups malt vinegar (tarragon or cider vinegar will substitute but malt is the traditional favorite)

1½ cups water

Other fish you can use with this recipe:

Mackerel and river herring

Yield: Serves 12

1. Preheat oven to 350°F.

2. Remove the backbone from fish if desired. Fish can be soused with or without the bones.

3. Sprinkle the fish with salt and pepper. Roll up boned fish and secure with a toothpick. If fish are not boned, place them in a shallow, non-metallic baking dish head to tail so they are well packed. (A metal dish will react with the acid in the vinegar).

4. Add bay leaves, peppercorns, allspice and onion slices. Mix the vinegar with the water and pour over the herrings.

5. Bake at 350°F. for 45 to 60 minutes. Allow to cool in the cooking liquid. Serve cold.

Approximate Nutrition Information per Serving:

Calories: 290   Fat: 15g   Sodium: 360mg

Protein: 34g   Cholesterol: 100mg

Heart Healthy Devilled Eggs

Turn that old favorite, devilled eggs, into a low cholesterol treat by stuffing the cooked whites with seafood. Crabmeat, herring, sardines, mussels, clams or oysters make ideal stuffing combined with any of the sauces given later. This version uses real or imitation crabmeat in cucumber dill sauce.

Ingredients:

6 ounces crabmeat, imitation crabmeat OR any of the seafoods suggested below

12 eggs, hard boiled and peeled

1 small cucumber, pared and cut in quarters

¼ cup reduced calorie mayonnaise

¼ cup plain lowfat yogurt

1 tablespoon freshly squeezed lemon juice

3 tablespoons fresh dill, chopped

½ teaspoon freshly ground black pepper

sprigs of fresh dill for garnish

Other fish you can use with this recipe:

crabmeat, herring, sardines, mussels, clams, oysters, imitation crabmeat and lobster

Yield: 12 servings

1. Several hours before serving, cut eggs in half. Remove and discard the yolks.

2. Finely chop the cucumber in a food processor or blender. Add the mayonnaise, yogurt, lemon juice, dill and pepper and blend.

3. Add the crabmeat to the cucumber mixture and blend, leaving fine chunks.

4. Fill the egg white halves with the cucumber-crab mixture and garnish with fresh dill sprigs.

Approximate Nutrition Information per Serving:

Calories: 40   Fat: 1g   Sodium: 85mg

Protein: 6g   Cholesterol: 10mg

Crabmeat Dip

Ingredients:

1 small onion, quartered
1 6 oz. can crabmeat OR 1 cup imitation crabmeat (about four sticks), chopped
8 oz. lowfat cottage or ricotta cheese

3 tablespoons freshly squeezed lemon OR lime juice
1 teaspoon grated lemon OR lime rind
1 tablespoon chopped chives
few drops Tabasco sauce

Other fish you can use with this recipe:
crabmeat, imitation crabmeat, shrimp and lobster

Yield: 2½ cups, 6 servings

1. In a food processor or blender, mince the onion. Add the cottage cheese and lemon juice and process until smooth.

2. Add the chopped crabmeat, chives, lemon rind and Tabasco and whirl until completely blended. Serve chilled or hot with crackers and crisp vegetables.

Variations: Use shrimp instead of crabmeat. ½ cup cheddar cheese may be added and the dip served hot. ¼ cup blue cheese also makes a tasty addition.

Approximate Nutrition Information per Serving:

Calories: 60   Fat: 2g   Sodium: N/A
Protein: 6g   Cholesterol: 20mg

Shrimp and Blue Cheese Dip

Ingredients:

1 6 ounce can shrimp or ½ lb. frozen shrimp, peeled and deveined

¼ lb. Roquefort or blue cheese

1 large clove garlic, minced

⅓ cup reduced calorie mayonnaise

⅔ cup plain lowfat yogurt

¼ teaspoon white pepper

few drops Tabasco sauce

Other fish you can use with this recipe:

shrimp, crabmeat and lobster

Yield: 2 cups, 8 servings

1. Cook frozen shrimp by plunging in boiling water for ½-1 minute. Drain and rinse canned shrimp.

2. In a food processor or blender mince the garlic. Add remaining ingredients and blend, leaving the mixture coarse.

3. Serve as a dip with raw broccoli, cucumber, celery, zucchini, carrots and bread sticks or use as a topping for crackers. The mixture also makes a tasty stuffing for cherry tomato halves, Belgian endive leaves or snow peas.

Approximate Nutrition Information per Serving:

Calories: 100   Fat: 6g   Sodium: >300mg

Protein: 9g   Cholesterol: 45mg

Raquel's Mediterranean Fish Stew

Ingredients:

1 lb. fish fillets

2 tablespoons olive oil

1 large onion, sliced

1-2 cloves garlic, minced

½ cup chopped celery with leaves

½ cup chopped green peppers

1 16 ounce can of tomatoes with 16 ounces of water

½ cup dry white wine

½ cup chopped fresh parsley

¼ teaspoon black pepper

2 threads saffron (optional and expensive but definitely character-giving)

1 cup cooked rice or potato slices

few drops Tabasco sauce

Other fish you can use with this recipe:

cod, pollock, grouper, lingcod, monkfish, whitefish, perch, ocean perch, whiting, orange roughy, haddock and cusk

Yield: 4 servings

1. In a large pot heat the oil and sauté the onion, garlic, celery and pepper. Add the tomatoes with their juice, water, wine, parsley and spices. Cover and simmer gently for 30 minutes. Thin with tomato juice or water if soup is too thick.

2. Cut fish into serving size chunks and gently lay them in the prepared hot broth. Simmer an additional 7-10 minutes until fish just flakes with a fork.

3. Add the cooked potatoes or rice merely to heat through, stirring ever so gently. Serve in deep bowls with Tabasco on the table.

Delicious with crusty French or Italian bread and a spinach salad.

Approximate Nutrition Information per Serving:

Calories: 280   Fat: 11g   Sodium: 100mg

Protein: 21g   Cholesterol: 50mg

Finnish Potato, Dill and Fish Soup

Simple yet elegant, this hearty soup makes an irresistible meal.

Ingredients:

1½ lb. moderately firm fish, fresh or frozen

2 tablespoons margarine

2 medium onions, sliced in rings

6 medium red skinned or new potatoes

1 14 ounce can chicken broth plus ¼ cup water OR 2 cups fish stock

12 peppercorns coarsely crushed with the flat of a knife

3 cups lowfat milk

3 tablespoons fresh dill, chopped, OR 1 tablespoon dried dill weed

6 sprigs fresh dill for garnish

Other fish you can use with this recipe:

cod, pollock, grouper, lingcod, monkfish, whitefish, perch, ocean perch, whiting, orange roughy and haddock

Yield: 6 servings

1. In a large heavy kettle melt the margarine and sauté the onions. Meanwhile, slice the potatoes ⅜ inch thick and add to the onions.

2. Add the chicken broth and water or the fish stock; cover and simmer until the potatoes are just beginning to soften, about 8 minutes.

3. Add the dill and pepper. Layer the fish across the potatoes and simmer covered for another 10 minutes or until the fish turns opaque. Stir gently to break up the fish.

4. Add the milk and heat until just below the boiling point for about 5 minutes. Serve at once. Garnish with fresh dill or finely chopped red onion.

Serve with crusty bread and cold bean salad.

Approximate Nutrition Information per Serving:

Calories: 300	Fat: 7g	Sodium: 430mg
Protein: 29g	Cholesterol: 55mg	

Joyce's Super Fish Chowder

I've been known to make this chowder at the last minute but the flavors are much better if the soup can mellow in the refrigerator overnight. It is thick with seafood and vegetables – a perfect one dish meal.

Ingredients:

1½ lb. firm fish, frozen or fresh
1 6 ounce can tiny shrimp, drained and rinsed
½ lb. bay scallops (optional)
¼ lb. lean bacon with the outside fat removed
4 large potatoes, scrubbed and coarsely diced (paring is optional)
3-4 stalks celery with leaves, chopped
2 large or 3 medium onions, chopped

4 bay leaves
12 peppercorns
2 cups fish stock, clam juice or water
1 12 oz. can corn kernels or 1 10 oz. package frozen corn kernels
4 cups lowfat or skim milk
¼ cup fresh parsley, chopped
1 10 oz. package frozen peas
¼ lb. sharp cheddar cheese, grated

Other fish you can use with this recipe:

cod, pollock, grouper, lingcod, monkfish, whitefish, perch, ocean perch, whiting, orange roughy, haddock and cusk

Yield: 6 servings as a meal

1. Slice the bacon into one inch pieces and sauté in a large heavy kettle. Layer the vegetables on top of the bacon as follows: potatoes, celery, onions.

2. Place the fish on top of the vegetables and add the bay leaves and peppercorns. Add the fish stock or water and cover. Simmer until the potatoes are tender but not mushy and the fish flakes.

3. Stir in the scallops, shrimp, milk and corn and keep on low heat for about 30 minutes. Do not boil or the mixture will curdle.

4. Just before serving stir in the peas, parsley and cheese. Stir until cheese melts. Taste for seasoning, adding pepper if necessary. To thin, add milk.

Serve with hot whole wheat biscuits and a tossed salad.

Variations: fresh or canned minced clams may be added to the chowder instead of shrimp.

Approximate Nutrition Information per Serving:
Calories: 460   Fat: 11g   Sodium: >550mg
Protein: 47g   Cholesterol: 140mg

Sweet and Sour Fish Soup

Ingredients:

1 lb. firm white fish cut into 2 inch chunks

3 tomatoes, chopped

2 carrots, sliced

3 green onions with tops, finely sliced

½ cup dry white wine

1 cup water

½ lb. mushrooms, washed, trimmed and sliced

2 tablespoons chopped, fresh parsley

3 tablespoons cider vinegar

1 tablespoon sugar

1 teaspoon tomato paste

1 tablespoon chopped fresh chives

Other fish you can use with this recipe:

cod, pollock, grouper, lingcod, monkfish, whitefish, perch, ocean perch, whiting, orange roughy, haddock and cusk

Yield: 4 servings

1. In a large saucepan simmer the tomatoes, carrots and onion in the wine and water for 5 minutes.

2. Add the fish and simmer another 5 minutes or until fish just turns opaque.

3. Stir in all remaining ingredients except chives. Let soup stand 10 minutes over very low heat to blend the flavors. Taste for sweetness adding 1-2 teaspoons more sugar if the soup is too sour. Serve in bowls and garnish with chives.

Approximate Nutrition Information per Serving:
Calories: 190   Fat: 1g   Sodium: 110mg
Protein: 22g   Cholesterol: 50mg

Mussel and Mushroom Soup

This soup was inspired by the Billibi soup from Maxim's in Paris. Our version is made with milk and wine instead of cream. The soup is a tasty first course for 4 or a meal for 2.

Ingredients:

2 lb. mussels in the shell or 1
  cup mussel meats
1 large cooking onion, sliced
1 bay leaf
2 teaspoons dried thyme leaves
6 parsley sprigs
1 clove garlic, quartered
½ cup dry white wine
1 tablespoon margarine

1 tablespoon vegetable oil
8 ounces fresh mushrooms,
  sliced – about 2 cups
3 green onions, finely sliced
2 tablespoons flour
½ cup dry white wine
½ teaspoon black pepper
1 cup lowfat milk
¼ cup chopped fresh parsley

Yield: 4 servings

1. In a sink of cold water scrub mussels with a brush and remove the beards. Discard any that do not close. Put the cleaned mussels in a large pot.

2. Add the onion, half the thyme leaves, garlic, bay leaf and parsley sprigs. Add ½ cup white wine, cover and steam over high heat until mussels open, about 5 minutes.

3. Pour off cooking liquid and reserve. Discard vegetables and herbs. Remove mussel meats from shells and set aside.

4. In medium saucepan lightly sauté mushrooms and green onions in margarine and oil. Stir in flour. Gradually stir in ½ cup white wine, remaining thyme leaves and pepper. Pour in broth from mussels, leaving behind any sediment in the bottom of the vessel. Stir over medium heat until thickened.

5. Gradually stir in milk. Do not not allow the soup to boil. Add the mussels and parsley and serve at once with crusty French bread.

Approximate Nutrition Information per Serving:

Calories: 220   Fat: 9g   Sodium: 250mg
Protein: 11g   Cholesterol: 40mg

Cioppino

Maxine Hegsted, a Wellesley, Massachusetts artist, makes a marvellous cioppino with a wide assortment of seafoods. This is her recipe just as she sent it to me. Plan ahead for this feast and watch it all disappear.

Ingredients:

1½ lb. fish of at least two different species

1 6-7 oz. can albacore tuna, drained and rinsed

1 lobster, cooked, shelled and broken into pieces OR ½ lb shrimp, peeled and deveined OR 1lb. squid, cleaned and sliced OR all three

16 clams or mussels in the shell, thoroughly scrubbed and debearded

1 large onion, chopped

1 medium green pepper, seeded and chopped

½ cup sliced celery

1 carrot, pared and shredded

3 cloves garlic, minced

3 tablespoons olive oil

1 28 oz. can crushed Italian plum tomatoes or 4 cups fresh tomatoes, diced

1 8 oz. can tomato sauce

1 teaspoon crushed basil

1 bay leaf

1 teaspoon salt (optional)

¼ teaspoon freshly ground black pepper

1 cup dry white wine

2 tablespoons minced parsley

Yield: 8 servings

1. In a large, non-reacting kettle sauté the onion, garlic, green pepper, celery and carrot in the olive oil until limp.

2. Stir in tomatoes, tomato sauce, basil, bay leaf, salt and pepper. Simmer an hour or more, then discard the bay leaf.

3. Remove any skin from the fish and cut into chunks. Stir the wine into the sauce and then add the fish. Do not stir. Simmer gently 10 minutes.

4. Add shrimp and squid and lobster. Place mussels or clams on top of fish and steam 5 minutes or until the shells have opened. Discard any shellfish that do not open.

5. Ladle into wide soup plates. Sprinkle with chopped parsley and serve with crusty French, Italian or sourdough bread.

Approximate Nutrition Information per Serving:

Calories: 260 Fat: 7g Sodium: >400mg
Protein: 32g Cholesterol: 100mg

New England Clam Chowder

The hearty clam chowder is usually made with quahogs and their juice, milk (or cream), potatoes, onions and whatever specialty the chef favors. Soft shelled clams or steamers also make an excellent chowder which has, as Sheryl Julian wrote in the Boston Globe, "a more subtle taste". Even canned clams will do if the fresh are not available. Here is Sheryl's recipe using steamers and Italian pancetta sausage.

Ingredients:

1 quart steamer clams
1½ cups water
1 cup clam juice
  (bottled will do)
3 ⅛ inch thick slices Italian
  pancetta, cut in strips
  (see Note)
3 tablespoons margarine or
  vegetable oil (see Note)

2 medium onions, chopped
3 tablespoons flour
3 cups lowfat milk
1 large potato, diced
handful fresh Italian parsley
  (the flat-leafed kind),
  chopped
freshly ground black pepper

Yield: 6 servings

1. Scrub the clams under cold tap water so that the shells are not gritty and pile them into a large deep kettle. Pour in the water, cover and bring to a boil over high heat. Cook clams for just a few minutes until all the shells are open.

   (Microwave: Following the manufacturer's directions, cook the clams in small batches in the microwave until they have just opened. Save all the juices that accumulate).

2. Remove clams from the broth, discarding any whose shells have not opened. Pluck the clam meats from the shells discarding the black skin from the necks of steamers.

3. Filter the clam broth through a towel or layers of cheesecloth and bring up to 3 cups volume with bottled clam juice. Wipe out the pot with a paper towel.

4. In the kettle, sauté the pancetta strips until they have rendered all their fat and are turning brown. Remove sausage from pan. Wipe out fat from pan and add margarine or oil.

5. Sauté the onions until soft but not brown, then stir in the flour. Cook over medium heat whisking constantly for 2 minutes.

6. Gradually stir in the 3 cups of clam broth and let the mixture boil. Stir in the milk and let the chowder just come to a boil, stirring constantly.

7. Reduce the heat and add the diced potato, parsley and a generous grating of black pepper. Cook the soup, barely simmering, until the potatoes are tender, about 15-20 minutes. Do not boil.

8. Chop the clams, catching the juice. When the potatoes are cooked, add the clams and juice. Heat thoroughly without boiling and ladle into bowls.

Serve with cornmeal muffins and spinach salad.

Note: If pancetta is not available use lean smoked sausage or chopped lean bacon, trimmed of fat.
Use 1½ tablespoons of margarine or oil for fewer calories.

Approximate Nutrition Information per Serving:
Calories: 210   Fat: 9g   Sodium: >300mg
Protein: 14g   Cholesterol: 20mg

Cod, Corn and Tomato Soup

Here's a perfect supper made in a hurry from either fresh or frozen fish. The Rhode Island Seafood Council has used it in many seafood demonstrations and it is one of many tasty recipes in their excellent collection. Any lean white fish that doesn't fall apart in cooking will do.

Ingredients:

1 lb. firm fish fillets

2 slices lean bacon with the outside fat removed

1 medium onion, chopped

1 tablespoon margarine or vegetable oil

2 tablespoons flour

1 28 oz. can crushed Italian tomatoes with juice

1½ cups water

1 medium green pepper, chopped

1 12 oz. package frozen corn or 1 16 oz. can cream style or corn kernels

½ teaspoon salt (optional)

1 tablespoon chili powder

Other fish you can use with this recipe:

cod, pollock, grouper, lingcod, monkfish, whitefish, perch, ocean perch, bass, sablefish, halibut, orange roughy and haddock

Yield: 4 servings

1. Cut trimmed bacon into one inch pieces and sauté in a large heavy kettle until lightly browned. Drain fat or remove with paper towels.

2. Add margarine or oil and sauté onions until they become transparent. Stir in flour and cook one minute.

3. Add tomatoes and their juice, water and green pepper. Simmer 5 minutes. Add corn, fish, salt and chili powder and simmer over low heat until fish turns opaque, about 15 minutes. Gently break fish into bite sized pieces, being careful not to mash it. Serve at once.

Serve with crusty French or sourdough bread and a tossed salad.

Note: The soup will be thicker if using creamed corn. To make it thicker with niblet style corn, add two tablespoons of tomato paste.

Approximate Nutrition Information per Serving:

Calories: 260   Fat: 6g   Sodium: 390mg

Protein: 25g   Cholesterol: 50mg

Calamari Salad

Served as an appetizing first course or as a main meal, this colorful salad shows how versatile calamari is.

Ingredients:

1 lb. squid, cleaned, peeled and sliced into ½ inch rings and soaked briefly in ice water to whiten

1 tablespoon olive oil

1 cup thinly sliced celery

½ cup red onion, diced

2 cups finely sliced red cabbage

1 Granny Smith apple, cored and thinly sliced

¼ cup fresh parsley, chopped

1 teaspoon dried oregano leaves

1 clove garlic, minced

¼ cup freshly squeezed lemon juice

2 tablespoons olive oil

grated rind of ½ lemon

½ ripe avocado, diced

¼ lb. feta cheese, crumbled

Other fish you can use with this recipe:

squid, mussels, shrimp, sardines, herring, mackerel, crab, scallops, lobster, tuna, swordfish, monkfish, snapper and shark

Yield: 4 servings

1. In a large skillet or wok, stir-fry the squid rings in 1 table-spoons of olive oil. Be careful that the squid has been dried or the oil will splatter. Cook briefly, 2-3 minutes and set aside.

2. Combine the remaining ingredients except feta cheese in a large bowl. Add the squid and mix well. Chill and serve on Boston lettuce leaves topped with feta cheese.

Serve with pumpernickel bread.

Approximate Nutrition Information per Serving:

Calories: 390   Fat: 28g   Sodium: 370mg
Protein: 22g   Cholesterol: 370mg

Seafood Tabouli

A popular whole grain salad, tabouli is made from cracked wheat or bulgur seasoned with lemon juice, mint and parsley. Combining tabouli with leftover cooked fish, shellfish or canned fish makes a meal. Make it a day ahead and use as a pocket bread stuffer too.

Ingredients:
1 cup boiling water
1 cup bulgur wheat – available in most large supermarkets or in health food stores. Bulgur comes in different sized grinds: fine, medium or coarse and I prefer the coarse grind in salads.
1 quart mussels, steamed in ½ cup white wine and shelled OR 1 cup mussel meats
1 6-7 oz. can shrimp OR 1 cup imitation crabmeat, chopped
1 3½ oz. can sardines OR herring OR kippers cut in bite sized pieces, drained and rinsed

¼ cup fresh mint, chopped OR 2 tablespoons dried mint
¼ cup fresh parsley, chopped
3 green onions with tops, finely sliced
2 cloves garlic, minced
½ pint cherry tomatoes, halved
¼ cup freshly squeezed lemon or lime juice
rind of ½ lemon
3 tablespoons olive oil
½ teaspoon freshly ground black pepper

Other fish you can use with this recipe:

mussels, shrimp, sardines, herring, mackerel, crab, scallops, lobster, squid, tuna, swordfish, monkfish, snapper, shark, amberjack, or any leftover cooked fish or shellfish

Yield: 6 servings

1. In a large bowl add boiling water to bulgur wheat. Allow to stand until water has been absorbed. For firmer grains, use only 3/4 cup water.

2. When bulgur has cooled add all remaining ingredients. Mix thoroughly but gently, then refrigerate the salad.

Serve with cucumbers in yogurt.

Approximate Nutrition Information per Serving:
Calories: 270   Fat: 10g   Sodium: >200mg
Protein: 17g   Cholesterol: 75mg

Superb Ceviche

With the tenderness of uncooked seafood and the cooking effects of lime juice, scallops are at their finest in this classic preparation. Serve alone or combined with tomatoes, avocado, wilted spinach, fresh chili peppers or other cold seafood such as salmon, tuna or mackerel.

Ingredients:

1 lb. bay scallops or sea scallops cut with the grain into small pieces
1 small onion, finely chopped, about ⅓ cup
1 cup lime juice
grated rind of one lime

freshly ground black pepper
1 tablespoon olive oil
½ lb. fresh spinach leaves, washed and stems removed
½ medium red onion thinly sliced in rings

Yield: 6 servings

1. The day before serving or, if time is short, at least three hours before: put scallops, chopped onion and lime rind in a glass bowl and add a good grating of black pepper. Cover with the lime juice, adding more juice if the scallops are not completely covered. Refrigerate overnight.

2. Just before serving, drain the scallops, reserving 1 tablespoon of the marinade. Whisk the lime juice with the olive oil and pour over the scallops. Mix.

3. To serve, spoon scallops on a bed of raw spinach leaves and top with red onion rings OR spoon into individual glass bowls or plates and top with barely wilted spinach leaves. To wilt the leaves, put spinach in a saucepan over high heat using only the water which clings to the leaves. Stir until leaves begin to collapse and remove from heat at once. Place on top of ceviche servings.

Serve as a first course or as a buffet style appetizer with toothpicks.

Approximate Nutrition Information per Serving:

Calories: 100   Fat: 3g   Sodium: 90mg
Protein: 13g   Cholesterol: 25mg

German Style Tuna Potato Salad

Ingredients:

2 7 ounce cans of albacore (white) tuna packed in water

4 medium white or red potatoes, cooked in their skins, about 3 cups

¼ lb. bacon trimmed of fat

1 medium cooking onion OR 4 green onions finely chopped, about ½ cup

3 large stalks of celery with leaves, sliced

1 medium cucumber, peeled and diced

¼ cup chopped fresh parsley

¼ cup reduced calorie mayonnaise

¼ cup plain lowfat yogurt

2 teaspoons celery seed

½ teaspoon salt (optional)

2 teaspoons dijon mustard

½ teaspoon freshly ground black pepper

Other fish you can use with this recipe:

mackerel, salmon, herring, pilchard and sardine

Yield: 4 servings

1. With kitchen shears or a sharp knife, trim away the outside fat from the bacon and cut strips crosswise into one inch pieces. Sauté until lightly browned.

2. If using a cooking onion, sauté the onion with the bacon until pieces are transparent. Be careful not to burn the onion.

3. Drain the tuna and rinse lightly with cold water. In a large bowl, combine tuna with potatoes, bacon, onion, celery, cucumber, and parsley.

4. Mix together the mayonnaise, yogurt, celery seed, salt, mustard and pepper and toss with the salad.

Serve with corn on the cob and sliced tomatoes in basil vinaigrette.

To make a simple creamy cucumber dressing for this salad, mince one clove of garlic in a blender or food processor, add one medium cucumber, peeled and quartered, and process; then add ¼ cup plain lowfat yogurt, ¼ cup reduced-calorie mayonnaise, ½ teaspoon pepper, 1 tablespoon lemon juice and 2 teaspoons dried dill weed. Blend and serve.

Approximate Nutrition Information per Serving:

Calories: 290   Fat: 7g   Sodium: >300mg

Protein: 33g   Cholesterol: 45mg

Oriental Sprout and Sardine Salad

Finely chopped sardines mingle with tasty greens and tangy dressing in this delightful salad. Use as a first course, lunch or brunch salad for heart healthy good eating.

Ingredients:

2 cans sardines in mustard, water or oil. If packed in oil or water, drain and rinse.

2 cups bean sprouts

1 small green pepper finely sliced lengthwise

1 small tomato, seeded and chopped OR eight cherry tomatoes cut in half

¼ cup or 2 medium green onions, chopped

3 tablespoons olive or vegetable oil

¼ cup white wine OR cider vinegar

2 teaspoons low sodium soy sauce

1 tablespoon dijon mustard

1 head Boston, Romaine or other leaf lettuce

Other fish you can use with this recipe:

sardines, mackerel, herring, tuna, pilchard, salmon and squid

Yield: 4 servings

1. **About an hour and a half before serving,** wash lettuce leaves, remove coarse ends and drain. Pat dry with paper towels, a linen tea towel or spin dry in a salad spinner. Refrigerate.

2. Combine vegetables in a bowl.

3. In another small bowl, whisk together the oil, vinegar, soy sauce and mustard. Pour over the vegetables and refrigerate the mixture for an hour or more.

4. Just before serving remove vegetables from the refrigerator, drain and reserve the marinade. Open the sardines and add the extra mustard sauce to the cold vegetables. Chop the sardines into small pieces and toss with the vegetables.

5. To serve, line salad plates or shallow bowls with lettuce leaves and heap the sardine vegetable mixture in the center. Serve the marinade on the side if additional dressing is desired.

Approximate Nutrition Information per Serving:

Calories: 130   Fat: 16g   Sodium: 380mg
Protein: 11g   Cholesterol: 25mg

Seafood and Barley Salad

Ingredients:

½ lb. cooked shrimp OR 1 7 oz. can shrimp, drained and rinsed

½ lb. crabmeat or imitation crabmeat, chopped

1½ cups barley

2 tablespoons vegetable oil

2¼ cups water

1 cup peanuts or pine nuts

½ lb. fresh mushrooms, sliced

2 cups cherry tomatoes cut in half

2 green onions with tops, thinly sliced

½ green pepper, chopped

½ red pepper, chopped

¼ cup fresh parsley, chopped

2 tablespoons olive oil

3 tablespoons lemon juice or white wine vinegar

2 teaspoons dijon mustard

freshly ground black pepper

Other fish you can use with this recipe:

shrimp, crab, scallops, mussels, clams, lobster, squid, crab, monkfish, tuna, shark, swordfish, scallops and salmon

Yield: 4 servings

1. In a heavy saucepan sauté the barley in 2 tablespoons oil until lightly browned. Turn down heat and add water. Cover saucepan and cook barley over low heat until grains are tender but not split, about 25 minutes.

2. With a whisk, blend the olive oil, lemon juice, mustard and pepper. Sprinkle half the dressing over the barley and mix.

3. Add the nuts, vegetables, seafoods and parsley. Mix and add the remaining dressing. Let salad mellow before serving. It may be served either warm or chilled.

Serve with gazpacho soup and slices of Swiss cheese.

Approximate Nutrition Information per Serving:

Calories: 720   Fat: 33g   Sodium: >250mg
Protein: 40g   Cholesterol: 130mg

Northwest Crab Salad

Using fresh, canned or imitation crabmeat, this salad will garner raves.
It is embarrassingly simple to make – a good reason to make it often.

Ingredients:

For the salad: 12 ounces fresh, canned or frozen crabmeat or imitation crabmeat

2 tomatoes cut in 6 or 8 wedges

1 cup corn chips

1 cup pitted ripe (black) olives, sliced, plus a few whole olives for garnish

2 green onions with tops, sliced

½ ripe avocado, chopped

6 cups mixed lettuce leaves torn in bite-sized pieces

For the dressing:

½ ripe avocado

¼ cup plain lowfat yogurt

¼ cup reduced calorie mayonnaise

2 tablespoons freshly squeezed lime juice

1 teaspoon chili powder

½ cup grated natural cheddar or Monterey jack cheese

Other fish you can use with this recipe:

crab, shrimp, scallops, lobster, mussels, clams and squid

Yield: 4 servings

1. Drain or thaw crabmeat if necessary and cut into bite-sized pieces if chunks or pieces are large. If using imitation crabmeat, shred and chop it into small bits.

2. Mix together the crabmeat, tomatoes, corn chips, olives, onion and the half chopped avocado. Toss lightly with the lettuce pieces.

3. In a food processor or blender, process the other avocado half until smooth. Add the yogurt, mayonnaise, lime juice and chili powder and blend.

4. Toss the salad with the avocado dressing and top with the grated cheese and whole ripe olives.

Serve vichyssoise as a first course, then the crab salad and hot herbed garlic bread, with fresh strawberries or melon to finish.

Approximate Nutrition Information per Serving:

Calories: 350   Fat: 22g   Sodium: 530mg

Protein: 22g   Cholesterol: 80mg

Whole Dressed Fish with Bacon and Mint

The combination of bacon and mint brings outdoor freshness inside. Prepared on the outdoor grill, baked or broiled this quick recipe will become a favorite.

Ingredients:

4 dressed trout or other dressed fish, about 8 ounces each

2 tbsps. dried mint or ½ cup fresh mint leaves, packed

¼ teaspoon salt

2 tablespoons dry white wine

1 tablespoon vegetable oil

4 lean strips of bacon trimmed of outside fat

Other fish you can use with this recipe:

trout, whiting, bass, perch, scup, baby salmon, butterfish and chub

Yield: 4 servings

1. Light barbecue coals and heat until white hot OR preheat outdoor gas grill OR preheat oven to 450°F. OR preheat broiler.

2. Rinse fish and pat dry with paper towels.

3. Mix together the mint, salt and wine and add the vegetable oil.

4. Spread ¼ of the mint mixture in the cavity of each fish.

5. Wrap one bacon slice diagonally around each fish and secure the ends with a toothpick if necessary.

6. Grill, bake or broil the fish for 10 minutes for each inch of thickness. Turn once during the cooking period. Remember that overcooking will dry and toughen the fish.

Serve with baked potatoes and peas.

Approximate Nutrition Information per Serving:

Calories: 360   Fat: 19g   Sodium: 260mg
Protein: 44g   Cholesterol: 130mg

Broiled Fillets with Nuts

Originally created for the Hawaiian fish mahimahi, this recipe is tasty with virtually any fish large enough to cut into steaks.

Ingredients:

1¼ – 1½ lb. fish fillets
grated rind of ½ lime
juice of ½ lime
1 tablespoon olive or vegetable
  oil
2 tablespoons chopped parsley
½ teaspoon freshly ground black
  pepper

½ cup chopped Macadamia nuts
  (plain, unsalted pistachios,
  pinenuts, walnuts or almonds
  may be used instead)

Other fish you can use with this recipe:

cod, pollock, haddock, halibut, lingcod, grouper, snapper, rockfish, seatrout, whiting, ocean perch, mahimahi, monkfish, bass, orange roughy, flounder, sole, swordfish, pike, lake whitefish, catfish, perch, fluke, shark, black sea bass, bream, buffalo, carp, chub, cusk, drum, snook, muskellunge, skate, weakfish, tautog, sterlet, striped bass, tarakihi, tilefish, tripletail, turbot, wahoo and wrasse

Yield: 4 servings

1. Preheat broiler.

2. Rinse fish fillets under cold water and pat dry with paper towels. Place fish on lightly greased or foil-lined broiler pan.

3. In a small bowl, whisk together the olive oil, lime juice, lime rind, parsley and black pepper. Spoon just enough sauce over fish to cover the surface.

4. Broil close to the heat source for 10 minutes per inch of thickness. When fish is just beginning to turn opaque, sprinkle with nuts and add a small amount of remaining sauce. Broil until fish has just turned opaque. Remove from heat at once.

5. Spoon any remaining sauce and pan juices over the fish at serving time.

Serve with rice or pasta and green beans.

Approximate Nutrition Information per Serving:

Calories: 260   Fat: 14g   Sodium: 110mg
Protein: 30g   Cholesterol: 70mg

Pan-Dressed Fish with Mushrooms

If you are puzzled by what to do with a whole or headless fish, this is the recipe to try. The mushroom sauce is a favorite.

Ingredients:

4 pan-dressed whiting or other dressed fish about 8 ounces each
½ teaspoon vegetable oil
⅔ cup low-fat milk
¼ cup flour
½ teaspoon black pepper
1 teaspoon paprika
1 tablespoon vegetable oil or melted margarine

1 medium cooking onion finely chopped
½ lb. fresh mushrooms
1 stalk finely sliced celery
1 tablespoon margarine
½ teaspoon freshly grated or ground nutmeg
juice and rind of 1 lemon
2 tablespoons chopped fresh parsley

Other fish you can use with this recipe:

porgy, mullet, snapper, perch, catfish, trout, whiting, salmon, smelt, haddock and bass

Yield: 4 servings

1. Preheat oven to 450°F. Oil a baking dish with ½ teaspoon oil.

2. Rinse fish under cold water and pat dry with paper towels.

3. Pour milk into a shallow pan or pie plate. Mix the flour, pepper and paprika together in a second pie plate.

4. Dip each fish into the milk and coat thoroughly in the flour mixture. Put the fish in the baking dish. Drizzle with 1 tablespoon of vegetable oil.

5. Bake fish for 10 minutes per inch of thickness at 450°F.

6. While fish is baking, sauté onions, mushrooms and celery in one tablespoon of margarine. Sprinkle with nutmeg.

7. About 3 minutes before fish is cooked, remove from oven and top with the mushroom mixture. Drizzle with lemon juice and rind and return to oven for last minutes of baking. Sprinkle with chopped parsley just before serving.

Serve with whole baby carrots and potato slices.

Variations: Instead of using flour to coat the whiting, try fine bread crumbs or half cornmeal and half flour. Finely chopped green or red pepper can replace the celery in the topping, and ¼ cup of dry white wine can be used in place of the lemon juice. Dill makes a noticeable difference when used instead of parsley.

Approximate Nutrition Information per Serving:
Calories: 300   Fat: 9g   Sodium: 200mg
Protein: 42g   Cholesterol: 100mg

Scrunchy Baked Fish Fillets

Even children like fish prepared this way. It has all the crunch of fried fish and none of the oil. Best of all, it is fast.

Ingredients:

1½ lb. lean fish fillets
1 cup unsweetened flaked
  wheat or bran cereal
2 tablespoons sesame seeds
1 teaspoon ground ginger

1 egg
1 tablespoon Teriyaki sauce or
  water
½ teaspoon vegetable oil

Other fish you can use with this recipe:
cod, pollock, haddock, grouper, catfish, flounder, sole, rockfish, bass, ocean perch, snapper, halibut, seatrout, whiting, monkfish, mahimahi, orange roughy, pike, lake whitefish, lingcod and turbot

Yield: 4 servings

1. Preheat oven to 450°F. Lightly oil a pan with ½ teaspoon oil.

2. Wash fish fillets and pat dry with paper towels.

3. Crush cereal in a clean paper bag using the heel of your hand. Leave the cereal fairly coarse. Add sesame seeds and ginger.

4. In a shallow pan, beat egg with Teriyaki sauce or water.

5. Dip fish in egg and then in cereal, coating all sides. Put fish in baking dish. Tuck under thin ends so the pieces are of even thickness. Bake 10 minutes per inch of thickness.

Serve with sliced potatoes and snow peas.

Approximate Nutrition Information per Serving:
Calories: 210   Fat: 5g   Sodium: 200mg
Protein: 31g   Cholesterol: 140mg

Rolled Fillets in Vermouth

This version of fish roll-ups is easy because there is no filling to make. Prepare the simple sauce while the fish steams. The rolls hold their shape well and the sauce is surprisingly assertive. Use small pieces of fish or thin fillets. Fish may be steamed or baked.

Ingredients:

1¼ – 1½ lb. any thin lean fish fillets
½ teaspoon vegetable oil
white pepper
paprika
1 tablespoon margarine
1 tablespoon vegetable oil

2 tablespoons flour
½ teaspoon salt
¼ teaspoon cayenne pepper
½ cup dry vermouth
3 tablespoons lowfat milk

Other fish you can use with this recipe:

cod, pollock, haddock, lingcod, rockfish, seatrout, whiting, ocean perch, bass, orange roughy, flounder, sole, lake whitefish, catfish, perch, fluke, bream, buffalo, cusk, drum, weakfish, tautog, tarakihi and turbot

Yield: 4 servings

1. Rinse fillets under cold water and pat dry with paper towels. Cut large fillets into serving pieces about 6 inches long by 2 inches wide. Sprinkle surface lightly with white pepper and paprika. Roll fish pieces and secure with a wooden toothpick.

2. Grease a vegetable steamer, baking rack or shallow pan with ½ teaspoon oil.

3. Stand rolls on end in steamer. Sprinkle each with white pepper and a generous amount of paprika. Place steamer in a pan containing about ¾ inch water and cover. Bring water to a boil, cover and simmer gently for 10 minutes per inch of thickness. Begin timing the cooking period when the water comes to the boil. For thin fillets about 10 minutes is sufficient (see Note).

4. While fish is cooking, combine oil and margarine in a saucepan. Over medium heat whisk in flour, salt and cayenne pepper. Gradually add the vermouth, stirring constantly. Cook the sauce gently until no trace of raw starch remains, about 5-8 minutes. Add the milk.

5. When fish is cooked, transfer to a serving dish if necessary, and cover with the sauce.

Serve with brown rice and snow peas sautéed with mushrooms.

Note: The fish may be baked in a 450°F. oven for each inch of thickness or cooked in a microwave according to the manufacturer's directions.

Approximate Nutrition Information per Serving:
Calories: 240   Fat: 8g   Sodium: 440mg
Protein: 29g   Cholesterol: 70mg

Baked Fish with Pesto

The combination of fresh basil, garlic and cheese is superb with fish. Pesto sauce keeps well in the refrigerator or freezer. If freezing, omit the cheese until ready to use.

Ingredients:

1½ lb. fish fillets or steaks   ½ cup pesto sauce (available
   rinsed and patted dry   ready made or see below
½ teaspoon vegetable oil   under Sauces)

Other fish you can use with this recipe:

cod, pollock, haddock, halibut, lingcod, grouper, snapper, rockfish, flounder, sole, swordfish, pike, lake whitefish, catfish, perch, fluke, shark, black sea bass, bream, catfish, buffalo, carp, chub, cusk, drum, snook, muskellunge, skate, rockfish, weakfish, tautog, sterlet, striped bass, tarakihi, tilefish, tripletail, turbot, wahoo and wrasse

Yield: 4 servings

1. Preheat oven to 450°F. OR preheat broiler.

2. Oil a baking dish OR broiler pan with ½ teaspoon oil.

3. Put fish fillets in baking dish OR foil and spread with pesto sauce. Bake for 10 minutes per inch of thickness or broil until fish just turns opaque.

Serve with baked butternut squash and julienned zucchini.

Approximate Nutrition Information per Serving (including 2 tablespoons of pesto):
Calories: 250   Fat: 12g   Sodium: 210mg
Protein: 31g   Cholesterol: 75mg

Baked Pike with Wild Rice

Ingredients:

2¼ cups boiling water
½ teaspoon salt
1½ lb. pike or any lean fish fillets
2 teaspoons dried leaf thyme
1 teaspoon black pepper
½ teaspoon vegetable oil
2 tablespoons margarine or
  vegetable oil

½ cup finely sliced celery with
  leaves
½ cup onion, finely chopped
½ lb. mushrooms, sliced
⅔ cup brown rice
⅓ cup wild rice
¼ cup chopped walnuts or whole
  sunflower seeds

Other fish you can use with this recipe:

pike, lake whitefish, bass, trout or any other lean white fish

Yield: 4 servings

1. Prepare rice as follows: to 2¼ cups boiling water and ½ teaspoon salt add the brown rice and cook covered over low heat for 15 minutes. Add the wild rice and cook an additional 15 minutes. Leave covered and set aside.

2. Preheat oven to 450°F.

3. Wash fish fillets and pat dry. Lightly oil a shallow baking dish with ½ teaspoon oil and place fillets in a single layer in the bottom. Sprinkle with thyme and black pepper.

4. In a small skillet sauté the onion and celery in 2 tablespoons of margarine or oil. Add the mushrooms and sauté until the mushrooms have just changed color, about 2 minutes.

5. Combine the sautéed vegetables with the rice and add the walnuts. Top the fish fillets with the rice mixture and cover the baking dish with aluminum foil.

6. Bake at 450°F. for 10 minutes per inch of thickness of the fish or until the fish just begins to turn opaque. Remove the cover and brown the topping by leaving in the oven another 5 minutes.

Serve with horseradish sauce (see Sauces) on the side, fresh asparagus or whole green beans and sliced tomatoes.

Approximate Nutrition Information per Serving:

Calories: 440
Protein: 39g

Fat: 14g
Cholesterol: 85mg

Sodium: 180mg

Fish with Onions and Parmesan

This simple and savory recipe was adapted from **Gourmet Magazine.**

Ingredients:

1½ lb. fish fillets

3 small onions sliced crosswise
and separated into rings

2 tablespoons unsalted
margarine

2 tablespoons reduced calorie
mayonnaise

¼ cup freshly grated parmesan
cheese

½ cup fine fresh bread crumbs

2 tablespoons reduced calorie
mayonnaise

freshly ground black pepper

Other fish you can use with this recipe:

cod, pollock, haddock, halibut, lingcod, grouper, snapper, rockfish, seatrout, ocean perch, mahimahi, monkfish, bass, orange roughy, flounder, sole, swordfish, pike, lake whitefish, catfish, perch, fluke, drum, snook, muskellunge, skate, rockfish, weakfish, tautog, sterlet, striped bass, tarakihi, tilefish, wahoo and wrasse

Yield: 4 servings

1. Preheat broiler.

2. In a skillet sauté onions in margarine over moderately high heat until they are brown and tender.

3. Rinse fillets under cold water and pat dry with paper towels. Sprinkle with freshly ground black pepper.

4. Spread fillets with 2 tablespoons of mayonnaise and broil about 4 inches away from the heat for 3 minutes.

5. Combine parmesan cheese with breadcrumbs.

6. Remove fish from heat and place onions over fillets. Spread remaining 2 tablespoons of mayonnaise over the fillets and top with cheese and crumb mixture.

7. Broil fillets 2-3 minutes more or until they just flake when tested with a fork and topping is golden brown.

Serve with brown rice pilaf and lima beans.

Approximate Nutrition Information per Serving:

Calories: 290   Fat: 11g   Sodium: 310mg
Protein: 32g   Cholesterol: 75mg

Spinach Stuffed Sole

Ingredients:

1½ lb. fish fillets
½ teaspoon oil
1 10 oz. package fresh spinach
  or 1 pack frozen chopped
  spinach, thawed
1 large clove garlic

3 green onions, sliced
¼ cup pinenuts or walnuts
¼ cup grated Parmesan cheese
½ teaspoon black pepper
¼ teaspoon ground nutmeg
2 teaspoons olive oil

Other fish you can use with this recipe:

sole, turbot, flounder, cod, haddock, rockfish, seatrout, whiting, ocean perch, bass, orange roughy, catfish, perch, fluke, black sea bass, bream, buffalo, drum, snook, rockfish, weakfish, tautog, tarakihi, tripletail and wrasse

Yield: 4 servings

1. Preheat oven to 450°F. Lightly oil a baking dish with ½ teaspoon oil.

2. Wash spinach and remove stems. Using just the water clinging to the leaves, steam spinach until wilted, about ½ minute. Put cooked or thawed spinach in a sieve and press out excess water. Finely chop the leaves.

3. In a blender or food processor mince the garlic. Add nuts and chop finely.

4. Combine by hand all ingredients except fish. The mixture will be coarse and somewhat crumbly but it holds together during cooking.

5. Place 2 tablespoons or more of mixture on each fillet and roll up. Secure ends with a toothpick. Transfer rolls to a baking dish and sprinkle with a little more parmesan cheese if desired.

6. Bake for 10 minutes or until fish has just turned opaque.

Serve with butternut squash and red-skinned potatoes.

Approximate Nutrition Information per Serving:

Calories: 190   Fat: 5g   Sodium: 190mg
Protein: 33g   Cholesterol: 75mg

Baked Halibut with Dill and Vegetables

Ingredients:

4 small halibut steaks about 6
ounces each or 2 large ones
about 12 ounces each
½ teaspoon vegetable oil
⅔ cup thinly sliced onion
1½ cups sliced fresh mushrooms
1 medium tomato, diced, about
½ cup
¼ cup finely chopped green
pepper, about ½ pepper
¼ cup chopped fresh parsley
¼ cup chopped red pepper OR 3
tablespoons chopped canned
pimento
½ cup dry white wine
2 tablespoons lemon juice
grated rind of ½ lemon
½ teaspoon salt
2 tablespoons chopped fresh dill
OR 2 teaspoons dried dill
½ teaspoon freshly ground black
pepper

Other fish you can use with this recipe:

cod, pollock, haddock, halibut, lingcod, grouper, seatrout, bass, swordfish, pike, lake whitefish, catfish, shark, black sea bass, buffalo, carp, chub, cusk, drum, snook, muskellunge, rockfish, tautog, sterlet, striped bass, tilefish and wahoo

Yield: 4 servings

1. Preheat oven to 450°F.

2. Oil a baking dish with ½ teaspoon vegetable oil. Arrange sliced onion on the bottom of the baking dish. Place fish steaks on the onion slices.

3. Combine vegetables and spread generously over the top of the fish.

4. Mix together the wine, lemon juice, rind and seasonings and pour over the vegetables.

5. Bake at 450°F. for 10 minutes per inch of thickness of the fish. The vegetable topping may require a little extra time.

Serve with spaghetti squash and broccoli flowers.

Approximate Nutrition Information per Serving:

Calories: 260   Fat: 7g   Sodium: 130mg
Protein: 35g   Cholesterol: 80mg

Country Steve's Spicy Farm-Raised Catfish

Steve Smith of Providence, Rhode Island won a prize in the 1986 catfish cooking contest with this tasty recipe, using fresh herbs. The recipe works well with many fish, a good reason for keeping it close at hand. The spice and herb mixture is superb.

Ingredients:

2 lb. catfish fillets
1 tablespoon vegetable oil
1 clove garlic, minced
1 tablespoon whole fennel seed (optional)
1½ teaspoons freshly ground black pepper
½ teaspoon salt
¾ teaspoon paprika
dash of ground thyme or thyme leaves

3 tablespoons chopped fresh or 1½ teaspoons dried basil
2 tablespoons chopped fresh or 1½ teaspoons dried oregano
2 tablespoons chopped fresh parsley
1 tablespoon chopped fresh or freeze-dried chives (optional)
2 tablespoons freshly squeezed lemon juice
fresh watercress sprigs

Other fish you can use with this recipe:

catfish, cod, pollock, haddock, halibut, lingcod, grouper, snapper, rockfish, seatrout, whiting, ocean perch, mahimahi, monkfish, bass, orange roughy, flounder, sole, swordfish, pike, lake whitefish, bass and perch

Yield: 6 servings

1. Preheat oven to 350°F. (see Note).

2. Combine oil and garlic and spread over the bottom of a large baking dish, about 9 by 1 inches.

3. Combine fennel, pepper, salt, paprika and thyme and spread one third of the mixture over the oil in the baking dish.

4. Combine basil, oregano, parsley and chives and sprinkle one third of the herb mixture over the oil and spices in the baking dish.

5. Rinse fish fillets, pat dry and arrange on top of spices and herbs in the baking dish. Sprinkle with lemon juice.

6. Top fish with remaining spices and herbs and bake 15-18 minutes until almost done. The fish should begin to separate with a fork, but should not separate easily. Remove from oven and turn on broiler.

7. Finish cooking fish by broiling about 4 inches from the heat source, about 4 minutes. Fish should flake easily but should not be dry. The broiling gives the fish a crisp surface.

8. To serve, transfer fish to a serving platter, pour the pan juices over it and top with watercress for garnish.

Note: The cooking directions are given just the way Steve prepared the fish. We tried it with the Canadian cooking rule of 450°F. for ten minutes per inch of thickness without the broiling and thought it turned out very well with one less preparation step.

Approximate Nutrition Information per Serving:
Calories: 190   Fat: 9g   Sodium: 290mg
Protein: 27g   Cholesterol: 80mg

Salmonburgers

These burgers re-define the classic burger as both tasty and healthy.
Variations are endless and delicious. Try these on your next barbecue.
Miniatures make excellent hors d'oeuvres too.

Ingredients:

1 15½ oz. can red or pink salmon
1 egg white, slightly beaten
⅓ cup finely diced onion
⅓ cup finely diced green pepper
½ cup whole wheat bread crumbs
1 tablespoon freshly squeezed
  lemon juice

grated rind of ½ lemon
½ teaspoon dried rosemary
  leaves, crushed (optional)
½ teaspoon freshly grated black
  pepper
2 tablespoons finely chopped
  fresh parsley

Yield: 4 servings

1. Drain salmon and reserve liquid. Remove any skin but keep the bones and mash with the fish.

2. Combine salmon with remaining ingredients and blend well. Add 2 tablespoons reserved liquid to moisten, using more if the mixture appears dry.

3. Form into 4 patties and broil without turning. Patties may also be baked at 450°F. for 15-20 minutes or microwaved.

Serve on hamburger rolls, English muffins, sourdough rolls, taco shells or soft tortillas.

Variations: Hot pepper – Add Tabasco sauce to the salmon mixture and top with grated hot pepper cheese.

All American – Top with reduced calorie mayonnaise, a dab of mustard, a slice of tomato, cucumber pickles and lettuce.

Mexican – Top with salsa verde or guacamole and shredded lettuce.

Approximate Nutrition Information per Serving

Calories: 200   Fat: 9g   Sodium: 540mg
Protein: 24g   Cholesterol: 35mg

Steamed Salmon Steaks
with Fresh Basil

Steam these foil packets on the outdoor grill with the lid on. It is easy and tasty and the fish stays moist. The fish is also easily done in the oven or a vegetable steamer.

Ingredients:

4 small salmon steaks, about 1½ lb.

freshly ground black pepper

8 clusters fresh basil leaves, about 4-6 leaves per cluster OR 4 teaspoons dried basil leaves

2 medium tomatoes, thinly sliced

½ lb. fresh mushrooms, sliced

¼ cup dry vermouth, dry sherry or dry white wine

heavy aluminum foil or parchment paper

Other fish you can use with this recipe:

salmon, swordfish, tuna, shark, halibut and cod

Yield: 4 servings

1. Place each fish steak or serving piece on a large square of aluminum foil.

2. Sprinkle generously with pepper and then add a layer of 4-6 basil leaves. Next add the tomato slices, followed by a second layer of basil leaves. Top with freshly sliced mushrooms and 1 tablespoon of vermouth or wine for each serving.

3. Seal the edges of the foil to make a tightly closed packet. Steam the fish on an outdoor grill, OR in a vegetable steamer set in a large saucepan OR bake the packets in a hot oven, 450°F. Timing depends on the thickness of the fish. Check for doneness after 10 minutes cooking per inch of thickness. Fish is cooked when it just turns opaque. Slight undercooking is preferable to any overcooking.

Serve with tabouli salad and fresh wax or green beans.

Approximate Nutrition Information per Serving:

Calories: 260   Fat: 10g   Sodium: 70mg

Protein: 34g   Cholesterol: 100mg

Broiled Fish with Green Chilies

The influence of Mexican cuisine makes this preparation zesty. Wear rubber gloves while handling the raw chilis to prevent irritating your hands. The flavor mellows with cooking leaving a pleasant tang. This recipe was adapted from a **Gourmet Magazine** *recipe for bluefish.*

Ingredients:

1½ lb. fish cut in four servings
1 medium onion, chopped
½ cup seeded, chopped semi-hot green chili peppers
2 garlic cloves, minced
½ cup water
1 tablespoon olive OR vegetable oil
½ cup chopped tomato

1 tablespoon white wine vinegar
¼ teaspoon salt (optional)
1 tablespoon olive OR vegetable oil
½ teaspoon freshly ground pepper
lime wedges or slices for garnish

Other fish you can use with this recipe:

bluefish, mackerel, herring, salmon, tuna, trout, halibut, swordfish and shark

Yield: 4 servings

1. In a food processor or blender, purée the onion, chili peppers and garlic with ½ cup water.

2. In a stainless steel or enameled skillet heat 1 tablespoon oil until hot. Carefully add the purée and cook, stirring, for 5 minutes.

3. Add the tomato, vinegar, salt and pepper and cook sauce over low heat, stirring, for 10 minutes. Keep warm.

4. Rinse fillets and pat dry. Arrange them skin side down on the lightly oiled rack of a broiler pan.

5. Sprinkle fillets with remaining tablespoon of oil and freshly ground black pepper. Broil 4 inches from heat for 10 minutes per inch of thickness or until fish just turns opaque.

6. To serve, top fish with the green chili sauce and garnish with lime wedges or slices.

Serve with hot corn bread and cheddar-topped cauliflower.

Approximate Nutrition Information per Serving:
Calories: 270   Fat: 12g   Sodium: 60mg
Protein: 35g   Cholesterol: 100mg

Raquel's Poached Mackerel with Tarragon

Raquel Boehmer, one of the finest seafood cooks in Maine published this recipe as "Shopping Night Mackerel." I didn't believe a recipe so simple could be truly fine but this has become a favorite.

Ingredients:

1 whole mackerel, split in half or filleted

1 teaspoon oil

About 1½ cups lowfat milk

2 teaspoons dried tarragon leaves

½ teaspoon freshly grated black pepper

Other fish you can use with this recipe:
bluefish, herring and mullet

Yield: 2 servings

1. Preheat oven to 400°F. Lightly oil a baking dish with 1 teaspoon oil.

2. Put mackerel in baking dish and sprinkle generously with black pepper and tarragon leaves.

3. Add milk until the fish is almost covered.

4. Bake 10 minutes per inch of thickness of the fish, about 10-15 minutes. Baste the fish at least once during baking to keep it moist and flavor the juices with the tarragon. Serve at once.

Serve with boiled potatoes and carrots, spooning the juices over the potatoes.

Note: If you use a split fish, the bones will float to the surface when the fish is cooked, making it easy to remove them before serving.

Approximate Nutrition Information per Serving:
Calories: 510   Fat: 30g   Sodium: 170mg
Protein: 48g   Cholesterol: 200mg

Granny Smith Fish with Mustard

The tart apples, onions and tangy sauce make an inimitable combination that is perfect for bluefish and other rich fish. I use this recipe with lean fish too.

Ingredients:

1½ lb. fish fillets or steaks

2 Granny Smith apples, cored and sliced with skin on

1 tablespoon white wine vinegar or lemon juice

1 large red onion, chopped

1 tablespoon margarine

2 tablespoons white wine

1 tablespoon dijon mustard

1 tablespoon olive or vegetable oil

½ teaspoon freshly ground black pepper

fresh dill sprigs for garnish

Other fish you can use with this recipe:

bluefish, mackerel, herring, salmon, tuna, trout, swordfish, shark, bass, halibut and kingfish

Yield: 4 servings

1. Preheat oven to 450°F. OR light barbecue coals about 30 minutes before cooking time, OR preheat grill or broiler.

2. Toss sliced apple with vinegar or lemon juice to keep it from turning brown.

3. Lightly sauté onions and apples in margarine about 1-2 minutes. Place on a baking dish OR on to a large piece of aluminum foil.

4. Place fish skin side down on top of onions and apples. Combine wine, mustard, oil and pepper and spoon over bluefish. Bake, grill or broil for 10 minutes per inch of thickness or until fish just turns opaque.

5. To serve, transfer fish to a serving dish and top with apples and onions and remaining sauce. Garnish with sprigs of fresh dill. Baked fish can be served directly from the pan.

Serve with spinach fettucine and sliced summer squash.

Variations: 1 teaspoon of caraway seeds can be sautéed with the apples and onions and additional caraway seeds sprinkled on top of the fish at serving time. If desired, 1 tablespoon of chopped fresh dill or 1 teaspoon dried dill weed may be added to the mustard sauce.

Approximate Nutrition Information per Serving:
Calories: 330   Fat: 11g   Sodium: 320mg
Protein: 35g   Cholesterol: 100mg

Grilled Fresh Tuna with Ginger

Ingredients:

1 lb. fresh tuna or other rich fish

1 tablespoon freshly grated ginger root

2 tablespoons dry white wine

2 teaspoons low sodium soy sauce

1 teaspoon sesame oil

2 small green onions with tops, finely sliced

Other fish you can use with this recipe:

tuna, shark, halibut, bluefish, salmon, lake whitefish, mackerel, herring, amberjack and yellowtail

Yield: 4 servings

1. Preheat outdoor grill or light barbecue coals.

2. Combine all ingredients except fish in a small bowl and whisk together.

3. Pour sauce over tuna and allow to marinate while the coals are heating or the grill is preheating. Leave the ginger and vegetables on the top.

3. Grill the tuna over white hot coals for 10 minutes per inch of thickness. With tuna, it is especially important not to overcook the fish as it quickly becomes dry and tough. Serve it slightly underdone.

Serve tuna with brown rice and mushroom pilaf and sautéed red peppers.

Approximate Nutrition Information per Serving:
Calories: 210   Fat: 9g   Sodium: 360mg
Protein: 29g   Cholesterol: 50mg

Yogurt-Marinated Bluefish

Don't be put off by the dark blueish gray appearance of fresh bluefish fillets. They cook up light. Bluefish has a strong flavor, but is moist and tender. While it is ideal for the barbecue, it bakes or broils nicely too. This recipe was adapted from **Gourmet Magazine** *and is superb.*

Ingredients:

1½ lb. bluefish fillets
½ cup fresh lemon juice
2 tablespoons peeled and
 grated ginger root
1 tablespoon minced garlic
½ teaspoon salt (optional)
2 teaspoons coriander seed
 (optional)

1 teaspoon cumin seed
 (optional)
1 cup plain lowfat yogurt
¼ cup peanut or other vegetable
 oil
sweet paprika
lemon wedges for garnish

Other fish you can use with this recipe:

bluefish, mackerel, herring, salmon, tuna, trout, swordfish and shark

Yield: 4 servings

1. The night before serving: Combine the lemon juice, ginger root, garlic, salt, coriander and cumin seeds in a blender or processor and mix well.

2. Transfer mixture to a bowl. Stir in the yogurt and oil.

3. Arrange the fillets in a shallow ceramic or glass baking dish and pour the marinade over them. Cover and refrigerate, turning occasionally, if possible.

4. To cook, light barbecue OR preheat grill OR preheat oven to 450°F. OR preheat broiler. Just before cooking, drain the fillets. Reserve the marinade.

5. Grill or broil the fillets skin side down about 4 inches from the heat, basting occasionally with the reserved marinade. Cook 6-8 minutes or until they just turn opaque when tested with a fork. If baking, cook 10 minutes per inch of thickness until just opaque.

6. To serve, sprinkle the fillets with the paprika. Garnish with lemon wedges.

Serve with red-skinned potatoes, wilted spinach and fresh cucumbers.

Approximate Nutrition Information per Serving:
Calories: 330   Fat: 19g   Sodium: 95mg
Protein: 37g   Cholesterol: 100mg

Kay's Creole Shark

Ingredients:

2 lb. shark or other firm-fleshed fish cut into 1½ inch cubes
2 tablespoons vegetable oil
1 cup chopped onion
1 cup chopped green pepper
2 cloves garlic, minced

¼ cup chopped parsley
1 cube OR 1 teaspoon chicken bouillon granules
few drops hot pepper sauce
1 28 ounce can whole tomatoes with juice

Other fish you can use with this recipe:

monkfish, tuna, pollock, grouper, halibut, swordfish, scallops and shrimp

Yield: 6 servings

1. Preheat oven to 400°F.

2. Heat oil in a skillet. Sauté fish over medium heat until lightly browned. Transfer fish to a non-metallic baking dish.

3. To the skillet add the onions, peppers, garlic, parsley, bouillon, hot pepper sauce and tomatoes. Simmer 5 minutes.

4. Pour sauce over fish and bake 10 minutes or until fish has just turned opaque.

Suggested accompaniments: rice and steamed green beans

Approximate Nutrition Information per Serving:
Calories: 340   Fat: 22g   Sodium: 490mg
Protein: 25g   Cholesterol: 70mg

TGIF Mussels

It is our custom to initiate summer with a big mussel feed on the front porch. With friends, wine and lots of French bread, this supper is standard Friday fare to usher in the weekend.

Ingredients:

2 quarts mussels, about 3 lb.
1 large onion, sliced
4 bay leaves
6 sprigs parsley or more
2 cloves garlic, sliced

1 teaspoon each: thyme leaves, oregano, marjoram leaves, black pepper
½ cup dry white wine or just enough to cover the bottom of a large pot

Other fish you can use with this recipe:

littleneck or steamer clams

Yield: 2 servings for hungry mussel lovers

1. With a vegetable brush or rough cloth scrub mussels in a sink of cold water and remove beards with a sharp pull. Discard any mussels that do not close or have broken shells.

2. Put scrubbed mussels in a large pot. Add onion, garlic, seasonings and wine. Cover.

3. Steam over high heat 5-7 minutes until all shells have opened. Shake the pot once during cooking to mix the mussels. Overcooking makes the meats tough.

Serve at once directly from the pot or ladle into soup plates. Have plenty of crusty bread to soak up the broth. Finish with a salad and fruit.

Approximate Nutrition Information per Serving:

Calories: 300   Fat: 6g   Sodium: 690mg
Protein: 31g   Cholesterol: 160mg

Maxine's Scalloped Oysters

My professor's wife first introduced me to the splendors of baked oysters with this fine recipe. This is divine.

Ingredients:

1 quart shucked oysters with their liquor
1 teaspoon vegetable oil
½ teaspoon freshly ground black pepper
½ cup finely chopped celery
½ cup finely chopped green pepper

2 cups coarsely crushed soda crackers with unsalted tops
Several drops Tabasco sauce
2 teaspoons unsalted butter or margarine
reserved oyster liquor, about ½ cup
1 cup lowfat milk

Yield: 6 servings

1. Preheat oven to 350°F. Oil a shallow 2 quart baking dish with 1 teaspoon oil. Sprinkle baking dish with half the crushed crackers.

2. Spread half the oysters over the cracker layer and sprinkle with black pepper.

3. Spread half the celery and half the green pepper over the oysters. Repeat the layers starting with the crackers, then the oysters and remaining vegetables. Sprinkle generously with Tabasco sauce.

4. Combine the reserved oyster liquor, milk and butter. Heat until butter melts. Do not boil. Pour hot milk over the oysters and bake at 350°F. for 45 minutes.

Suggested accompaniments: whole wheat rolls and Boston lettuce salad.

Approximate Nutrition Information per Serving:

Calories: 170   Fat: 6g   Sodium: 250mg
Protein: 7g   Cholesterol: 30mg

Calamari Marsala

Calamari is especially tasty in tomato or wine based sauces. It is economical, very low in fat and quick to prepare. Even if you have never tried squid before, I think you will like this version.

Ingredients:

1½ lb. squid, cleaned and peeled
1 cup chopped onion
1 clove garlic, minced
2 tablespoons olive oil
2 tablespoons flour
2 medium tomatoes
½ cup water

½ teaspoon freshly ground black
  pepper
2 bay leaves
1 cinnamon stick
1 lb. mushrooms, washed and
  sliced
¼ cup Marsala wine

Other fish you can use with this recipe:

squid, scallops, shrimp, halibut, monkfish, shark and tuna

Yield: 4 servings

1. Soak squid in ice water for a few minutes to whiten. With a sharp knife, cut squid into 1 inch pieces.

2. In a large skillet, sauté onion in oil and add garlic. Add squid and sauté for about 5 minutes. Sprinkle with flour. Add tomatoes, water and seasonings and mix well.

3. Add mushrooms and cook until the mushrooms are just moistened, 2-3 minutes. Add Marsala wine and stir. Thin sauce with water if necessary.

Suggested accompaniments: spinach fettucine and wax beans.

Approximate Nutrition Information per Serving:

Calories: 330
Protein: 27g

Fat: 8g
Cholesterol: 510mg

Sodium: 300mg

Gingered Shrimp and Broccoli Stir-Fry

Ingredients:

1 lb. peeled shrimp
¼ cup dry white wine
2 tablespoons freshly grated
  ginger
2 cloves garlic, minced
½ teaspoon freshly grated
  pepper
¼ teaspoon cayenne pepper
1 teaspoon sesame oil

4 cups broccoli, chopped
1 tablespoon vegetable oil
2 cups fresh mushrooms, sliced
1 cup celery, sliced diagonally
1 large red or white onion,
  sliced in rings
1 red pepper, seeded and sliced
  in thin strips

Other fish you can use with this recipe:
scallops, squid, halibut, monkfish, shark, tuna and swordfish

Yield: 4 servings

1. Combine wine, ginger, seasonings and sesame oil in a medium bowl. Add shrimp or fish and stir gently to coat all pieces. Marinate shrimp while preparing vegetables.

2. Add 1 tablespoon oil to wok or large frying pan and heat. Add vegetables and cook, stirring until vegetables are bright in color and tender crisp, about 1 minute.

3. Drain shrimp, reserving liquid. Add shrimp to vegetables and cook over high heat until shrimp is opaque, just a few minutes. Pour reserved marinade over vegetables and serve at once.

Suggested accompaniments: brown rice and a tossed salad.

Approximate Nutrition Information per Serving:

Calories: 220   Fat: 6g   Sodium: N/A
Protein: 24g   Cholesterol: 170mg

Curried Shellfish

Curry complements the sweetness of shellfish. This recipe is a simplified version of an authentic Indian curry I used to make for student parties. Omit the cayenne if you want it mild. Yogurt also cuts the fire. You can use just curry powder but it will not be as hearty.

Ingredients:

1½ lb. shellfish or firm fleshed
   fish cut in cubes
2 tablespoons vegetable oil
1 cup chopped onion
1 cup chopped tomato, fresh or
   canned
2 cloves garlic, minced
2 teaspoons curry powder

1 teaspoon turmeric (optional)
1 teaspoon ground ginger
1 teaspoon ground cumin
½ teaspoon black pepper
¼ teaspoon cayenne pepper
½ teaspoon ground cardamom
   (optional)
1 cup plain lowfat yogurt

Other fish you can use with this recipe:

shrimp, scallops, clams, mussels, lobster, crab, halibut, monkfish, swordfish, squid and lake whitefish

Yield: 4 servings

1. Heat the oil in a large skillet. Add the curry powder and remaining spices and cook thoroughly over medium heat at least 5 minutes.

2. Stir in the onion, garlic and tomatoes and simmer about 10 minutes to blend flavors.

3. Add the shellfish and simmer until seafood is just cooked. Serve with yogurt on the side or stir in half the yogurt just before serving.

Suggested accompaniments: brown rice or egg noodles, steamed whole green beans and a tossed salad.

Approximate Nutrition Information per Serving (using bay scallops):

Calories: 260   Fat: 9g   Sodium: 190mg
Protein: 29g   Cholesterol: 65mg

Scallop Kebobs

Ingredients:

1 lb. bay scallops or sea scallops cut in 1 inch pieces
½ cup lowfat milk
¼ cup fine bread crumbs
¼ cup yellow corn meal
6 slices lean bacon with the outside fat cut away
2 green peppers cut in 1 inch squares

32 small mushroom caps
8 wooden or bamboo skewers 8-12 inches long
2 tablespoons vegetable oil
1 tablespoon white wine vinegar
1 teaspoon tomato paste
1 tablespoon water

Other fish you can use with this recipe:

scallops, shrimp, halibut, swordfish, tuna, shark, monkfish and lake whitefish

Yield: 4 servings

1. Pour milk into a small bowl. Combine bread crumbs and corn meal in a shallow pan or pie plate. Cut bacon into 1 inch pieces.

2. Dip scallops in milk and then crumb mixture, coating evenly. Coat all the scallops at once.

3. Preheat broiler or outdoor grill.

4. Assemble the kebobs by arranging the ingredients in the following order: mushroom cap, green pepper, bacon, scallop. Allow 4-6 scallops per skewer. Arrange skewers on a foil-lined broiler pan.

5. In a small bowl whisk together the oil, vinegar, tomato paste and water. Add more water if the sauce is too thick. Brush sauce over kebobs.

6. Broil kebobs about 4 inches away from the heat. Broil about 1-2 minutes as scallops cook very quickly. The vegetables will be crisp yet hot. Turn once during cooking to brown both sides.

Suggested accompaniments: rice pilaf, broiled tomato halves and braised celery.

Approximate Nutrition Information per Serving:

Calories: 300	Fat: 12g	Sodium: 220mg
Protein: 24g	Cholesterol: 50mg	

Linguini with Clam Sauce

Ingredients:

18 large cherrystone or 24
   littleneck clams
2 tablespoons olive oil
2 large cloves garlic, minced
½ cup chopped parsley leaves
¼ teaspoon freshly ground black
   pepper
pinch of cayenne pepper or few
   drops Tabasco sauce

1 teaspoon dried oregano leaves
4 medium tomatoes, chopped
1 tablespoon tomato paste
2 tablespoons dry red wine
   (optional)
1 lb. linguini

Yield: 4 servings

1. Wash clams and discard any that are open or broken. Steam clams in ¼ inch water until all the shells have opened and clams are barely cooked, about 8-10 minutes. Remove meats from half the clams, reserving the rest. Reserve the clam broth. Clams may also be cooked in the microwave for five or more minutes depending on size. Arrange clams in a circle on a large plate with the hinges out. Microwave on high until barely cooked. Exact time depends on your microwave and the size of the clam.

2. Mince clam meats and set aside.

3. In a skillet heat the oil and add garlic, parsley, black and cayenne pepper and oregano. Cook slowly about 5 minutes.

4. Add the tomatoes, tomato paste, reserved clam broth and wine. Simmer slowly about 10 minutes.

5. While sauce simmers, cook linguini according to package instructions until it is "al dente", still firm to the tooth.

6. Add minced clams to the sauce. Adjust thickness of the sauce with water or tomato juice. Add clams in shell to the pan and heat another 2 minutes. Serve hot over linguini or spaghetti with freshly grated parmesan cheese.

Suggested accompaniments: sautéed zucchini and mushrooms

Approximate Nutrition Information per Serving:

Calories: 550	Fat: 10g	Sodium: 90mg
Protein: 24g	Cholesterol: 25mg	

Oysters Rockefeller

Ingredients:

12 live oysters in the shell, freshly shucked

½ lb. fresh spinach, washed and trimmed of stems

1 minced clove garlic

1 tablespoon olive oil

1 tablespoon unsalted butter

¼ cup bread crumbs (optional)

black pepper

Yield: 3 servings

1. Have fish dealer shuck oysters saving one large shell from each; OR shuck oysters at home using a stiff dull knife. Wear a glove over the hand that holds the oyster. Pry open shell at the hinge keeping the shallow shell on top; OR open oysters in the micro-wave for just a few seconds on high. Reserve meats and liquor separately.

2. Preheat broiler.

3. Place one oyster in each shell and place on a foil-lined broiler pan or shallow pie pan. Keep shells from tipping by loosely crumpling foil around the base of each shell.

4. Broil oysters for one minute and remove from heat.

5. In a small skillet wilt the spinach over high heat using just the moisture clinging to the leaves. Remove spinach from heat before the leaves have completely collapsed. Top each oyster with the hot spinach and sprinkle with pepper.

6. In the same skillet melt the oil and butter and stir in the garlic. Cook until garlic is just soft, about half a minute. Top each oyster with ½ teaspoon of the garlic butter. If desired top each with a teaspoon of bread crumbs.

7. Return oysters to broiler until each bubbles, about 1 minute. Overcooking will toughen the oysters.

Suggested accompaniments: a fine white wine

Approximate Nutrition Information per Serving:

Calories: 135   Fat: 8g   Sodium: 150mg

Protein: 9g   Cholesterol: 35mg

Any of the following sauces can be used atop baked, broiled or steamed fish or served cold on the side. Each is fast to make, especially in a food processor or blender. They are always better made with fresh herbs but dried ones will work too.

Horseradish Sauce

Ingredients:

¼ cup reduced calorie
  mayonnaise
5 tablespoons plain lowfat
  yogurt

½ teaspoon leaf thyme
4 teaspoons prepared
  horseradish (in vinegar)

Yield: ⅔ cup, 5 servings

1. Mix all ingredients together and chill. If desired, the sauce can be thinned with a little lemon juice.

Approximate Nutrition Information per serving:
Calories: 25   Fat: 2g   Sodium: 30mg
Protein: 1g   Cholesterol: 0mg

Joyce's Lime and Dill Sauce

Ingredients:

1 tablespoon olive oil
1 tablespoon freshly squeezed
  lime juice
grated rind of ½ lime

2 teaspoons dijon mustard
1 tablespoon dry white wine
¼ cup chopped fresh dill
freshly ground black pepper

Yield: 4 servings

1. Whisk together the oil, juice, mustard, wine and rind in a small bowl. Stir in the dill and black pepper.

2. Use to marinate fish, to top fish for baking, broiling or steaming or serve on the side.

Approximate Nutrition Information per serving:
Calories: 35   Fat: 3g   Sodium: 75mg
Protein: 0g   Cholesterol: 0mg

Pesto Sauce

Ingredients:

1 well packed cup of fresh basil
   leaves – dried basil doesn't
   work in making pesto
2 large cloves garlic

½ cup pine or walnuts
¾ cup grated Parmesan cheese
⅓ cup olive oil

Yield: About 1 ½ cups, 6 servings

1. Mince the garlic in a food processor or blender. Add the basil leaves and process until finely chopped. Add the nuts and process until the mixture is fine.

2. Add the cheese. Slowly add the oil mixing gradually until just blended.

Approximate Nutrition Information per serving:

Calories: 120   Fat: 10g   Sodium: 95mg
Protein: 3g   Cholesterol: 5mg

Orange Mustard Sauce

*This sauce was adapted from one published in **Gourmet Magazine**. It is an all-purpose sauce suitable for both mild and robust flavored fish.*

Ingredients:

2 tablespoons margarine
2 teaspoons dijon mustard
2 tablespoons chopped fresh
  parsley
1 teaspoon dried thyme leaves

½ cup fresh orange juice
rind of ½ orange grated or cut in
  thin strips with a zester
¼ cup fresh lemon juice

Yield: About 1 cup, 4 servings

1. In a medium saucepan melt the margarine and whisk in the mustard, parsley and thyme. Gradually stir in the orange juice, rind and lemon juice. Cook gently for about 3 minutes and remove from heat.

2. Use to marinate and baste fish for baking, broiling and barbecuing.

Approximate Nutrition Information per serving:

Calories: 70   Fat: 5.8g   Sodium: 140mg
Protein: <1g   Cholesterol: 0mg

Horseradish Chili

The tang of horseradish is often used with shrimp, though it lends itself to many other fish recipes. Combined with tomatoes and parsley, it is one of the quickest ways to enhance baked or steamed fish.

Ingredients:

2 teaspoons olive oil
1 small onion, finely chopped
2 teaspoons chili powder
2 medium tomatoes, chopped

¼ cup fresh parsley, chopped
2 tablespoons prepared
   horseradish (not the creamed
   variety)

Yield: 1 cup, 4 servings

1. In a small pan, sauté the onion and chili powder in the oil until onion becomes transparent.

2. Add the tomatoes, parsley and horseradish and simmer just until tomatoes soften. Use directly as is to top baked or steamed fish or process in a blender or food processor until smooth.

Approximate Nutrition Information per serving:

Calories: 50
Protein: 1g

Fat: <1g
Cholesterol: 0mg

Sodium: 15mg

Watercress Sauce

Watercress has a slightly pungent taste that is particularly refreshing. It is especially suited to fish cookery as well as salads and its ruffled leaves are attractive for garnishes. Its only disadvantage is its relative scarcity.

Ingredients:

¾ cup watercress, washed and patted dry
½ cup reduced calorie mayonnaise
½ cup plain lowfat yogurt
½ teaspoon celery seed
1 tablespoon freshly squeezed lemon juice
grated rind of half a lemon
freshly ground black pepper

Yield: 1½ cups

1. In a food processor or blender, coarsely chop the watercress.

2. Add the remaining ingredients and blend. Serve cold.

Variations: You can add a small clove of garlic, minced, or 2 small green onions, finely sliced. Just be careful not to overwhelm the flavor of the watercress with these powerful additions.

Approximate Nutrition Information per serving:
Calories: 40   Fat: 3g   Sodium: 25mg
Protein: 1g   Cholesterol: 0mg

Cucumber Dill Sauce

I made this sauce on the spur of the moment one hot summer evening and have been making it ever since for salads and seafood. It is also good spread on pocket bread sandwiches – especially fish ones.

Ingredients:

1 medium cucumber, pared and quartered
1 clove garlic
⅓ cup reduced calorie mayonnaise
⅓ cup plain lowfat yogurt

1 tablespoon freshly squeezed lemon or lime juice
grated rind of ½ lemon or lime
¼ cup fresh dill, chopped
dash of white pepper

Yield: About 1¼ cups, 5 servings

1. In a food processor or blender, mince the garlic. Add the cucumber and process until finely chopped.

2. Add the remaining ingredients and blend.

Variations: This sauce can be spiced by adding dijon mustard or Tabasco sauce.

Approximate Nutrition Information per serving:

Calories: 30
Protein: 1g
Fat: 2g
Cholesterol: 0mg
Sodium: 30mg

The Fishmonger's Mustard and Dill Sauce

*This recipe appeared in the **Boston Globe** in Sheryl Julian's weekend food column with her suggestion to use it with mackerel gravlax. It complements such a variety of fish and is so easy to make that we thought you would like it too. The Fishmonger is a seafood shop in Cambridge, Mass.*

Ingredients:

⅓ cup dijon mustard
2½ teaspoons dry mustard
¼ cup sugar
3 tablespoons white wine
    vinegar

⅓ cup olive or vegetable oil
¼ cup chopped fresh dill

Yield: About 1 cup, 4 servings

1. In a blender or food processor blend the mustards, sugar and vinegar.

2. Slowly add the oil in a thin stream, blending until emulsified. Stop mixing and add the dill. Turn on the machine just to incorporate the dill or stir in by hand.

3. Check the sauce for thickness, thinning it with a little warm water if necessary. Refrigerate the sauce for several hours to allow the flavors to blend.

The sauce can be used to baste fish before broiling or grilling or served separately with hot or cold fish.

Approximate Nutrition Information per serving:

Calories: 225   Fat: 18g   Sodium: 590mg
Protein: <1g   Cholesterol: 0mg

Salsa

Thanks to the popularity of Mexican cuisine and the wider availability of the fresh ingredients that make authentic salsa, you can turn just about any fish preparation into a Mexican treat. Try topping the fish with salsa, baking at 450° F. for 10 minutes per inch of thickness and topping with shredded Monterey Jack or sharp cheddar cheese. Olé!

Ingredients:

2 tomatillos (small green tomato-like vegetable with a green husk) husked and chopped

¼ cup water

3 medium tomatoes, finely chopped

1 small red onion, finely chopped

1 shallot, minced

2 medium mild green chili peppers, chopped (1 can green chilis will do)

1 small hot serrano or jalapeño pepper, minced (wear rubber gloves to protect your hands from the chili juice)

¼ teaspoon salt (optional)

Yield: About 1½ cups, 6 servings

1. Combine tomatillos with ¼ cup water in a small saucepan and cook over high heat until just tender, not mushy, about 5 minutes.

2. Mix tomatillos with the remaining ingredients and serve as a cold sauce to accompany cooked fish or use as a topping for baked fish Mexican style.

Note: For a finer sauce, purée the mixture in a blender or food processor. The salsa will be less piquant if the entire mixture is cooked for a few minutes, but the texture is softer.

Variations: Add minced garlic or sliced green onions instead of the red onion. If you cannot obtain fresh hot chili peppers use Tabasco sauce or cayenne pepper instead.

Approximate Nutrition Information per serving:

Calories: 33   Fat: <1g   Sodium: <10mg

Protein: 2g   Cholesterol: 0mg

Salsa Verde

Like the red and green common salsa, this chili sauce is made from fresh chilis, but just the green ones. Tomato may be added but not so much as to mask the lovely green color of this sauce. If you cannot find the fresh ingredients, most will be available in canned form in the specialty foods section of the supermarket. They make an acceptable sauce too.

Ingredients:

1 tablespoon olive oil
1 small onion finely chopped
1 clove of garlic, minced
4 tomatillos, husked and chopped OR 1 10 oz. can tomatillos
2 fresh mild green chilis, seeded and finely chopped OR 1 can green chilis (see Note)
1-2 fresh hot green chilis, either jalapeño or serrano

1 tablespoon chopped fresh cilantro (coriander) (optional) (see Note)
2 tablespoons chopped fresh parsley
½ teaspoon freshly ground black pepper
1 small tomato (optional)
cayenne pepper or Tabasco (optional)

Yield: About 1¼ cups, 5 servings

1. In a skillet, sauté the onion, garlic, tomatillos and chili peppers in olive oil until just tender.

2. Stir in cilantro, parsley, pepper and tomato if desired. Put all ingredients in a food processor or blender and whirl until blended but not puréed. Mixture should still be chunky. Taste for piquancy and add cayenne pepper or Tabasco to fire.

Note: Fresh green peppers will make a green sauce but completely different in flavor. They are not an adequate substitute for chili peppers; use canned chilis instead.

Fresh cilantro has a pleasing slightly bitter taste and should be used cautiously. If not available use dried coriander but cook it well with the onion and garlic. It can be omitted entirely.

Approximate Nutrition Information per serving:
Calories: 60   Fat: 3g   Sodium: 5mg
Protein: 2g   Cholesterol: 0mg

Glossary

Allergen: a substance capable of provoking a bothersome inflammatory response; for example, ragweed pollen.

allergic response: an acute or chronic inflammatory response upon exposure to an allergen; such a response occurs in hypersensitive individuals repeatedly exposed to the allergen; the symptoms of hayfever are an example.

antibody: a specific protein made by the body that combines with an allergen. Its purpose is to help eliminate or make harmless foreign particles that have entered the body.

antigen: in the strict sense, an antigen is a substance which stimulates the production of antibody; in the general sense, antigens are substances that stimulate any type of adaptive immune response; antigens are frequently proteins.

arachidonic acid: a polyunsaturated fatty acid containing twenty carbon atoms and four double bonds. Because the first double bond is located six carbon atoms away from the omega or methyl end of the fatty acid, it is classed as an omega-6 (n-6) fatty acid. Arachidonic acid is essential in cell membranes. It is the starting material for making prostaglandins, thromboxanes and leukotrienes – powerful hormone-like substances that regulate many cellular activities. The body makes arachidonic acid from linoleic acid and we obtain small amounts from food, especially meat.

arteriosclerosis: a group of diseases in which the walls of arteries thicken and lose their elasticity; atherosclerosis is the most common disease of this kind.

atherosclerosis: a slowly developing condition where the lining of arteries (blood vessels carrying blood to the heart) becomes laced with lipid deposits containing cholesterol and other substances; the result is narrowing and scarring of the blood vessel that impairs the flow of blood.

cholesterol: a lipid belonging to the class of substances known as sterols. Cholesterol is made mainly of carbon and hydrogen atoms arranged in ring structures. Cholesterol is part of every animal cell and is made in the body. We need it for cell membranes and hormones. It is found only in animal foods, especially eggs, liver and squid. It is not found in plants.

DHA: docosahexaenoic acid, one of two major polyunsaturated fatty acids in fish oil. DHA has twenty-two carbon atoms and six double bonds. DHA is important in nervous tissue and photoreceptors in the eye.

double bond: the common name for the position in a fatty acid chain where two hydrogen atoms are missing. Double bonds change the shape of the fatty acid molecule, thus affecting its behavior in cells. A fatty acid with one or more double bonds is called unsaturated. Omega-3 fatty acids in fish oil have five or six double bonds whereas vegetable fatty acids usually have one or two.

eicosanoid: a general term for all products containing 20 carbon atoms made from the fatty acid arachidonic acid. The two major kinds of eicosanoids are prostaglandins and leukotrienes.

EPA: eicosapentaenoic acid, one of the two major polyunsaturated fatty acids in fish oils. EPA has twenty carbon atoms and five double bonds. It competes with arachidonic acid to be made into prostaglandins and leukotrienes. The products made from it are similar to those made from arachidonic acid but have less pronounced metabolic effects.

epithelial: describes the cells covering the internal and external surfaces of the body such as the skin, blood vessels and intestinal tract. Epithelial cells differ in size, shape, number of layers and function.

essential fatty acid: those fatty acids that cannot be manufactured by the body and must be obtained from the diet. They are essential for normal growth and development. The main essential fatty acid is linoleic acid, found in vegetables and grains and in small amounts in animal foods. Arachidonic acid is the second fatty acid we require, but our bodies can make it from linoleic acid. For this reason, arachidonic acid does not count as an essential fatty acid. There is evidence that linolenic acid is probably essential, at least in children. It is less abundant in foods but is present in small amounts in some vegetable oils, especially soybean oil. Greater amounts are found in rapeseed and linseed oil but these are not widely consumed by people.

A saturated fatty acid. It has no double bonds. This type predominates in meats, dairy foods, coconut and palm oils and avocado.

A monounsaturated fatty acid. It has one double bond where a pair of hydrogenations is missing. It predominates in olive oil.

A polyunsaturated fatty acid. It has two double bonds. It predominates in most vegetable oils.

A polyunsaturated fatty acid from fish oils. It has five double bonds and is found only in seafood.

fat: the simple term for a triglyceride. Triglyceride is the main fat in food and the body and it contains three fatty acids. When the body "burns" fat for energy it obtains more than twice the energy as it does from burning carbohydrate or protein; fat yields about 9 calories per gram.

fatty acid: a molecule made of a long chain of carbon atoms with hydrogen attached to the carbons; the carbon at one end has two oxygens and is acidic. It can combine with other molecules such as cholesterol.

food allergy: an immunologic response to ingesting a food or food additive. Such responses occur only in some people. Allergy to shrimp is an example.

glycerol: a molecule composed of three carbon atoms with an "alcohol" (OH) group attached to each carbon. Each alcohol group reacts with a fatty acid to form a triglyceride.

hazard: the ability of a substance to produce injury under the circumstances of exposure. The idea contained in the term hazard is that a substance may have the intrinsic capacity to be toxic but does no harm as we are customarily exposed to it. Arsenic is an example of a toxic substance present in tiny amounts in some foods but is not a hazard in the food supply.

HDL: high density lipoproteins. HDL lipoproteins are thought to transport cholesterol away from tissues. High blood HDL levels are believed to be a favorable indicator of reduced risk of heart disease.

heart attack: a block in blood flow through a vessel in the heart. As a result, part of the heart muscle is damaged and the heart is less able to pump blood. Blockage of a major heart vessel can be fatal.

high blood pressure: see hypertension

hypercholesterolemia: means literally, too much cholesterol in the blood. This is a clinical condition that increases risk of heart disease. People with high levels of cholesterol in the LDL fraction of the blood have an increased risk of heart disease. Hypercholesterolemia tends to run in families.

hyperlipidemia: A general term for too much lipid in the blood. The term includes high levels of cholesterol and triglyceride and does not distinguish among different types of hyperlipidemia.

hypertension: the medical term for high blood pressure. Blood pressure is the push of the blood against the blood vessel walls. When it is consistently too high there is excessive strain on the heart, kidneys and blood vessels. Untreated high blood pressure can cause strokes, heart attack and kidney disease. Blood pressure is considered "high" when measurements exceed 140 mm mercury (pressure) for systolic pressure (heart contraction), or 90 mm mercury for diastolic pressure (heart relaxation).

immune response: defense mechanisms triggered by the presence in the body of "foreign" materials or those recognized as being not part of oneself; a typical foreign material is bacteria and a common immune response is the production of antibodies to those bacteria.

inflammatory response: an adaptive response to injury or infection characterized by redness, warmth or fever, swelling and pain. It is brought about by the immune system and prostaglandins.

LDL: low density lipoproteins. LDL are the main carriers of cholesterol in the blood. They transport cholesterol to the tissues. High levels of LDL cholesterol increase risk of heart disease.

leukotriene: a class of twenty-carbon compounds made from arachidonic acid. Leukotrienes are powerful agents in producing inflammatory responses. Only a few cells make leukotrienes – leukocytes, lung tissue, platelets and a few others. Omega-3 fatty acids lead to the generation of a type of leukotriene that has less pronounced effects than those made from arachidonic acid with the result that inflammatory symptoms are less severe.

linoleic acid: an essential fatty acid we obtain from food. It is abundant in seeds, grains and most vegetable oils. Linoleic acid is a polyunsaturated fatty acid with 18 carbon atoms and 2 double bonds. Like nearly all vegetable fatty acids, linoleic acid has the omega-6 structure. It can be converted to arachidonic acid in the body.

linolenic acid: Like linoleic acid, linolenic acid is an 18-carbon fatty acid. It is different from linoleic in having 3 double bonds and the omega-3 structure. It is abundant in linseed oil, after which it is named, but is not widespread in other common seeds and grains. Soybean and canola (rapeseed) oil have considerable amounts of linolenic acid. Linolenic acid can be converted to EPA in the body.

lipid: a general term for substances that are insoluble in water but dissolve in organic solvents like ether and chloroform. Lipids include fats like triglyceride, sterols such as cholesterol, waxes, and other complex substances like phospholipids.

lipoprotein: a group of compounds made of proteins and a variety of lipids. Lipoproteins are the main carriers of triglyceride and cholesterol in the blood. They are distinguished from each other by density or weight. The lipoproteins involved in transporting triglyceride (fat) are chylomicrons and VLDL. Those carrying cholesterol are LDL and HDL. Fat soluble vitamins like vitamin A and D are also carried by lipoproteins. The pattern of lipoproteins in the blood is one indicator of risk of heart disease.

monounsaturated: describes fatty acids that are missing one pair of hydrogen atoms from their structure. In other words, these fatty acids have one double bond. The most common monounsaturated fatty acid is oleic acid which is abundant in olive oil. Monounsaturated fatty acids are also produced in the hydrogenation of oils to make margarine.

omega: the Greek name for the non-acidic end of a fatty acid molecule. The omega end of a fatty acid is also called the methyl end for the methyl group located there. Scientists prefer to call the omega end "n."

omega-3: a general description for the highly polyunsaturated fatty acids in fish oils. It refers to the position in the fatty acid chain three carbons away from the methyl or omega end of the chain. This is the position of the first double bond or pair of missing hydrogens in the major polyunsaturated fatty acids in fish oils. Fish oils are the richest source of omega-3 fatty acids. The major omega-3 fatty acids in fish oil are EPA (eicosapentaenoic acid) and DHA (docosahexaenoic acid). Linolenic acid is an omega-3 fatty acid found in small amounts in plants but it is not as long nor as unsaturated as fish oil omega-3 fatty acids. Scientists use the term n-3 instead of omega-3.

omega-6: describes fatty acids whose first double bond is located six carbon atoms away from the omega or methyl end of the fatty acid chain. Vegetable oil fatty acids are mainly of the omega-6 type. Linoleic acid, the main essential fatty acid is an omega-6 fatty acid. Omega-6 may also be written n-6.

peroxides: compounds formed by the chemical reaction (oxidation) between fatty acids and activated oxygen. Examples are hydrogen peroxide and ozone. Peroxide formation can be induced by air and light at room temperature. Peroxides break down into reactive compounds that destroy other molecules.

phytate: a chemical form of phytic acid. Phytic acid occurs mainly in the outer part or husk of seeds and grains. It is able to bind many minerals so that they are unavailable for absorption from the intestine.

plaque: literally a patch or flat area. Associated with heart disease it refers to deposits of lipid and cells that build up in the lining of blood vessels. Large plaques can eventually block the flow of blood through a vessel.

platelet: a small blood cell responsible for blood clotting. Platelets have a strong ability to clump together or aggregate under the appropriate stimulation. Their aggregation helps heal wounds. Platelets have no nucleus so they are incomplete cells.

poison: a substance causing structural or functional damage after it has been ingested, inhaled, absorbed, injected, applied or developed within the body; responses to poisons do not necessarily involve immune responses.

polyunsaturated: a description of fatty acids having two or more double bonds; that is, they are missing at least two pairs of hydrogen atoms in their structure. Polyunsaturated fats like corn and safflower oil are rich in polyunsaturated fatty acids. Polyunsaturated fats tend to lower blood cholesterol levels thereby reducing risk of heart disease. Fish oils are rich in the highly polyunsaturated fatty acids EPA and DHA which have five and six double bonds respectively.

prostacyclin: a particular prostaglandin (PGI_2) made from arachidonic acid. It is made by cells lining blood vessels and is the most potent inhibitor of platelet aggregation known.

prostaglandin: a general term for three groups or series of compounds made mainly from arachidonic acid or EPA (eicosapentaenoic acid) from fish oil. The prostaglandins made from arachidonic acid are the most prevalent in the body. Prostaglandins are potent, very short-lived substances that regulate cell function. They are prominent in immune/inflammatory responses. The two best known types of prostaglandins are thromboxanes and prostacyclin.

RDA: Recommended Dietary Allowances. These are recommendations of the average daily amounts of nutrients that all of us should consume. They include a safety allowance to ensure that they will meet the needs of virtually everyone. They are not individual requirements. The RDAs are published roughly every five years by the National Academy of Sciences. People use the RDAs to estimate the nutritional adequacy of the food intake of certain groups of people. There are no RDAs for several essential nutrients because of a lack of adequate data.

saturated: describes fatty acids that have all the hydrogen atoms in their structure they can hold – hence they are full or saturated. Saturated fats are those rich in saturated fatty acids. Saturated fats are abundant in meats, coconut oil, avocado, hydrogenated vegetable shortening and some margarines. Saturated fats tend to raise blood cholesterol levels which increases the risk of heart disease.

sterol: a compound composed mainly of carbon and hydrogen with some oxygen where the atoms are arranged in four adjoining rings with a side chain attached. Cholesterol and vitamin D are examples of sterols.

stroke: blockage of blood flow through a vessel in the brain. A stroke may damage the nervous system. A severe stroke can be fatal.

thromboxane: a powerful substance that promotes platelet clumping. Thromboxanes are made originally from arachidonic acid via the same pathway that makes prostaglandins. Platelets are the best known source of thromboxanes. Thromboxanes are one of the three major products of arachidonic acid metabolism.

toxin: another term for poison. Toxins are usually proteins and may be made by plants, animals and bacteria. Botulinus toxin is a deadly bacterial toxin produced by the bacterium, *Clostridium botulinum*. Pufferfish or fugu, a fish prized in the Orient is excluded from the USA because of its dangerous toxin, tetrodotoxin, which can be fatal.

triglyceride: the chemist's term for "fat". Triglycerides are made of three fatty acids attached to a three-carbon chain backbone called glycerol. Triglycerides differ from each other according to the kind of fatty acids they contain.

unsaturated: describes fatty acids that have one or more pairs of hydrogen atoms missing from their structure. Monounsaturated fatty acids are missing one hydrogen pair; polyunsaturated fatty acids miss two or more pairs. Unsaturated fats are those rich in unsaturated fatty acids. Fish oils are rich in highly unsaturated fatty acids.

US RDA: United States Recommended Daily Allowances. These are the amounts of vitamins, minerals and other nutrients from

Recommended Dietary Allowances, 1980 and the U.S. RDA*

Nutrient	RDA for an Adult Man	RDA for an Adult Woman	U.S. RDA**
These nutrients must appear on a nutrition label			
Protein, mixed protein	56 g	44	–
PER < casein	–	–	65 g
PER ≥ casein	–	–	45 g
Vitamin A, RE	1000	800	1000
Vitamin C, mg	60	60	60
Thiamin, mg	1.4	1.0	1.5
Riboflavin, mg	1.6	1.2	1.7
Niacin, NE	18	13	20
Calcium, g	0.8	0.8	1
Iron, mg	10	18	18
These nutrients may appear on a nutrition label			
Vitamin D, IU	200	200	400
Vitamin E, IU	15	12	30
Vitamin B_6, mg	2.2	2.0	2
Folic Acid, mg	0.4	0.4	0.4
Vitamin B_{12}, mcg	3.0	3.0	6
Phosphorus, g	0.8	0.8	1
Iodine, mcg	150	150	150
Magnesium, mg	350	300	400
Zinc, mg	15	15	15
Copper, mg	–	–	2
Biotin, mg	–	–	0.3
Pantothenic acid, mg	–	–	10

Abbreviations: U.S. RDA: U.S. Recommended Daily Allowances; PER: Protein Efficiency Ratio, an estimate of protein quality; RE: Retinol Equivalent, equal to 1 microgram retinol; I.U.: International Unit; mg: milligram or one thousandth of a gram; NE: Niacin Equivalent, equal to 1 mg niacin or 60 mg tryptophan; g: gram; mcg: microgram; <: less than; >: greater than

* In general, the RDA for infants and children are less than the values for adults; the RDA for adolescents, pregnant and lactating women are greater than for adults. RDAs never exceed the U.S. RDAs. RDAs for energy (Calories) vary with age, sex, height, weight and level of activity. There are no RDAs for several essential nutrients because we lack the necessary scientific data.

**U.S. RDA: For definition and difference from RDA, see glossary food that a person should eat every day to stay healthy. The US RDA were selected from the RDAs (see above) and include an excess to allow for individual variation in need. They are not minimum requirements. The US RDAs are the basis for nutrition labels on food.

VLDL: very low density lipoproteins. VLDL are the main carriers of triglyceride in the blood. They also carry small amounts of cholesterol. VLDL particles give rise to LDL particles, the main carriers of cholesterol in blood. Omega-3 fatty acids from seafood markedly reduce the VLDL levels of people with high triglycerides in their blood.

Bibliography

A. Nutrition and Seafood

1. Nettleton, J.A. *Seafood Nutrition: Facts, Issues and Marketing of Nutrition in Fish and Shellfish.* 1985. Osprey Books, Huntington, NY.

   A comprehensive volume about the nutrition in fish and shellfish. It includes basic nutrition information as well as detailed information on the healthful properties of seafood. The effects of processing and cooking are discussed as well as additives and contaminants. The author collected reliable and up-to-date data on the nutrient composition of fish and shellfish, including values for the omega-3 content of many species.

2. McClane, A.J. *Encyclopedia of Fish Cookery.* 1977. Holt, Reinhart and Winston, New York.

   The gold standard of fish cookery, this treasury gives information about fish species, handling, preparation and cuisine. Recipes vary from simple to elaborate with no hesitation about using cream, butter and salt. The book is a pleasure to read but requires effort to match a recipe with a species if you do not choose the ones recommended for the fish you have in hand.

3. Whitney, E.N. and Hamilton, E.M.N. *Understanding Nutrition.* 3rd edition. 1984. West Publishing Co., St. Paul, MN.

   An excellent basic textbook about nutrition that brings the excitement and fascination of nutrition to the reader. Explanations of terms, examples, illustrations and clear, clever writing make this book an enjoyable and authoritative reference.

4. MacDonald, H.B. *Eating for the Health of It: A new look at nutrition.* 1985. 3 S Fitness Group, Box 705, Santa Barbara, CA 93102

   A witty and accurate account of nutrition that dispels popular myths about eating and makes practical suggestions for meeting nutritional needs throughout the life cycle. This book makes reading about nutrition palatable and enjoyable.

5. Connor, S.L. and Connor, W.E. *The New American Diet.* 1986. Simon and Schuster, New York, NY.

This authoritative and practical book is designed to make it easy and delicious to have healthful eating habits. The book provides menus, recipes and lots of sound information about wise eating to discourage the development of the chronic diseases that predominate in affluent countries. The dietary recommendations favor low fat, low saturated fat and low cholesterol foods and emphasize the importance and enjoyment of eating seafood regularly.

6. DeBakey, M., Gotto, A., Scott, L. and Foreyt, J. *The Living Heart Diet*. 1984. Raven Press, New York, NY.

This book is directed toward healthful eating to reduce the risk of heart disease. It includes detailed discussion of heart disease and its causes as well as 500 recipes for heart healthy living.

7. Gorbach, S., Zimmerman, D. and Woods, M. *The Doctors' Anti-Breast Cancer Diet*. 1984. Simon and Schuster, New York, NY.

The authors present the case for women to eat less fat and more fiber-rich foods in order to reduce their risk of breast cancer. The authors are directing a national diet and breast cancer study among women to examine further the importance of low fat eating. The book includes menus and recipes to make it easier to adopt a low fat eating style. The book is clearly written and reliable.

8. Aronson, V. and Stare, F. *Rx:Executive Diet. Sensible Nutrition for Today's Health-Conscious Executive*. 1986. Christopher Publishing House, Norwell, MA.

A sensible, practical and easily understood guide to nutritious eating for busy people who travel and eat out often. Menus and tips for healthful eating as well as a variety of recommended references make this book a commonsense and reliable volume to use.

9. Pennington, J.A.T. and Church, H.N. *Bowes and Church's Food Values of Portions Commonly Used*. 14th edition. 1985. J.B. Lippincott Co., Philadelphia, PA.

For those who want the numbers, this manual gives the details of food composition. This book is one of the most widely respected and commonly used references for nutrient data.

10. Faria, S.M. *The Northeast Seafood Book*. 1984. Mass. Division

of Marine Fisheries, New England Fisheries Development Foundation and Northeast Marine Advisory Council. Boston, MA

This compendium describes the various types of seafood available, processed forms, nutrition, public health issues, buying and handling tips, cooking methods and extensive "how-to" information for fish and shellfish. While the title implies that the information is restricted to North Atlantic species, the majority of the facts pertain to seafood from all parts of the country. The reference is excellent.

B. Seafood Recipe Books

There are hundreds of recipe books devoted to seafood each with its own style and emphasis. Few, however, have been developed with both taste and nutrition principles in mind. Only a few include nutrition information. Some are most worthwhile for their culinary creativity. You can find inspiration in all of them, as I have. Here are some thoughts about a few.

1. Editors of Time-Life Books. *Fresh Ways with Fish & Shellfish*. 1986. Time-Life Books, Alexandria, VA.

   As part of their series on healthy home cooking, the editors of Time-Life Books have prepared an excellent volume on handling and cooking seafood. Exquisite photographs accompany each recipe. The recipes use unusual flavors, fresh ingredients and quick preparations that will have the most hesitant cook raving. Nutrition information is included and fat and cholesterol levels are low to moderate.

2. The Rhode Island Seafood Council. *Complete Guide to Seafood Cookery*. 1982. To obtain a copy, send $4.50 to: The Rhode Island Seafood Council, 387 Main Street, Wakefield, RI 02879.

   This handy little plastic covered book is probably the best value available. It is full of good recipes, facts and how-tos for fish and shellfish available in the East. Most of the recipes are adaptable for West Coast species. Some nutrition information is given. The recipes are inconsistent in their use of fat, type of fat and salt. A revised edition is planned.

3. Grunes, B. and Magida, P. *Fish on the Grill*. 1986. Contemporary Books, Inc., 180 N. Michigan Ave., Chicago, Ill. 60601.

   This is one of my favorites for its creative recipes and simple preparations. Some recipes are heart healthy, but many suggest flavored butters, heavy cream and egg yolks. The nutrition conscious cook can scale down the amount of fat suggested but it may be more difficult for the average person to make some of the sauces without the eggs or sour cream.

4. Walker, Charlotte. *Fish and Shellfish.* 1984. HP Books, P.O. Box 5367, Tucson, Arizona 85703.

This beautifully illustrated book has some of the most interesting recipes I've seen. There are many recipes for steaming, poaching, baking and microwaving with interesting flavor combinations. The author readily uses cream and half-and-half but you can adapt these fat rich choices for healthier eating.

5. Hurlburt, Sarah. *The Mussel Cookbook.* 1977. Harvard University Press, Cambridge, MA.

This delightful book not only informs but inspires. Its delicious recipes show off the immense versatility of mussels and most are simple to prepare. If you're not already a mussel devotee, you will be following Sarah's suggestions. Most recipes do not use large quantities of oil or butter, but there are some where the amounts could be halved.

6. Spinazzola, A. and Paimblanc, J-J. *Seafood As We Like It.* 1985. Globe Pequot Press, Chester, CT 06412.

This book is a delight to read as much for its witty style as for its delicious recipes. It has all the old world flavor one expects of its continental authors as well as a good deal of cream and butter. Each recipe has information about its calorie, fat, protein, carbohydrate and sodium content but no guide as to what level might constitute a low, moderate or high amount of fat or calories. The reader needs to ferret out the lean cuisine recipes but some are there.

7. Editors of Sunset Magazine. *Sunset Seafood Cook Book.* Lane Publishing Co., Menlo Park, CA 94025

Like the other fine cook books in this series, the seafood one covers all the bases. It has a useful series of pages giving a profile of the most commonly used fish and shellfish with suggestions for the most suitable ways of cooking. Flavor and texture information is included. Appealing photographs and drawings enhance the presentation of recipes and information. This book, like so many others, endorses the notion that butters and butter based sauces are the perfect complement for seafood, while nutritionists would suggest that less fat-dependent preparations can be equally tasty.

8. California Culinary Academy. *Fish and Shellfish*. 1985. Chevron Chemical Co., San Francisco, CA 94105.

    This recipe collection abounds with unusual culinary presentations and luxurious ingredients, especially the fresh herbs so readily available in California. If you cannot find exciting ideas and recipes here, cease your search. Bluefish with melon salsa is a fine example of the treasures in this volume. Beware all ye who seek trim waistlines, for this is the land of cream and butter, yea honey too. If we could just get these folks to do a lean cuisine version we would be all set.

9. Harsila, Janis and Hansen, Evie. *Seafood – A Collection of Heart-Healthy Recipes*. National Seafood Educators, P.O. Box 60006, Richmond Beach, WA 98160.

    Here's the book we nutritionists have been waiting for, and it is not disappointing. Nutrition information, heart-healthy tantalizing recipes in a clear readable layout make this book appealing. The preparations are straightforward with ingredients nearly everyone would have. Nearly all recipes have less than 300 calories and many are under 200.

    The authors designed the recipes around the American Heart Association's dietary guidelines so that they are low in calories, fat, saturated fat and cholesterol. They are also moderately low in sodium but high in flavor. Portions have 3½ – 4 oz. of seafood, amounts that meet nutritional needs but might call for seconds by many. Because most seafoods are low in calories, larger portions are often suitable and more pleasing. Calorie-rich preparations can be traded off against portion size and offer diversity. This flexibility is one of seafood's greatest advantages. The recipes might have been enhanced if the authors had suggested what else to serve along with the meal.

General Index

Index of Seafoods in the Recipes